D0985121

THE REVELS PLAYS

Founder Editor: Clifford Leech 1958–71

General Editor: F. David Hoeniger

'TIS PITY SHE'S A WHORE

'And here's my breast, strike home!'
Oliver Tobias as Giovanni in G. P. Griffi's film *'Tis Pity She's a Whore* (reproduced by kind permission of Miracle Films Ltd.).

'Tis Pity She's a Whore

JOHN FORD

EDITED BY

DEREK ROPER

THE REVELS PLAYS

Manchester University Press

Oxford Road Manchester M13 9PL

PR2524.T5 1975t

This edition first published 1975

This title is available in both hardbound and
paperback editions. The paperback edition is
sold subject to the condition that it shall not, by
way of trade or otherwise, be lent, resold, hired
out or otherwise circulated without the pub-
lisher's prior consent in any form of binding or
cover other than that in which it is published and
without a similar condition including this condition being imposed on the subsequent purchaser.

ISBN (hardbound) 0 416 67070 9
(paperback) 0 416 70350 X
Introduction, Apparatus Criticus, etc.
© 1975 Derek Roper
Printed in Great Britain by
W & J Mackay Limited, Chatham
Distributed in the U.S.A. by
HARPER & ROW PUBLISHERS INC.
BARNES & NOBLE IMPORT DIVISION

General Editor's Preface

The series known as the Revels Plays was conceived by Professor Clifford Leech. The idea emerged in his mind, as he tells us in the General Editor's Preface to the first of the Revels Plays, published in 1958, from the success of the New Arden Shakespeare. The aim of the series was, in his words, 'to apply to Shakespeare's predecessors, contemporaries, and successors the methods that are now used in Shakespeare editing'. We owe it to Clifford Leech that the idea has become reality. He planned the series, set the high standards for it, and for many years selected and supervised the editors. He aimed at editions of lasting merit and usefulness, that would appeal to scholars and students, but not to them alone; producers and actors were also much in his mind. 'The plays included should be such as to deserve and indeed demand performance.' And thus the texts should be presented in a form that is attractive and clear to the actor, with some space of the introduction devoted to records of productions, and some of the notes to comments on stage business.

Under his direction each editor of the series has of course been expected to apply certain basic principles to his editing and other aspects of method, and to follow as a model some of the best previous editions. But in many matters the guidelines have necessarily had to be flexible, for the series includes works from a period of two centuries, from *circa* 1500 to *circa* 1700, many with peculiar problems of text and interpretation. And it is best to allow the individual editor room to do justice to his peculiar gifts and interests, and to express his own convictions or hypotheses. It is indeed the editors themselves who in each instance deserve chief credit for any excellence that may be found in their editions, or who must be held responsible for certain weaknesses. Yet no one knows better than the past editors themselves how many suggestions they owe to

3C84283

Clifford Leech, and how often he kindly alerted them to weaknesses or saved them from error. It is fitting that he will now be known as Founder Editor of the Revels Plays.

The text of each Revels Play is edited afresh from the original text (in a few instances, texts) of best authority, but spelling and punctuation are modernized, and speech-headings silently normalized. The text is accompanied by collations and commentary, and in each volume the editor devotes one section of his introduction to a discussion of the provenance and trustworthiness of the 'copytext', the original on which he has based his edition, and to a brief description of particular aspects of his editorial method. Other sections of the introduction deal with the play's date and sources, its place in the work of the author, its significance as a dramatic work of literature in the context of its time and designed for a certain theatre, actors, and audience, its reputation, and its stage-history. In editions of a play by an author not previously represented in the series, it has been customary also to include a brief account of the author's life and career. Some emphasis is laid on providing available records of performances, early and modern.

Modernization has its problems, and has to be practised with care and some flexibility if the substance of the original is not to be distorted. The editor emends, as distinct from modernizing, the original text only in instances where error is patent or at least very probable, and correction persuasive. Archaic forms need sometimes to be retained when rhyme or metre demands them or when a modernized form would alter the required sense or obscure a play on words. The extent to which an editor feels free to adapt the punctuation will largely depend on the degree of authority he attributes to the punctuation of his copy. It is his task to follow the original closely in any dramatic or rhetorical pointing that can be trusted for good reason. Punctuation should do justice to a character's way of speaking, and to the interplay of dialogue.

In general, the manner of modernization is similar to that in the Arden Shakespeare. Yet in the volumes since 1968, the '-ed' form is used for non-syllabic terminations in past tenses and past participles ('-'d' in Arden and earlier Revels volumes), and '-èd' for syllabic ('-ed' earlier). Act divisions are given only if they appear in the original text or if the structure of the play clearly points to them. Those act and scene divisions not found in the original are provided unobtrusively in small type and in square brackets. Square brackets are also used for any other additions to or changes in the stage directions of the original. But in no instances are directions referring to locale added to scene headings; for the plays (at least those before the Restoration) were designed for stages whose acting area was most of the time neutral and where each scene flowed into the next without interruption; and producers in our time would probably be well advised to attempt to convey this characteristic fluidity of scene on whatever stage they may have at their disposal.

A mixture of principles and common sense also governs the collations accompanying the text. Revels plays do not provide a variorum collation; only those variants which require the critical attention of serious textual students. All departures of substance from 'copy-text' are listed, including any relineation and those changes in punctuation which involve to any degree a decision between alternative interpretations; but not such accidentals as turned letters, nor necessarily additions to stage directions whose editorial nature is already made clear by the use of brackets. Press corrections in the 'copy-text' are likewise included. Of later emendations of the text (or errors) found in seventeenth-century reprints of no authority or editions from the eighteenth century to modern times, in general only those are given which as alternative readings still deserve serious attention. Readings of a later text of special historical interest or influence are, in some instances, more fully collated.

One of the hallmarks of the Revels Plays is the thoroughness of their annotations. Besides explicating the meaning of difficult words and passages and alerting the reader to special implications, the editor provides comments on customs or usage, text or stage business—indeed on anything he judges pertinent and helpful. Glosses are not provided for words that are satisfactorily explained in simple dictionaries like the *Concise Oxford*. Each volume contains an Index to the Annotations, in which particular attention is drawn to meanings for words not listed in *O.E.D.*

By 1970, seventeen volumes had appeared in the series, and a fair number are well in progress. The series began with some of the best-known plays of the Elizabethan and Jacobean era. Some years ago it was decided to include also some early Tudor and some Restoration plays. But it is not our object to concentrate only on well-known plays. Some lesser-known plays of whose merit as literature and as drama we are convinced are being included in the hope that they will arouse the attention they deserve, both from students and in the theatre.

F. DAVID HOENIGER

Toronto, 1973

Contents

Illustrations

Preface

Grateful acknowledgements are due to many persons and institutions for help with this edition. Mr Nigel Bawcutt generously gave me the benefit of his earlier experience as an editor of *'Tis Pity*, and my discussion of the printing of the 1633 quarto owes much to him. Mrs Elsie Kemp Schmitz placed at my disposal her unpublished critical edition of the play (to which my collation owes several readings), besides much information about twentieth-century productions. Thanks are due to librarians in the U.S.A. who sent photocopies or Xerox prints of the quarto; to those nearer home who arranged for me to collate their copies; and to the staff of Sheffield University Library for much patient and courteous help. Mr Roy Wilson gave speedy and skilful assistance with the cover of the paperback edition. Grants from the Sheffield University Research Fund paid for photocopies and helped with travel expenses. Mr Denis Reidy translated Speroni's *Canace* into English for my benefit; so far as I know this is the only translation ever made. Valuable assistance came from Dr Christina Roaf, whose critical edition of *Canace* is shortly to be published at Bologna by the *Commissione per i testi di lingua*. Among those who replied to letters, helped with special problems or made useful suggestions were Professor Allardyce Nicoll, Dr James McManaway, Mr Thomas V. Lange, Professor Raymond Southall, Miss Roma Gill and Dr R. H. Robbins. Professor Brian Morris gave encouragement when it was needed, as well as the stimulus provided by his own editions of Ford. The General Editor gave vigilant assistance and some beneficial goading during the later stages. Earlier on the work profited from the scrutiny and constructive advice of Professor Clifford Leech, founder and first General Editor of the Revels Plays; but my debt to him goes back to a time (for there was such a time) before work on *'Tis Pity* began. His lectures at Durham, besides what they taught me of the Elizabethan and Jacobean drama, showed me what lectures should be—a model still unsurpassed. For this and much else, may this edition of a play which he has written about so well convey my thanks.

DEREK ROPER

Sheffield, 1973

Abbreviations

McIlwraith	*Five Stuart Tragedies*, ed. A. K. McIlwraith (1953). World's Classics.
Schmitz	'A Critical Edition of John Ford's *'Tis Pitty Shee's a Whore*', ed. Elsie Kemp Schmitz (unpublished typescript prepared at Cambridge, England, 1956–9).
Bawcutt	Edition of this play by N. W. Bawcutt, Lincoln, Nebraska, 1966, in the Regents Renaissance Drama Series.
Morris	Edition of this play by Brian Morris, 1968, in the New Mermaids Series.
Sturgess	*John Ford: Three Plays*, ed. Keith Sturgess (Penguin English Library, 1970).

OTHER WORKS

Abbott	E. A. Abbott, *A Shakespearian Grammar* (edit. 1874).
Bentley	Gerald Eades Bentley, *The Jacobean and Caroline Stage* (7 vols., Oxford, 1941–68).
Burton	Robert Burton, *The Anatomy of Melancholy*, ed. A. R. Shilleto (3 vols., 1893).
Christes Bloodie Sweat	*Christes Bloodie Sweat, or the Sonne of God in his Agonie*, by I.F. (1613). (Probably by Ford; see Introduction, p. xxi).
Don Quixote	Miguel de Cervantes, *The Life and Atchievements of the Renown'd Don Quixote de la Mancha*, trans. Peter Motteux, revd. John Ozell (Modern Library, New York, 1930).
Leech	Clifford Leech, *John Ford and the Drama of his Time* (1957).
Materialien	*Materialien zur Kunde des älteren Englischen Dramas*, ed. W. Bang (Louvain, 1902–14) and new series ed. H. De Vocht (1927–50). References are to line-numbers.

O.E.D.   *The Oxford English Dictionary* (13 vols.,
                       1888–1933).

Oliver   H. J. Oliver, *The Problem of John Ford*
                       (Melbourne, London and New York, 1955).

Perkin Warbeck   John Ford, *The Chronicle History of Perkin
                       Warbeck*, ed. Peter Ure (1968). Revels Plays.

Queen   *The Queen, or The Excellency of her Sex*, ed.
                       W. Bang (1906; Vol. XIII of *Materialien*).
                       Ascribed to Ford by Bang and generally
                       accepted as authentic. References are to
                       line-numbers.

Sargeaunt   M. Joan Sargeaunt, *John Ford* (Oxford,
                       1935).

Shakespeare's Bawdy Eric Partridge, *Shakespeare's Bawdy* (edit.
                       1961).

Shakespeare's England *Shakespeare's England: An Account of the
                       Life and Manners of his Age* (2 vols., Ox-
                       ford, 1916).

Tilley   Morris Palmer Tilley, *A Dictionary of the
                       Proverbs in England in the Sixteenth and
                       Seventeenth Centuries* (Ann Arbor, 1950).

Ford's other works are normally cited from the standard three-volume edition by Dyce. The reissue by A. H. Bullen (1895) follows Dyce for text and pagination, though some new material is added. Neither Dyce nor Bullen gives line-numbers, so references are by act and scene followed by volume and page.

Shakespeare quotations are from the one-volume *Complete Works* edited by Peter Alexander (London and Glasgow, edit. 1968). In this work lines are 'numbered as in the great Cambridge edition of Clark and Wright' (presumably the revised edition, 9 vols., 1891–3). This accounts for some anomalies: in Alexander's edition the prose is printed in shorter lines and more frequently divided than in Clark and Wright, so that his '45' may come seven lines after his '40' (as on p. 1); and this has an accumulative effect, as in *Two Gentlemen*, II. iii, where the line numbered '29' is the fortieth of the scene. But references given in the present commentary are accurate within a line or two.

Introduction

I. FORD AND HIS WORKS

John Ford came of an old Devonshire family and was the second son of Thomas Ford of Ilsington, a substantial country gentleman.[1] He was baptized on 17 April 1586, and either he or another 'John Ford Devon Gen.' matriculated at Exeter College, Oxford, on 26 March 1601. On 16 November 1602 Ford was admitted to the Middle Temple, where a number of men from both sides of his family had been members before him—most notably his mother's uncle, the Lord Chief Justice Popham, who was to preside at Raleigh's trial a year later. At this period the Inns of Court were esteemed not only for the legal training they slowly and unmethodically gave but as town residences for young gentlemen, centres of fashion and culture, where members might stay on indefinitely so long as they kept the rules and paid their dues. When Ford arrived at the Middle Temple Marston was in residence there, and had already 'created a precedent for other members of the gentry' by turning playwright;[2] John Davies, the author of *Orchestra* and *Nosce Teipsum*, had just been readmitted after three years' rustication; and Carew made an abortive attempt to study law there in 1612.[3] Other notable figures whose residence coincided with Ford's were John Pym (admitted a few months earlier) and, probably, the future Earl of Clarendon (from 1625). Ford remained at the Middle Temple for many years, indeed we have no indication that

[1] Authorities for the biographical statements in this paragraph are given by Sargeaunt, chaps. I and II.

[2] P. J. Finkelpearl, *John Marston of the Middle Temple* (Cambridge, Mass., 1969), p. 126. See this work generally for the Middle Temple at this period. Appendix A lists important figures at this and other Inns of Court 1590–1610.

[3] See *The Poems of Thomas Carew*, ed. Rhodes Dunlap (Oxford, 1949), p. xvii.

he ever left it. He was suspended for not paying his buttery bill early in 1606 and not reinstated until June 1608; this was a fairly common occurrence and may mean that he had outrun his allowance, or temporarily preferred lodging elsewhere. In 1610 his father died, leaving him £10, which suggests disapproval;[1] but it is possible that some other provision had been made for Ford, since in 1616 he surrendered his rights in some Devon land as a condition of inheriting an annuity of £20. He was never called to the Bar, but may have found other legal employment. In 1617 he was admonished for taking part in an organized protest against the compulsory wearing of caps in hall. In 1638 the commendatory poem prefixed to *The Fancies Chaste and Noble* still addresses him as '*Master Iohn* FORD, *of the middle Temple*'. Nothing certain is heard of him after the appearance early in 1639 of *The Lady's Trial*, the dedication of which he signed. The date of his death is unknown.

Contemporary references to Ford are few and uninformative. The much-quoted lines from William Heminges' *Elegy on Randolph's Finger*—

> Deep In a dumpe Iacke forde alone was gott
> Wth folded Armes and Melancholye hatt[2]—

tell us nothing about the man or his hat, but give a conventional portrait of the melancholy man in allusion to Ford's authorship of *The Lover's Melancholy*. Heminges amuses himself in this way with several other titles, and brings in another play by Ford when he adds 'that wee are troubled wth a broken hart.' *The Lover's Melancholy* is dedicated sociably enough to the members of Gray's Inn, some of whom are specified; among these Ford seems to have been on particularly close terms with the cousin, another John Ford, to whom he dedicated *Love's Sacrifice*. Presumably Ford

---

[1] The law student led astray by the distractions of town life is a frequent subject of contemporary satire (Finkelpearl, pp. 12–15); cf. the well-known bequest by Marston's father of his books and other chamber furniture 'to my s^d son whom I hoped would have profited by them in the study of the law but man proposeth and God disposeth &c.' (*ibid.*, p. 84).

[2] *William Hemminge's Elegy on Randolph's Finger*, ed. G. C. Moore Smith (Oxford, 1923), lines 81–2.

also enjoyed the society of the Middle Temple, since he remained
there so long. He contributed commendatory poems to plays by
several contemporaries, including Webster, Massinger and Shirley,
and received commendatory poems from Shirley and other writers
in return. From the dedication to 'Tis Pity we learn that the Earl
of Peterborough had benefited Ford in some way and had approved
of the play in performance; but with the other noblemen who figure
in his dedications Ford seems not to have been personally acquainted. These meagre facts apart, Ford must be sought in his
writings.

Ford's earliest known publications date from a period when
shortage of money may have 'strengthened the literary urge'.[1]
Fame's Memorial (1606) is an elegy of nearly 170 stanzas on the
death of the Earl of Devonshire, one of the Armada captains and
a successful soldier under Elizabeth; Ford takes occasion to praise
Devonshire's love (first illicit, then impolitic) for Lady Penelope
Rich, the 'Stella' of Sidney. Honour Triumphant (also 1606) is a
prose pamphlet occasioned by an entertainment for the King of
Denmark's visit, at which four noblemen had proposed to maintain 'at Point of Launce and Sword' four chivalrous propositions:
'1. That in Service of Ladies no Knight hath free Will. 2. That it
is Beauty maintaineth the World in Valour. 3. That no fair Lady
was ever false. 4. That none can be perfectly wise but Lovers'.[2]
Ford upholds these same propositions by arguments which, though
sometimes paradoxical or facetious, seem for the most part earnest;
and some of these arguments reappear in the mouth of Giovanni
in the present play (II. v. 14-26). His next known writings, published seven years later, show very different preoccupations.
Christes Bloodie Sweat (by 'I.F.', almost certainly Ford,[3] 1613) is
a long poem designed apparently to call sinners to repentance,
passing from a satirical survey of society to a rather confused but
sometimes powerful presentation of Christian (some would say

[1] Bentley, III, 435. For a complete list of writings attributed to Ford
with summaries of the evidence see Leech, pp. 124-32.

[2] Reported by William Drummond of Hawthornden in a letter of 1 June
1606, Works (Edinburgh, 1711), pp. 231-2.

[3] See M. Joan Sargeaunt, 'Writings ascribed to John Ford by Joseph
Hunter in Chorus Vatum', Review of English Studies, X (1934), 165-74.

Calvinist) doctrine. This poem too finds echoes in *'Tis Pity* (III. vi. 8–30, v. i. 1–30). *The Golden Mean* (also 1613) is a pamphlet of Stoical moralizing, less sombre in tone than *Christes Bloodie Sweat*. In 1615 a pamphlet, now lost, called *Sir Thomas Overburyes Ghost* was entered in the Stationers' Register as the work of 'John Fford gent'.; and Ford's interest in the Overbury affair is also shown by his verses contributed to *Sir Thomas Ouerburie his Wife* (1616). His only other considerable non-dramatic work was *A Line of Life* (1620), a pamphlet similar in substance and tone to *The Golden Mean*.

The plays of which Ford is claimed to have written the whole or a substantial share number eighteen, of which seven have been lost.[1] It is not known when or in what circumstances he began writing for the stage. The fact that no plays can be shown to have been written before 1621 has favoured the assumption that 'Ford's dramatic career began with his collaboration with Dekker'.[2] It is a little odd that he should have begun publishing at the age of twenty, yet made no experiments in the drama until he was thirty-five. Among several lost plays attributed to Ford by Humphrey Moseley in 1660 is a comedy called *An Ill Beginning has a Good End, and a Bad Beginning May have a Good End*; this seems likely enough to be the same lost play as *A Bad Beginning Makes a Good Ending*, which was acted by the King's men at court in the winter of 1612–13.[3] Moseley also ascribes to Ford two other comedies, *The Royal Combat* and *The London Merchant*, which are known only from his list and may have been written at any date. Unfortunately Moseley's attributions are unreliable. Ford's tragi-comedy *The Queen* (first published anonymously in 1653) may also be an early work, though some critics detect in it the influence of

---

[1] Leech, *loc. cit.*, includes some dramatic work attributed to Ford but omitted by Bentley, III, 433–64.

[2] Leech, p. 127; though Leech finds that 'a reasonable case has been made out' for Ford's share in a 'Beaumont and Fletcher' play, *The Laws of Candy*, which may date from 1619 (p. 131).

[3] See Bentley, III, 444–6. These attributions occur in a list of twenty-six plays with authors (sometimes wrongly) attached, entered to Moseley in the Stationers' Register. As Bentley remarks, 'the 1660 title seems foolishly redundant'; perhaps Moseley attempted to give alternative versions and his *and* (written '&') should have been 'or'.

Burton's *Anatomy of Melancholy* (1621).[1] The plays that we can date most precisely fall within a period of collaboration with several other dramatists; and the earliest of these is *The Witch of Edmonton*, written with Thomas Dekker and William Rowley between April and December 1621.[2] It is very likely that Ford wrote a substantial part of *The Spanish Gipsy*, a tragi-comedy licensed for performance in July 1623 and published in 1653 over the names of Rowley and Thomas Middleton.[3] Between the autumn of 1623 and that of 1624 Ford took part in at least four other collaborative works: *The Sun's Darling*, *The Fairy Knight*, *The Bristow Merchant* (all with Dekker), and *A Late Murder of the Son upon the Mother* (a catchpenny production, quickly put together by Ford, Dekker, Rowley and John Webster).[4] Of these four plays only the masque-like *Sun's Darling* survives. This burst of literary activity must have earned Ford some money, but the collaborations were probably enjoyable and we need not suppose that he was writing for bread.

The seven extant plays written independently by Ford were all published between 1629 and 1639. They are *The Lover's Melancholy* (1629), *The Broken Heart*, *'Tis Pity*, *Love's Sacrifice* (all 1633), *Perkin Warbeck* (1634), *The Fancies Chaste and Noble* (1638) and *The Lady's Trial* (1639). On the (perhaps rash) assumption that performance followed soon after composition we can date *The Lover's Melancholy* shortly before 24 November 1628, when it was licensed and acted by the King's men; and *The Lady's Trial* shortly before 3 May 1638, when it was licensed for 'Beeston's boys'.[5] The chronology of the other plays is obscure. *Perkin*

[1] E.g. G. F. Sensabaugh, *The Tragic Muse of John Ford* (Stanford, 1944), pp. 54–6.

[2] Bentley, III, 269–72.

[3] For argument on this point see H. Dugdale Sykes, *Sidelights on Elizabethan Drama* (1924), pp. 183–99; Sargeaunt, pp. 41–57; Oliver, pp. 29–34; Leech, pp. 32–4.

[4] Bentley, III, 459–61, 249–50, 247–8, 252–6. Ford's hand has also been found in two scenes of *The Welsh Ambassador*, for which Dekker is claimed as the main author and which was written about 1623. See Bentley, III, 267–8; Oliver pp. 34–7.

[5] Authority for all statements in this and the next paragraph about Ford's independent plays will be found in Bentley, III, 438–64.

Warbeck must have been written after the publication of Bacon's *History of King Henry VII* in 1622, but for the rest no such evidence is available. *'Tis Pity*, *The Broken Heart* and *Perkin Warbeck* are better plays than *The Lover's Melancholy*, but need not therefore have been written later.[1] The title-pages of *'Tis Pity*, *Love's Sacrifice*, *Perkin Warbeck* and *The Fancies* declare that these plays were 'acted by the Queen's Majesty's servants, at the Phoenix in Drury Lane'. This might seem at first glance to establish a *terminus a quo* in 1625, when Christopher Beeston, who owned the Phoenix theatre, formed the troupe known as Queen Henrietta's men. But this troupe inherited plays from the repertories of Beeston's earlier companies, who had been acting at the Phoenix since 1617; and as Bentley points out, 'the company named on the title-page is usually the one which produced the play most recently, not originally.'[2] Thus Massinger's *A New Way to Pay Old Debts* was, like *'Tis Pity* and *Love's Sacrifice*, published in 1633 as '*acted at the Phoenix in Drury-Lane, by the Queenes Maiesties seruants*'; but we know from its topical content that the play had been written as early as 1621 or 1622, and must have been first performed either by Prince Charles's men or by the Lady Elizabeth's men.[3] Nor, of course, was this an unusual interval to elapse between first performance and publication. Another Phoenix play published in 1633 was Rowley's *All's Lost by Lust*, which had been acted in 1619 or 1620.[4] *The Witch of Edmonton*, *The Spanish Gipsy* and *The Sun's Darling* had all been written for Beeston's early companies, were in the repertory of the Queen's men during

---

[1] On this point see Bentley, III, 449.

[2] Bentley, IV, 566.

[3] Bentley, IV, 801–3. For the Phoenix and its companies see Bentley, I, 158–259, 324–42; VI, 47–77. Beeston opened the theatre with Queen Anne's men, who were followed in turn by Prince Charles's (I) men, the Lady Elizabeth's men, Queen Henrietta's men and (from October 1637) Beeston's boys. In at least one case doubt exists as to whether 'her Maiesties Servants' on a title-page refers to Queen Henrietta's company or Queen Anne's (Bentley, I, 251).

[4] Bentley, V, 1018–20. Of nine datable plays from the Phoenix repertory published 1630–33 only three were less than six years old. The others included *The Jew of Malta* and Part I of Heywood's *Fair Maid of the West* (written before 1610), besides three plays written for Beeston's early companies (Bentley, I, 254–8).

the 1630s and remained unpublished till the 1650s.[1]

The Broken Heart, like *The Lover's Melancholy*, was acted by the King's men, though at what date is unknown; to these two Black-friars plays should perhaps be added the lost *Beauty in a Trance*, ascribed to Ford by Moseley and acted by the King's men in the winter of 1630.[2] H. J. Oliver and G. E. Bentley have suggested that these plays were written before the Phoenix plays, and that Ford made an agreement to switch from the King's men to the Queen's 'at least a year or so before 1633'.[3] This conjecture may of course be right, but seems to have met with rather more deference than it deserves.[4] The evidence which supports it is meagre and mostly negative. It perpetuates that 'huddling of [Ford's] dramatic development into the short period between 1628 and 1633' to which Bentley elsewhere objects.[5] And it neglects the fact (obscured perhaps by his supposed 'tutelage' to Dekker) that Ford had already written for Beeston and the Phoenix during the period 1621–4. We have no very strong grounds for supposing that Ford had successive regular engagements with these theatres: but if we are to suppose this, we may as easily suppose that he wrote *'Tis Pity*, *Love's Sacrifice* and *Perkin Warbeck* during what might be called his early Phoenix period, *before* writing anything for Black-friars. On this view *'Tis Pity* and *Love's Sacrifice* may have been written at any time between 1617 and 1628 (though 1624 should probably be excluded as too crowded a year), and *Perkin Warbeck* during the second half of this period.[6] There would be nothing

---

[1] Bentley, III, 270–2, 459–61; IV, 893–5.

[2] It has been argued that Ford wrote part of a 'Beaumont and Fletcher' play, *The Fair Maid of the Inn*, which was licensed for the King's men in January 1626; also that Robert Howard's *The Great Favourite, or The Duke of Lerma* (1668) is founded on a play Ford wrote for the King's men which may be identical with *Beauty in a Trance* (Leech, pp. 129–31).

[3] Bentley, III, 441–2; cf. Oliver, pp. 47–9.

[4] E.g. from Brian Morris, ed. *The Broken Heart* (1965), pp. ix–x and *'Tis Pity* (1968), pp. vii–viii. Even Leech, who on critical grounds sees *'Tis Pity* and *Love's Sacrifice* as early plays, hesitates to depart from Bentley's very tentative chronology (pp. 37, 49).

[5] Bentley, III, 449.

[6] It has been suggested that *Perkin Warbeck* is a product of the Dekker-Ford collaboration; for references and a discussion see the edition by P. Ure (1968), pp. xxviii–xxxv.

extraordinary about these plays having survived in the Phoenix repertory for sixteen years without any record of performance.[1] All that need have happened shortly before 1633 is that Ford decided to publish them, and came to some arrangement with Beeston for this purpose.[2] *The Fancies* and *The Lady's Trial* would then be seen as belonging to a later period of work for the Phoenix. But nothing is easier than to frame theories where so little is known.

2. SOURCES

In *'Tis Pity* Ford apparently keeps to no single source, but there are several tales of incest between siblings which may have influenced the construction and treatment of his main plot. The one which offers most parallels is that of François de Rosset, 'Des Amours Incestueuses d'vn Frère & d'vne Soeur', in *Les Histoires Tragiques de Nostre Temps* (Paris, 1615).[3] This story tells of Lyzaran and Doralice, son and daughter of a French country gentleman, identical in beauty (cf. *'Tis Pity*, I. ii. 237–8) and devoted to each other from infancy. Their love develops or reveals its sexual character when Lyzaran first revisits home after four years at 'college' (boarding-school), where, like Giovanni at the University of Bologna, he has been a brilliant student. Doralice, like Annabella, has many suitors, but her father arranges a marriage with the rich and elderly Timandre, who persists in his courtship despite many snubs (Doralice 'luy faisoit mille affronts, lors qu'il l'accostoit'; cf. Soranzo and Annabella at III. ii. 14–49). Lyzaran

---

[1] The Revels Office book survives only in incomplete transcription and includes no Jacobean entries earlier than 1622. It is silent as to the licensing and performance of *'Tis Pity*, *Love's Sacrifice*, *The Broken Heart*, *Perkin Warbeck* and *The Fancies*. See *The Dramatic Records of Sir Henry Herbert*, ed. Joseph Quincy Adams (New Haven and London, 1917).

[2] Companies did not, of course, favour the publication of plays, and it was a condition of Brome's contract with the Salisbury Court theatre in 1635 that he should publish none without permission (Bentley, III, 52–3; cf. IV, 566–7).

[3] Reprinted 1615, 1616, 1619; first pointed out as a source by Henry Weber, ed. *The Works of Beaumont and Fletcher* (1812), I, 179. Rosset's story is apparently based on an historical episode of 1603 recorded by Pierre Matthieu in his *Histoire de France . . . durant Sept Annees de Paix* (Paris, 1606), II, 617 ff. For extracts from Rosset see Appendix I.

comforts Doralice by assuring her of his continued love; like Giovanni, he is present at his sister's wedding; he takes up lodging with Doralice and Timandre, and after some inner conflict on Doralice's part she and her brother become lovers. The affair remains unsuspected until they are caught 'sur le faict' by a servant woman, who reproaches Doralice and warns her of the risk she is running. Doralice abuses, beats and dismisses the servant, an incident Rosset dwells upon with some indignation. The servant reveals the affair to Timandre, who hides his feelings until his own observation confirms the story; and even then he suppresses his desire for vengeance and merely forbids Lyzaran his house. This leads to a violent scene between Doralice and Timandre (cf. IV. iii.) in which he accuses her of shameful, filthy behaviour, but offers complete forgiveness if she will repent. Meanwhile Lyzaran has returned to his parents' house. After some months the lovers can bear their separation no longer and by a concerted arrangement flee the district, taking Doralice's jewels. Hearing the news from Timandre, their father falls prostrate with shock and their mother almost dies (cf. the death of Florio). Lyzaran and Doralice are eventually discovered in Paris and are arrested one night as they lie in bed; Doralice is four months pregnant by her brother. The pair are condemned to be executed, though Doralice seeks to take all the blame upon herself (cf. v. i. 21–3). At their execution Doralice makes a moving speech of repentance, and both brother and sister impress the onlookers by their courage, youth and beauty.

I find it easy to believe that Ford had this story in mind, though perhaps only at the back of his mind, when he wrote 'Tis Pity. Besides the more obvious resemblances it seems significant that the shrewish side of Annabella's nature, which appears rather extraneous to the play (it is seen in her taunting of Soranzo in III. ii and in the 'waspish perverseness and loud fault-finding' reported by Vasques at IV. iii. 165–6), is also present in Doralice. Rosset's story also resembles 'Tis Pity in its provincial setting ('Tis Pity is the only independent play by Ford which has no concern with the court or courtiers) and in some domestic touches (Doralice, like Annabella, has music lessons). Emil Koeppel has suggested that

Rosset's erroneous reference to the identical brother of Ariosto's heroine Bradamante by the name of 'Richardet' provided Ford with a name for Richardetto.[1] If Ford was remembering Rosset, then he may have thought of Giovanni's return from Bologna less than three months before the action begins (I. i. 48) as following an uninterrupted absence of some years, like Lyzaran's return from 'college', which would make the development of a violent passion between brother and sister somewhat more credible. It is even possible that Annabella's failure to recognize Giovanni when she first sees him on stage at I. ii. 131-5 (confusedly explained as the result of his having been reduced by grief to the 'shadow of a man'—though she has just described him as the 'blessed shape Of some celestial creature') may survive from an earlier conception of Ford's, in which she was to have fallen in love with her brother on his return (like Lyzaran, 'si beau, si scauant, & desia grand') in the moments before she identified him.

Another story of incest is related in the eleventh of Ovid's *Heroides*,[2] which would almost certainly have been known to Ford. Macareus and Canace, son and daughter of Eolus, love each other secretly for nine months, after which time a child is born. Canace's nurse tries to smuggle the baby out of Eolus's palace, but its cries are heard by Eolus, who orders it to be put to death by exposure and sends Canace a sword with which to kill herself. Before doing so she writes a letter to Macareus (who has fled to sanctuary), under the form of which their story is related. Ovid creates compassion for Canace by emphasizing her youth and ignorance—she knows nothing of sexual love or of childbirth until fatally involved in them—and the whole narrative is coloured by her anguish and remorse. The role of Putana is prefigured by Canace's accomplice-nurse, and Annabella's letter to her brother (v. i) by Canace's. Parthenius in his *Erotica*[3] tells a less well-known story in which

---

[1] *Quellen-Studien zu den Dramen George Chapman's . . . und John Ford's* (Strasburg, 1897), p. 181; see below, p. 125.

[2] Or *Epistolae Heroidum*; available in many editions and in the translation by George Turbervile (1567, repr. several times).

[3] The Greek text and a Latin translation were published as *Parthenii Nicaensis de Amatoriis Affectionibus Liber* (Basle, 1531); a French version as *Les Affections de Divers Amans, Faictes et Rassemblées par Parthenius de*

interest is concentrated on the brother. Leucippus, a renowned young warrior, earns the enmity of Aphrodite, who causes him to fall in love with his sister. He strives to overcome his passion, fails, dramatically confesses his feelings to his mother, and threatens suicide if she does not help him. It is here if anywhere that Ford takes a hint from Parthenius, for neither Ovid nor Rosset focuses attention upon the moment when the incestuous passion has to be revealed. The mother of Leucippus persuades the girl to take her brother as a lover. The affair is discovered by the girl's fiancé, who without telling the full story leads her father to her room when brother and sister are together. The girl tries to escape but is stabbed to death by her father in mistake for the supposed seducer; and in the confusion which follows the father is killed by Leucippus. The most likely place for Ford to have found this story is in the compilation by Thomas Heywood called *Gunaikeion: or, Nine Bookes of Various History concerning Women* (1624), which also includes a version of the story of Canace.[1] It is tempting to see the *Gunaikeion* as a source for *'Tis Pity*, not least because it would provide a *terminus a quo* for the date. Some resemblances of treatment can be found. Heywood makes Leucippus the victim not of Aphrodite but of psycho-physiological causes, in a way that would have interested Ford: 'want of action, in a stirring braine, and bodie, wrought this distemperature'. He also represents Leucippus as 'ashamed . . . to court his sister . . . because he knew her modest' (Parthenius does not discuss this problem), and makes her fiancé into 'a gentleman of a noble familie' (Parthenius says nothing of his status). His version of Canace's story is meagre, but when describing her 'passionate letter to her brother' he adds the non-Ovidian detail that 'she first besought him to have a care of

Nicée (Paris, 1555); an English version in 1624 (see text, below). Parthenius was first pointed out as a possible source by W. Bang and H. de Vocht in *Englische Studien*, xxxvi (1906), 392–3. For a literal modern translation see *The Love-Romances of Parthenius*, ed. and trans. S. Gaselee (Loeb Classical Library, 1916), pp. 268–73.

[1] Bang and de Vocht, *op. cit.* (pp. 429–31, 169), draw attention to the *Gunaikeion* but do not mention that it includes the story of Canace as well as that of Leucippus.

his safety' (cf. '*Tis Pity*, v. i. 46–52). His description of the nurse as 'acquainted with all their wicked proceedings' also seems more suggestive of Putana than does Ovid's. But these resemblances may very well be coincidental, and Ford need not have known the story of Leucippus in any version.

S. P. Sherman has argued[1] that Ford found inspiration in an Italian tragedy based on Ovid's story—*Canace* (1546), by Sperone Speroni. No translation of *Canace* seems ever to have been published, and from Ford's attempt at IV. iii. 59–63 of '*Tis Pity* to simulate an Italian song it does not look as though he would have been able to read the original; though a friend or colleague could have translated all or some of it for his benefit. As a play *Canace* is utterly unlike '*Tis Pity*, being a series of monologues, dialogues and choruses in the Senecan manner arranged so that Macareo and Canace never speak to each other, or even appear together. The plot can have given Ford nothing that he would not more readily have found in Ovid. What Sherman chiefly insists on, however, is a similarity of outlook between the two writers, both of whom he takes to be glorifying sexual love in terms of a 'decadent and vicious idealism':

> Speroni, like Ford, bends all his energies to the task of soliciting pity and admiration for the unnatural lovers. . . . He, too, makes his hero a Renaissance Platonist, identifying the good and the beautiful and the worship of beauty with the love of virtue. Macareo, like Giovanni, regards his love as a proof of his intelligence:
>
> > Amo infinitamente, e volentieri
> > Le bellezze, i costumi, e le virtuti
> > Di mia sorella, e parmi
> > Che indegnamente degno
> > Saria di sentimento, e di ragione
> > Chi si rare excellenze non amasse
> > Ovunque ei le trovasse.

These lines mean 'I love, infinitely and willingly, the beauty, manners and virtues of my sister; and I hold him unworthy of feeling and reason who would not love such rare excellences

[1] Sherman, pp. xlvii–liii.

wherever he found them.' But for a full statement of Macareo's
views we must read the continuation of this passage, which
Sherman leaves unquoted:

> Ma degnamente indegno
> Sarei desser mai nato,
> Se con vile intentione
> A dishonesto fine
> Mosso fossi ad amare
> Le sue doti divine.
> Vili seco, io nol nego,
> E dishoneste fur le opere mie:
> Ma nhebbi quel, che non pur non sperai
> Ma mai non disiai.
> Spinse alhor le mie membra
> Non propria elettione,
> Ma uno impeto fatal, che intorno al core
> Mi s' avolse in quel punto, e in vece dalma
> Mosse il mio corpo frale,
> E sforzollo affar cosa
> Horribile a chi lode:
> A chi la fe odiosa.
> Da quel tempo io son visso
> Vile, e grave a me stesso, e se non fosse
> Che io son caro a colei che mi e si cara;
> Gia con la propria mano
> Harei di vita scosse
> Queste mie membre ardite, e scelerate.
> Hor vivo, e con lempiezza
> Del mio grave peccato,
> Che spense il nome, e la ragion fraterna,
> Do cagione a mio padre
> Di divenir spietato. . . .

(But I would be unworthy of ever having been born if I had been
moved to love her divine gifts with an evil intention and to shameful ends. Vile and shameful, I do not deny it, were my actions
with her; but from them I had that which I neither hoped for nor
even desired. My limbs were guided, not by my own choice, but
by a fatal impulsion which captured my heart at that time, and in
the place of my soul moved my frail body, and forced it to act a
deed horrible to him who hears of it and hateful to him who has
done it. Since that time I have lived an odious burden to myself,
and were it not that I am dear to her who is so dear to me I should

already with my own hands have shaken the life from these
daring and wicked limbs of mine. Now I live, and with the
impiety of my grave sin, which took from me the name and
nature of a brother, I give my father cause to become merciless.
...[1]

Far from justifying incest, Macareo (a better Platonist than
Giovanni) believes and feels that coition with his sister has been
something shameful, unworthy of the spiritual love he feels for her.
Sherman further writes (p. xlix):

> Both lovers die unrepentant and in unshaken loyalty to each
> other. Canace, on her deathbed, says that her one consolation is
> the knowledge that her name and face will live in the heart of her
> brother, to whom she sends this message:

> > Moriamo volentieri
> > Tu per esser fedele, io per amare.

This is precisely the spirit of Annabella's

> Che morte più dolce che morire per amore?

In fact these words of Canace's ('Let us die willingly, you for being
faithful, I for loving') are addressed not to Macareo but to the
nurse, condemned to die for her complicity. It is true that the
brother and sister speak movingly of their continuing love, but to
call them 'unrepentant' is romantic falsification: both express
bitter regret for their physical relationship, neither seeks to justify
it, and the predominant mood of the play is one of grief and remorse for irremediable error, mingled with pity for the doomed
pair.[2]

The only person in *Canace* who defends or excuses incest is
Deiopea, mother of the lovers, when pleading with Eolus for their

---

[1] Text supplied by Dr Christina Roaf from *Tragedia di Ms Sperone
Speroni* (Valgrisi, Venice, 1546), sigs. 13ᵛ, 14; translation by Mr. D. V.
Reidy and Dr Roaf.

[2] Rymer compares *Canace* favourably with Beaumont and Fletcher's
King and No King because instead of giving an offensive display of
incestuous passion Speroni begins his action when punishment is about
to overtake the lovers, so that the audience is able to feel pity for them
(*Tragedies of the Last Age*, 1677; p. 49 in *Critical Works of Thomas Rymer*,
ed. Zimansky, New Haven and London, 1956).

lives. She does so strictly in terms of the classical mythology which makes one dimension of the play (Eolus himself is the god of winds). First, the children have been driven on by malicious Venus, who is avenging old wrongs done by Eolus to her son Aeneas: this story is mentioned several times in the play, and explains why Macareo describes his impulse of lust as though it were an external force. Second, incest is practised by important gods such as Jupiter and Juno and therefore does not deserve to be punished by death when practised by mortals. These arguments have some dramatic validity, but it is plain that they would not have been offered to sixteenth-century readers as a general defence of incest. The controversy which followed the appearance of *Canace* was not about whether incest was a great sin—which was common ground—but about whether the incestuous lovers were so wholly wicked as to fall below Aristotle's definition of a tragic character. In short, the supposed similarity of treatment between *Canace* and '*Tis Pity* rests upon a drastic misreading of one, if not both, of these plays; and there is really no evidence that Ford used *Canace* as a source.

There are interesting parallels between '*Tis Pity* and Middleton's *Women Beware Women*. In each play a half-witted young heir, with some elementary sexuality but a preference for childish games, accompanied by a servant who is half-playmate and half-keeper, is propelled by his guardian towards marriage with a beautiful young girl who is involved in an incestuous relationship elsewhere (Isabella becomes the mistress of her uncle). The comic scenes are often very similar:

Guar. Do you hear, sir ? follow me; I must new school you.
Ward. School me ? I scorn that now; I am past schooling.
        (*Women Beware Women*, ed. Roma Gill, 1968, I. ii. 126–7)

Don. Get you home sir, and look you keep within doors till I
    return.
Ber. How! that were a jest indeed; I scorn it i'faith.
                ('*Tis Pity*, II. iv. 37–9)

One of these dramatists may well have been recalling the work of the other, but we cannot tell which play was written first: *Women Beware Women* may have been written at any time between 1610 and 1627, though a late date is favoured by recent critical opinion. The source for the story of Isabella and her uncle is *Les Amours Tragiques d'Hypolite et Isabelle* (Paris, 1610), translated in 1628 as *The True History of the Tragicke Loves of Hipolito and Isabella, Neapolitans*. If Ford knew this tale he may have found a prefiguring of Vasques in the treacherous servant planted to spy upon the incestuous love-affair:

> Hipolito . . . let passe no occasion that might binde him to him; but vnder the disguize of a fained affection to their seruice, and acknowledgment of his obligation (this crafty malitious fellow) soothes, and lulles them a sleepe.
>
> (*Tragicke Loves*, p. 105; cf. *'Tis Pity*, IV. iii. 243–54)

But this source includes no group corresponding to Donado-Bergetto-Poggio or Guardiano-Ward-Sordido. The existence of two such similar comic groups may suggest a reference to contemporary personages.[1]

In two scenes Ford may have been remembering the Beaumont and Fletcher play *A King and No King* (licensed 1611). This play centres on the love of Arbaces and Panthea, who until the final scene believe themselves to be brother and sister. Like *'Tis Pity*, it includes a scene of mounting sexual tension in which the pair walk hand in hand:

> *Arb.*   Brothers and Sisters may
>   Walke hand in hand together; so will we:
>   Come neerer: Is there any hurt in this?
> *Pan.* I hope not.
> *Arb.*   Faith theres none at all.
>
> (*A King and No King*, IV. iv. 142–5[2])

---

[1] There are some parallels with the forced marriage made in 1617 between Frances Coke and John Villiers, the mentally unstable brother of the reigning favourite (for a summary see L. Stone, *The Crisis of the Aristocracy, 1558–1641*, Oxford, 1965, p. 596).

[2] Quotations from *The Dramatic Works in the Beaumont and Fletcher Canon*, gen. ed. F. Bowers (Cambridge, 1966–   ), II.

Gio. Come sister, lend your hand, let's walk together.
 I hope you need not blush to walk with me;
 Here's none but you and I.
Ann. How's this?
Gio. Faith, I mean no harm.   (*'Tis Pity*, I. ii. 176–80)

And when Arbaces, tormented by passion and guilt, asks the coward soldier Bessus for help, Bessus cheerfully replies 'O you would have a bout with her? Ile do 't, Ile do 't Ifaith. . . . and when this is dispatcht, if you have a minde to your Mother tell me, and you shall see Ile set it hard' (III. iii. 147–69). This recalls Putana's role and outlook and her speech at II. i. 48–50: 'I say still, if a young wench feel the fit upon her, let her take anybody, father or brother, all is one.'

It has not previously been noticed how closely the attempted murder of Soranzo and its sequel (III. vii, ix) resembles a famous historical episode, the attempted murder of Paolo Sarpi in Venice on 5 October 1607. Sarpi, a Servite friar, had championed the rights of the Venetian state against the claims of the Pope during the disputes of 1605–7. Shortly after these disputes had been settled Sarpi was ambushed late one evening, stabbed with a weapon that was at first thought to be poisoned, and left for dead. The leader of the attack was Ridolfi Poma, reputed a 'man of honour' and an intimate of the Pope's nephew, Cardinal Borghese. Sarpi's friend and biographer Fulgenzio Micanzio, who was in Venice at the time, records that after the attack Poma and his accomplices

> saved themselves in the house of the Popes Nuncio, then resident at *Venice*, and from thence the same night they past to the shore, where having prepared a flat Boat . . . they went therein towards *Ravenna*, or (as some said) to *Ferrara*. But it being divulg'd, and understood that the *Assasines* had first sheltred themselves in the Nuncios house, the insurrection and concourse of the people was so great, that although it were very late at night, the house was surrounded, and what with reproachful words, and popular clamours, the person of the *Nuncio* himself was seen to be in manifest danger. . . .[1]

[1] 'The Life of the Most Learned Father Paul', prefixed to *The History of the Council of Trent* by 'Pietro Soave Polano' [Sarpi], trans. N. Brent,

This affair made a great stir when Ford was twenty-one years old, and though the involvement of the Papal Nuncio may be apocryphal[1] it is the kind of detail that would have been readily believed in Protestant countries. In 'Tis Pity Grimaldi is a Roman gentleman 'greatly in favour with the Cardinal' (II. iii. 44), who in this case is also the Nuncio. He ambushes Bergetto in mistake for Soranzo, kills him with a poisoned rapier, takes refuge in the Nuncio's house and thence escapes to Rome, after a scene in which angry citizens assemble about the Nuncio's gate but are contemptuously dismissed. Ford's memory may have been stimulated by the pseudonymous publication of Sarpi's History of the Council of Trent (1619, 1620), or his History of the Interdict (1626).[2] The preface to the English version of the latter work briefly alludes to the attack on Sarpi, and some verses on the subject are appended to the Latin version; but neither gives the historical details Ford seems to have remembered and used.

Lastly, when Ford came to organize his material into a play he incurred a large and obvious debt to Shakespeare. His thematic pattern follows that of Romeo and Juliet in its contrast of joyful, but forbidden and finally tragic, love with a background of malice and strife. His grouping of secondary figures about the lovers recalls the same play. Friar Bonaventura is modelled on Friar Laurence, combining as he does the roles of affectionate confidant

---

edit. 1676, p. lviii. This biography by Micanzio was written soon after Sarpi's death in 1622, though not published until 1646 or translated until 1651. For contemporary accounts of the attack on Sarpi see the sentence on Poma and his accomplices passed by the Council of Ten and translated into French and English (text in Arabella Campbell, Life of Fra Paolo Sarpi, 1869, pp. 240–3); also The Life and Letters of Sir Henry Wotton, ed. L. P. Smith (Oxford, 1907), I, 404–8.

[1] That the Nuncio sheltered the murderers is mentioned by Micanzio alone among the early sources I have seen, and is accepted by later biographers on his authority. Whatever the truth, it is extremely likely that a rumour to that effect became current in Venice and elsewhere.

[2] Historia del Concilio Tridentino, London, 1619; trans. N. Brent, London, 1620; The History of the Quarrels of Pope Paul V with the State of Venice, trans. C[hristopher] P[otter], London, 1626; Interdicti Veneti Historia, recens ex Italico conversus [by William Bedell], Cambridge, 1626.

and spokesman for the traditional moral order—perhaps also in the lack of success which follows his attempts to help. Putana may have her original in Ovid, but is developed as a more cynical and depraved version of Juliet's Nurse; Florio is 'like Capulet in his more expansive moods'[1]; and Soranzo corresponds roughly in the grouping to County Paris. Echoes of *Hamlet* and *Othello* occur in the play (II. ii. 146–7, v. v. 84), and the death of Bergetto in III. vii has been likened by Weber to that of Roderigo (*Othello*, v. i).

3. DATE

Neither the facts of Ford's career nor the sources of the play give much help in dating *'Tis Pity*, as the above discussions will have made clear. Not even the opening of the Phoenix theatre in 1617 provides a firm *terminus a quo*, for the company with which Beeston opened that theatre had already been in existence for many years;[2] and of course Ford may have written the play any length of time before offering it for performance. The latest work we can regard as a very probable source is Rosset's (1615). Such evidence as the text provides is likewise inconclusive. In the dedication to the Earl of Peterborough Ford refers to the play as '*These First Fruites* of my leasure'. Until twenty years ago this was usually taken to mean that it was his earliest piece of writing, or rather the earliest that in 1633 he cared to remember or acknowledge: to insist on its precedence over the occasional pieces of 1606 or the shares in unpublished collaborative plays would be taking a dedication too literally.[3] On this construction *'Tis Pity* could be seen as the first-written of the series of independent plays Ford had begun to publish in 1629, and was so seen by Reed, Weber (who dated it 1623–4), Gifford, Fleay (c. 1626), Sargeaunt (1625–8) and Davril (1626–7).[4] But in 1953 Oliver called all in doubt by

[1] Oliver, p. 87.

[2] Bentley, I, 158–60; for Ford's supposed engagement with the Phoenix see above, pp. xxiv–xxvi.

[3] Cf. Shakespeare's dedicatory description of *Venus and Adonis* as 'the first heire of my invention'.

[4] Reed, VIII, 3, 7; Weber, I, x–xi; Gifford in *Quarterly Review*, VI (1811), 465; F. G. Fleay, *A Biographical Chronicle of the English Drama*,

interpreting the phrase to mean 'only that the play was the first product of a particular period of leisure following some special employment' (p. 47). This is certainly a possible reading, but it seems to me that if Ford had been referring to a period which was now past he would have written 'my late leisure' or 'my leisure of ten years since'. The phrase will naturally bear Oliver's construction only if the leisure is still being enjoyed and is, moreover, something Peterborough may be expected to know about. Conceivably Peterborough himself had created the leisure by providing Ford with a small income or procuring him a sinecure: Ford goes on to acknowledge some undefined obligation, and one possible meaning of 'first fruits' is the tribute due to a patron from whom a place is held. In that case one would expect the leisure to have begun comparatively recently, which would mean a late date for the play. But all this is very speculative, and on balance the traditional reading of the phrase seems the more likely of the two. Ford liked to emphasize his amateur status as a writer—the dedication to *The Lover's Melancholy* describes it as the result of 'some leisurable houres'—and '*Fruites* of my leasure' is probably no more than a gentlemanly periphrasis for 'writings'.

It seems probable from references in this dedication and in the apology for misprints which follows the play that a performance of *'Tis Pity* had taken place not very long before publication. Thus in the dedication Ford acknowledges Peterborough's 'Noble allowance of [the play] in the Action', i.e. his approval of it in performance; and the apology appeals to 'the generall Commendation deserued by the Actors, in their Presentment of this Tragedy'. Bentley rightly observes (III, 463) that if this note has any meaning at all it must refer to a production recent enough for the reader to recall. But there is no reason to suppose, as Bentley does, that this production was the first. Plays which had been many years in repertory were regularly furnished with dedications of this kind

---

1559–1642 (1891), I, 233; Sargeaunt, pp. 21–3; Robert Davril, *Le Drame de John Ford* (Paris, 1954), pp. 68–71. Reed and Weber seem to have read '*Fruites* of my leasure in the Action' together as meaning dramatic recreations or performances; but 'in the Action' almost certainly qualifies 'Allowance' (see below pp. 3–4).

when they eventually appeared in print,[1] and the production
referred to may quite well have been a revival. In support of a late
date Sherman (p. xxxvi) points out that on 12 May 1631 Sir Giles
Alington was heavily fined by the Court of High Commission for
going through a form of marriage with the daughter of his half-
sister. The few facts that are known about this affair[2] show no
resemblance to the story of Giovanni and Annabella except in
the general fact of incest, which had been treated by dramatists
long before. The scandal may, as Sherman suggests, have inspired
Ford to write *'Tis Pity*; but it may equally well have inspired
Beeston to mount a new production of the most striking play about
incest in his repertory. These references to recent performance
therefore give no safe clue to the date of composition.[3]

Most recent writers on *'Tis Pity* have nevertheless favoured a
late date, *c.* 1629–33.[4] The rather tenuous hypothesis (discussed
above, pp. xxv–xxvi) that Ford's 'Phoenix plays' were written after
his 'Blackfriars plays' has been widely accepted; also, where facts
are few the publication date acquires a strong gravitational pull.
Yet the title-page is almost the only link between this play and its

---

[1] Cf. Massinger's *A New Way to Pay Old Debts* (1633), the dedication
of which gives no hint of its previous repertory life of from ten to twelve
years.

[2] According to a contemporary letter quoted by Sherman 'it was the
solemnest, the gravest and the severest censure that ever, they say, was
made in that court'. Yet within two months Alington's fines and other
punishments were remitted (*Calendar of State Papers, Domestic, 1631–33*,
pp. 41–2, 62, 90–1, 108). The affair remains obscure owing to the destruction of the Court's records. But it may be that marriages within the tables
of affinity took place less seldom than one would suppose, for the sake of
property rather than of passion, and that offenders were being prosecuted
at this time out of ecclesiastical and financial policy. Strafford writes to
Carlisle on 24 October 1632: 'hear was one Payler fined by the hie Commission 1000£ for an incest, this fine, upon a sute of this Churche [York
Minster] was by his Ma^{ty} bestowed upon them, for buying a paire of
Organs, adorning the Altar, and such sacred uses' (*Facsimiles of National
Manuscripts*, ed. Sir Henry James, Part IV, 1868, p. 55).

[3] In discussing Rider's *The Twins* Bentley recognizes the possibility
that 'the applauded performances noted on the title-page were not the
original ones' (V, 1009).

[4] E.g. Oliver, p. 48; Bentley, III, 463–4; Mark Stavig, *John Ford and the
Traditional Moral Order* (1968), p. 208 n. 1.

supposed period. Ford's presentation of Giovanni owes something to Elizabethan and Jacobean notions of morbid psychology, but there is no specific debt to Burton's *Anatomy of Melancholy* (1621) such as we find in *The Lover's Melancholy*; Ford may have been drawing on earlier books such as Bright's *Treatise of Melancholy* (1586, repr. 1613), or simply on received ideas. The Neoplatonic glorification of love and beauty had been anticipated by Ford himself in *Honour Triumphant* (1606), and gives no ground for connecting *'Tis Pity* with the love-cult fostered by Henrietta Maria. The debt to Heywood's *Gunaikeion* is dubious. But there are many certain or highly probable links between *'Tis Pity* and the years before 1616: echoes of *Tamburlaine* and *Dr. Faustus*,[1] *Hamlet* and *Othello*; borrowings from *Romeo and Juliet*, from Florio,[2] probably from Rosset and from *A King and No King*; recollections of the attack on Sarpi. Another small pointer to an early date may be Bergetto's 'codpiece-point' at III. i. 11–12, for codpieces had been obsolescent since the beginning of the century.[3] On critical grounds, Clifford Leech has argued that among Ford's plays *'Tis Pity* is peculiarly 'Jacobean' in its character:

> Ford learned much, of course, from Shakespeare, but only in one play, *'Tis Pity She's a Whore*, which may have been his first independent work for the theatre, did he attempt to reproduce the tragic manner of the opening years of the century. In that play the characterization is complex in the Jacobean fashion: Giovanni is hero and villain, arousing at once sympathy and revulsion, led by fate or circumstance to a catastrophe that is both a punishment for sin and a predestined doom. We are bound to regard Giovanni as we regard Macbeth or Webster's Vittoria Corombona, seasoning our admiration with horror, our horror with a sense of kinship. It may be that this is Ford's best play: certainly it is the one that most easily wins the attention of the reader who first knows his Shakespeare. But it is not Ford's most characteristic play.

[1] v. i. 19–20, v. 11–12, 45–7, and many other Marlovian lines which have no specific parallels (e.g. I. i. 64–5).

[2] IV. i. 72–3; IV. iii. 59–63, 167–8.

[3] See C. W. and P. Cunnington, *English Costume in the Sixteenth Century* (1954), p. 118.

Leech further describes '*Tis Pity* as 'the play in which he came closest in style and thought to his major predecessors, to Shakespeare and Webster and Chapman'; and again as 'this last, belated Jacobean tragedy.'[1] Verbal and metrical tests applied by Frederick E. Pierce confirm the impression that '*Tis Pity* differs markedly in style from most of Ford's plays. In the use of certain kinds of diction '*Tis Pity* stands at one extreme and the bulk of Ford's drama at the other, with *Love's Sacrifice* in an intermediate position; while in several characteristics of verse and rhyme '*Tis Pity* and *Love's Sacrifice* stand together and are as unlike Ford's other plays as the work of another man might be.[2] On these grounds E. H. C. Oliphant has argued, perhaps too confidently, that both these plays must have been written before 1621.[3] Pierce's findings might possibly be explained otherwise than by differences of date, but in the general context of this problem they deserve not to be ignored.

So far as facts go, '*Tis Pity* may have been written at virtually any date before 1633, or, if Rosset is accepted as a source, between 1615 and 1633. It may quite easily have been a Jacobean play in fact as well as in spirit.

4. THE PLAY

Ford's writings show more imaginative power than intellectual consistency. Human beauty, exalted sexual love are themes he can render in convincing verse; so too are sin, hell-fire, penitence, the notion of lust as a foul infection which must be cleansed by tears and grace. The Marlovian superman impresses Ford, and so does the idea of man controlled by his temperament, or by fate. Even within a single, evidently sincere poem—*Christes Bloodie Sweat*—Calvinist beliefs and attitudes jostle with confessions, incense and beads. It does no real service to Ford's reputation to expound his work in terms of one or two of these ideas and claim that he is only

[1] Leech, pp. 11, 37, 64.
[2] F. E. Pierce, 'The Collaboration of Dekker and Ford', *Anglia*, XXXVI (1912), 141–51.
[3] *Shakespeare and his Fellow-Dramatists* (New York, 1929), II, 18–19.

'satirizing' the rest.[1] In itself, the power of entering into widely
different attitudes and experiences is obviously a great asset to a
playwright; and if Ford sometimes seems unable to assert order,
to resolve contradictions or even notice them, he is not alone
among the dramatists of his age.

The main design of the present work is coherent enough. *'Tis
Pity She's a Whore* is the first English play to take fulfilled incestuous love as its main theme. The subject often provokes a peculiarly strong revulsion, for reasons Freud seems to have explained.[2] When Speroni's *Canace* appeared in 1546 it was attacked
chiefly on the grounds that such a vice could be knowingly
practised only by monsters who deserved no pity: since pity was
needed for tragic catharsis, incest was no fit subject for tragedy.[3]
Ford's play might have been designed to test this proposition. It is
not a 'problem play' making out a case for incest, nor a satirical
melodrama mocking the excesses of heroic love.[4] It is an attempt to
raise this theme to the level of tragedy by creating compassion for
the lovers while enforcing the necessary judgements against them.
Giovanni and Annabella are brave, beautiful, eloquent and
accomplished. Like fruit-picking in Eden, their love is evil only
because misplaced. It is expressed in poetry which is sensuous and
passionate, but also at times exalted, imaginative, even idealistic.
They delight in their affinity and their 'united hearts'; each appre-
hends the other's beauty as something angelic or divine; yet at
relaxed moments they can talk to each other like quite ordinary
lovers, with a mixture of teasing and tenderness. What is good or
simply human about their love is thrown into relief by the hypo-

[1] As Mark Stavig does in *John Ford and the Traditional Moral Order*
(Madison and London, 1968). Rejecting the romantic view of Ford as a
moral rebel, Stavig goes to the other extreme and interprets his work as
strictly orthodox.

[2] By describing 'taboo' as the social equivalent of neurotic repression:
we dread that which represents what we unconsciously desire. Some such
explanation seems in order because incest creates so much more horror
than what might rationally seem greater crimes, e.g. murder.

[3] The main documents in this controversy are to be included in Dr
Christina Roaf's edition of *Canace*, which is soon to be published at
Bologna.

[4] The views respectively of S. P. Sherman and (substantially) of Professor Stavig.

crisy and murderous malice of the conventionally Italian setting.
But the wrongness of incest was something no seventeenth-century
writer was likely to question, and is a basic assumption of the play.
Giovanni's arguments in defence of the relationship (I. i, II. v) are
not only stage arguments, they are stage bad arguments, plainly
intended to seem self-interested and spurious and reveal his
'ignorance in knowledge'. As the play progresses Annabella is
driven to compound incest with adultery; Giovanni's love finally
expresses itself in murder. Their inevitable destruction is felt to
be just, perhaps the result of divine intervention (IV. ii. 8–9, v. i.
58–9), though repentance seems to have saved Annabella's soul. It
says much for Ford's powers of detachment that he could in his day
present incest, not as an incomprehensible abomination, but as a
tragic error.

Giovanni's intellectual brilliance is vouched for by the Friar's
report of his career at Bologna, though within the play he uses
only the sophomore[1] logic that suits Ford's purpose. Pride in his
wit and learning leads him, like Faustus, to presumptuous inde-
pendence of mind and hence to heretical speculations: he begins by
justifying incest and ends by denying the existence of Heaven and
Hell. At the same time his 'melancholy' temperament (characteristic of a scholar), hard study and solitary habits (I. iii. 5–6,
II. vi. 122–4) make him a prey to psychological disorders. When
the play opens he is already a victim of love-melancholy or
heroical love—so called, according to Burton, 'because commonly
Gallants, Noblemen, and the most generous spirits are possessed
with it', yet apt to lose this honourable title and become 'burning
Lust, a Disease, Phrensy, Madness, Hell' which 'begets rapes,
incests, murders'.[2] Frustration reduces him to the state in which
he launches on his fatal course (I. ii). Making love with his sister
brings them both a damnable happiness; Giovanni, instead of
repenting, defends their actions by more false logic; passion and
intellectual pride, each reinforcing the other, pervert his reason
and will to the end of the play and by v. vi have brought him to

---

[1] *Sophomore:* literally 'wise fool'; in the U.S.A., a second-year university
student.

[2] Burton, III, 43, 54, 60.

madness. Annabella is contrasted with Giovanni rather as in *The White Devil* Vittoria is contrasted with Flamineo: each woman is a passionate creature who sins from 'blood', but can repent because she lacks her brother's self-deluding pride. Giovanni's love culminates in murder, Annabella's in earnest attempts to save his life and soul. But her part, like Vittoria's, is fragmentary and exploited for different purposes in different scenes. She initiates little; she has no long speeches until IV. iii, where Ford is chiefly interested in working up a climax of rhetorical violence; her only soliloquy is the plaintive meditation upon sin and death in V. i. If her first repentance (III. vi) is to be taken as genuine, we should expect her to have been faithful to Soranzo for at least a short period after marriage; but she continues to be Giovanni's mistress (V. iii. 1-12), and at V. v. 15 he reproaches her as though she were turning 'honest' for the first time. Perhaps Ford did not think the story through. But conceivably the first repentance is a blind to encourage the Friar to marry her to Soranzo, which she now needs as a screen for her pregnancy. This would make her a less pathetic, more actively wicked figure than she is usually taken to be, but would agree with her contemptuous taunting of Soranzo before and after marriage and with what looks like an ironical promise at III. ii. 61-2.

Within certain limits Ford's handling of the theme of forbidden passion is masterly. The movement of Giovanni's feelings in the early part of the play—from attempts at rationalization, through despair, overmastering desire and intolerable tension, to rapturous success and post-coital contentment—is superbly presented; and Ford conveys passion and sensuality without the pornographic gloating found in *A King and No King*, and in some work of his own. (Despite its catchpenny title *'Tis Pity* is not a titillating play.) But too much should not be claimed for the piece as a study specifically of incest. As Eliot points out, 'the passion of Giovanni and Annabella is not shown as an affinity of temperament due to identity of blood'[1]; nor is Ford curious about other psychological peculiarities of the double relationship; nor does he explain how

[1] 'John Ford', *Selected Essays* (edit. 1951), p. 197 (for extracts see below pp. 140-1).

this brother and sister, presumably brought up together, can appear to be experiencing love at first sight. (He could have solved or avoided some of these problems by emphasizing Giovanni's long absence at Bologna.[1]) In a sense the play is not about incest: it is about passionate love which demands a unity more complete, more self-sufficient than human life permits.[2] For such love incest can provide a type without being rendered in psychological detail. Giovanni regards the exchange of vows in I. ii as a unique and particularly sacred form of marriage. Thus when the Friar urges him to persuade his sister to take a husband, he cries

> Marriage? Why, that's to damn her; that's to prove
> Her greedy of variety of lust. (II. v. 41–2)

And at II. vi. 35–41 we find that the ring destined for Annabella's husband is being worn by Giovanni himself. Both in their vow (which is actually formulated by Annabella) and in later speeches (especially II. i. 26–7) he demands total loyalty in love; he kills Annabella for denying this loyalty; he dismembers her to obtain it, by a crazy symbolism to 'possess her heart'. What seems inconsistent with this fiercely exclusive passion is that the murder does not take place on Annabella's wedding-day. Instead, Giovanni sees her married with only a few expressions of jealousy and ill-will; Professor Stavig reproves him (p. 113) for his rudeness. Still more surprising, at V. iii. 1–12 he declares himself perfectly happy to be sharing Annabella's bed with Soranzo! If the rest of Ford's presentation of Giovanni and his kind of love has any validity at all, it is hard to imagine him content with such an arrangement.[3]

[1] In the cinema adaptation of 'Tis Pity by G. P. Griffi (see below, p. lxii), when Annabella asks who Giovanni is, at I. ii. 131–4, Putana replies 'That's your brother, just back from Bologna'. For something similar in a probable source see above, p. xxviii.

[2] This and other ideas are interestingly developed by R. J. Kaufmann in 'Ford's Tragic Perspective', Texas Studies in Literature and Language, I (1960), 522–37; repr. in Elizabethan Drama: Modern Essays in Criticism, ed. Kaufmann (New York, 1961).

[3] In Griffi's film Annabella for some time remains faithful to Giovanni by refusing to consummate the marriage. (This provides a way, though not an easy way, of interpreting her words at IV. iii. 48–9.) She betrays her brother, not by repenting, but by making love with Soranzo when he succeeds in arousing her desire; so that Giovanni's accusation at V. v. 1–3 is true. This of course is departing some way from the play.

One must recognize that Ford is writing not only a tragedy of incest but also an Italianate tragedy of intrigue, or what might better be called a stage thriller; and that the two do not always work well together. From the point of view of his main tragic theme nothing of the first importance would have been lost if Giovanni *had* murdered Annabella on her wedding-day, and the action would have been simple, logical and expressive. Instead, Ford has contrived a complicated plot requiring two repentances by Annabella and two sets of murderous revels. The relationship between Giovanni and Annabella does not develop between II. i and v. v—they are alone together on-stage only at II. vi. 130–6—and is obscured apparently for some months (v. vi. 39–41).[1] Meanwhile the sub-plots thicken. Hippolita's intrigue provides some brisk melodrama and adds something to Ford's presentation of Soranzo, perhaps of Parma; but the plottings of Richardetto and Grimaldi are irrelevant and perfunctory. Despite some effective scenes (the Friar's hell-fire sermon, Bergetto's death, the Cardinal's rebuke to the citizens), much of the material which fills up the middle of the play is of very secondary interest. To wind up one revenge plot and dispose of Philotis, Ford conscientiously writes a short scene in verse (IV. ii) which is very hard to act without causing laughter ('Uncle, shall I resolve to be a nun?'). In Act v the relationship of the lovers becomes central again and the play returns to the tragic level. But it may be questioned whether Ford quite recaptures the control, or the unifying inspiration, of the early scenes. The needless letter in blood, the 'policy' of Vasques, the chorus of Banditti properly belong to the stylized world of the sub-plots. This context explains how in v. iii Ford can sacrifice consistency about one of his major themes—Giovanni's possessiveness—to gain the immediate dramatic effect of confident delight shattered by ominous messages.

Ford's verse, of course, dignifies even the more mechanical parts of the play. It is clear, melodious, rhythmically sensitive and often finely expressive (as in the last thirty lines of I. ii, most of II. v, much of v. v). But its musical and emotional effects are some-

---

[1] The main action of *'Tis Pity* uses a slower kind of time than Richardetto's sub-plot, though the two are almost coterminous.

times gained at the expense of meaning, which is thinned down or evacuated (Ford's poetry was much admired by Swinburne). Sometimes this matters very little, as when a solemn but absurd couplet closes IV. i. At other times it matters more:

> Fair Annabella, should I here repeat
> The story of my life, we might lose time.   (v. v. 52–3)

Well, they would; but why *should* Giovanni repeat the story of his life, here or elsewhere? The lines have the dying fall, the vague nostalgic emotion that Ford wants ('Fair . . . life . . . time' bids farewell to beauty), but the sentence is not meaningful even as madness. The rest of this speech has a haunting lyrical movement, but is appropriate only in the most general way to the speaker and scene. Someone beautiful and beloved is to die, but from lines 61–2 we should suppose it was a child;[1] and when Giovanni, who has just rejected the notion of an after-life, sends Annabella to 'a throne Of innocence and sanctity in Heaven', we cannot be sure whether Ford intends a meaning or is being absent-minded. Another strain Ford sometimes indulges rather uncritically is that of heroic defiance in the Tamburlaine manner. At I. i. 64–5 Giovanni says

> It were more ease to stop the ocean
> From floats and ebbs, than to dissuade my vows.

These thunderous lines must surely express resolution, however misdirected; but eighteen lines later Giovanni agrees to try and discipline his 'vows' by penitential exercises. Possibly Ford intends this contradiction to show Giovanni's unsettled state of mind; possibly his comparison of himself to 'a well-grown oak' at v. iii. 77 is meant to seem as ridiculous as it does; possibly the inflated hyperboles at v. iii. 58–62 and v. v. 9–14 convey incipient madness: but it is hard to be sure. What Stavig believes is being satirically presented, as heroics, T. B. Tomlinson thinks is being offered uncritically as heroism.[2] These uncertainties blur the edges of Ford's ambitious tragic design.

---

[1] The same hyperbole is more appropriately used at the beginning of Milton's 'On the Death of a fair Infant dying of a Cough'.

[2] Tomlinson, *A Study of Elizabethan and Jacobean Tragedy* (Cambridge, 1964), p. 273 (see also pp. 266–8); Stavig, pp. 118–19.

It is the beginning and the end of this love-affair that seem most strongly to have possessed Ford's imagination. For the first four scenes almost everything is alive and sensitively controlled. The exposition is swift, shocking and poignant: the incest theme is fully explicit by line 37, and Giovanni's passion has driven two men who love and admire each other into irreconcilable conflict. After a convincingly authoritative rebuke the Friar descends to pleading and to practical counsels. His religion, his distress and his concern for Giovanni are all felt as genuine, and his grave compassionate speeches command our assent as Giovanni's do not. His view of Giovanni as one whose understanding and will are corrupted by passion is confirmed by Giovanni's own language: from the controlled pathos of lines 12–19 Giovanni passes to the extravagance of 20–3, and thence to a climax of unreason with the illogical violence of 'Curse to my joys!' and the wild claim that religion itself justifies incest. He reveres the Friar but disregards most of what he has to say, fears the rod of vengeance but is on the way to rejecting religion (84) because it stands in the way of his desires. As Robert Ornstein writes, 'it requires a peculiar insensitivity to the nuances of characterization and verse in 'Tis Pity to treat Giovanni as Ford's spokesman'.[1] His intelligence is vouched for by the Friar's praise, his energy and will-power by the rhythmic drive of his speeches; everything else proclaims his disordered and dangerous state of mind, warns us that his next step may take him over a precipice.

Without losing momentum Ford switches from the confessional to the street, from emotional to physical violence and from verse to harsh idiomatic prose. Parma is more meanly contentious than the Verona of Romeo and Juliet: Annabella's two noble suitors speak proud words but behave as cowards, Soranzo is known to be the lover of a married woman, and the third suitor (equally cowardly) is an idiot. Putana too is a simpler and coarser creature than Juliet's nurse: the terms *charge*, *tutress*, become ironical almost at once as she reviews the candidates in terms of the dearth of flesh and a capacity for standing upright. The most im-

---

[1] *The Moral Vision of Jacobean Tragedy* (Madison and Milwaukee, 1965), p. 207.

portant fact about Annabella is that she is in love with Giovanni, and this fact Ford skilfully keeps in reserve until the crisis forced by Giovanni's declaration. In the early part of the scene she therefore says little. But it is not entirely fanciful to interpret her silence somewhat as Kaufmann does: 'these suitors [and Putana] create a predisposition in favor of the girl's need for love; we grow sensitive to her isolation and learn to justify her despair of beauty and dignity in her life'.[1]

Giovanni's second appearance is more impressive than his first, and not only by contrast with Putana's cackle. He does not now justify his passion by sophistries, but sees himself as 'lost'; the knelling repetition in line 144, the heavy, wearied movement of the lines which follow make suffering actual, and 'fate' something more than a refuge from responsibility. Nevertheless there is a touch of Pistolian swagger about his rallying of courage in lines 160-2. His wooing is not an easy or efficient piece of seduction: an approach by way of brother-and-sister intimacy (176, 188) is abandoned in impatience; the ardent speeches which follow give some outlet to his feelings, but all the response he receives is astonishment ('D'ee mock me, or flatter me?'). When he offers Annabella his dagger it is inconceivable that she should use it, yet in context this does not operate as a piece of play-acting but as an expression of frustration and despair, an attempt to force home the life-and-death seriousness of what she has treated as a joke. From then on Giovanni's speech is eloquent, urgent and (except for the equivocation at 241-2) sincere. That lie shows the unscrupulousness of the passion by which Giovanni is driven, and helps to limit the stature he achieves in this scene; yet it seems born of desperation, not of cunning, and is apparently neither sustained nor believed. Ford's verse makes it difficult for us to feel anything but relief when the long suspense of the wooing, the tension of Giovanni's speeches culminating in the broken rhythms of lines 243-4, are dissolved in Annabella's reply and the peace of line 246. Then, as Brian Morris writes (p. xi), 'their sense of the solemnity, the awfulness, of their love is brilliantly captured in the marvellous delicacy of the ritual which follows'. Yet the dread crime of incest

---

[1] *Op. cit.*, p. 366 in *Elizabethan Drama*.

is humanized. The last phrases of the scene are simple and exqui-
sitely natural, and make their love seem equally so. When Giovanni and Annabella depart to 'kiss and sleep' we do not feel
revulsion but compassion, perhaps even something like fascinated
admiration, for the pair whose lovemaking is so simple, yet so
dangerous that they ask each other for reassurance until almost the
last moment. The close of this scene marks the high point of
Ford's dramatic art.

The opening of the third scene swiftly changes our perspective.
Florio and Donado personify the bourgeois life which, equally
with the Friar's creed, the lovers have rejected: prudent, peace-
able, reasonably honest, kindly, even generous (as at II. vi. 53–6,
115–18). These virtues are rooted in real life, we know and depend
on them. Florio's language, so straightforward and yet so tactful,
makes us momentarily share his point of view—which means
thinking of the lovers as outsiders. Florio is not, of course, quite so
straightforward as he appears. He implies that the competition for
Annabella's hand is completely open, whereas in fact he is backing
Soranzo[1] (just as Donado is not above bribing Putana to put in a
good word for Bergetto at II. vi. 17–19). This is a venial piece of
hypocrisy, perhaps no more than politeness requires. If we
assume that Florio knows about Soranzo's affair with Hippolita
(as 'Parma' does, IV. i. 43), then we must take it that he is con-
doning adultery so as to forward an ambitious match; Ford's
presentation of bourgeois life would then seem a good deal darker.
But Florio never refers to this affair, nor has the play such consistency of detail that we have to infer that he knows of it. Ford's
intention is, I think, not to portray a mercenary father or a corrupt
society,[2] but to keep his play in touch with the world of workaday
virtue and common sense and to contrast this with the intense

[1] See I. ii. 53–6. Ford seems not too deeply concerned about Florio's
hypocrisy, for these lines are spoken with Donado on-stage.

[2] Any play which presents a number of characters living in one place
can, of course, be discussed as a portrayal of 'society'; and if several of the
characters are wicked, then 'society is shown as corrupt'. What we see of
society in 'Tis Pity is imperfect, but I do not think this an important
theme—as it is in Jonson's comedies, The Revenger's Tragedy or The White
Devil. For a different view see Irving Ribner, Jacobean Tragedy (1962),
p. 164 ff.; Kaufmann, pp. 366–9; Morris, pp. xvi–xxii.

private world of the lovers, rather as the experience of Polonius is contrasted with that of Hamlet. Yet the one wholly sincere and innocent person in Parma is Bergetto, endearingly associated here with May-games, hobby-horses, puppet-shows and other unsophisticated delights.

When Giovanni and Annabella reappear, the most noticeable effect of their sexual intercourse is that it has made them happy. Giovanni, as usual, has most to say, and his mood encompasses both the exaltation of II. i. 1–5, 16–20 and the playfulness of 9–15; when he gets a bit above himself Annabella can tease him with a reminder of his previous anguish—'*Now* you can talk'. His bawdy is part of a delighted exploration of their new intimacy. The whole conversation is tenderly imagined, and Annabella brings it to a close with a quiet couplet of affection and trust that would serve for the chastest heroine (39–40). Putana's entrance strikes a jarring note, and her speech at 48–50 has a crudeness not found in Giovanni's jokes. We have seen that a forbidden sexual relationship can be personal and loving; Putana reduces love to sex, and sex to an itch that anyone can scratch. Yet her 'natural' attitude is like enough to Giovanni's (9–12) to act as a hostile parody, which is the more disconcerting as coming from an ally. One's response is partly protective, partly dismayed: 'It isn't like that—but perhaps it comes to that.' And Annabella is now bound to Putana in strict complicity, emphasized by their reaction to Florio's voice. The schoolgirlish adroitness with which she hides her appalling secret is both realistic and pathetic. Florio and his guests enter, the normal world reasserts itself, and the talk is all of domestic affection and courtesy—punctuated by phrases recalling Annabella's new incompatible experience ('your virtue . . . parts I love . . . touch an instrument, she could have done 't').

The next scene brings Soranzo into prominence, his conventional poeticizings almost comically interrupted by 'love's annoys' in the person of Hippolita. Surface sentiment and morality are disturbed to reveal egotism, brutality, lust; Soranzo's masterpiece of hypocrisy is to justify his vices in terms of his affected virtues (II. ii. 86–101). Then from II. ii. 102 onwards Ford allows the sub-plots to proliferate, as Hippolita, Vasques, Grimaldi and

Richardetto plot complicated crimes involving treachery and poison. For a while the lovers are kept fairly well in view, and it is clear that until Annabella is found to be pregnant their affair is perfectly happy. Giovanni's confession (II. v) shows him still passionately in love and no longer troubled by fears: his real reply to the Friar's warnings is not the parade of false logic (13–26) but the rapturous description of Annabella (45–58, 67), glowing with joy, pride and confidence. At the end of the following scene Giovanni and Annabella are briefly alone together; he is wearing the ring intended for her husband; she teases him with the ring given by Donado and he responds by being 'jealous', but none of this is very serious, and Act II closes with the lovers looking forward to another 'sweet night'. When in III. ii Soranzo comes to court Annabella, who dislikes him (II. i. 28–30), she has no difficulty at all in showing the loyalty Giovanni demands. But from the time Annabella hears the Friar's 'lecture' their relationship is obscured, apparently for a period of months. As already noted, it is not clear whether Annabella's first repentance is to be taken as genuine, nor how the affair is supposed to have developed after her marriage. From IV. iii onwards events are consistent on the assumption that he has continued to be her lover, though this is not stated until IV. iii. 215. Soranzo has now discovered that she is pregnant by another man; in keeping with his behaviour towards Hippolita he regards himself as an injured innocent and maltreats Annabella, who defies him and, literally, sings the praises of her absent lover. By the beginning of Act v Soranzo has discovered who this lover is, and Ford focuses once more on the relationship between Giovanni and Annabella as it moves into its last phase under threat of retribution.

He does not, however, bring them together until v. v, and it soon becomes clear that they are separated by more than physical distance. In v. i Annabella appears in a new role. She is now genuinely repentant and takes the orthodox view of their past conduct ('My conscience now stands up against my lust'). Logically though not chronologically v. i seems the direct sequel of III. vi, the expected response to the Friar's sermon. Coming where it does in the play this mood is rather unexpected. True, Annabella's

feelings towards Soranzo were softened by the play-acting at IV.
iii. 106–46, but she has since discovered that his kindness was
false: he has imprisoned her and is planning revenge. Her speeches
in V. i have nothing about them characteristic of the passionate
partner of Giovanni's love, the virago who has just been taunting
her husband. They convey sorrow and weariness, but not the
sharp self-disgust that we find in (say) Beatrice's last speeches in
The Changeling. Interpreted psychologically, this musical mourn-
ing might seem a little self-indulgent; the moral maxims at v. i.
12–13, 28–9 might even sound complacent. But in this scene
Annabella is not a person so much as a personification—an alle-
gorical figure of Repentance.

Giovanni meanwhile has remained, in essentials, the same figure
as in Act I. He knows nothing of his sister's transformation, and
an ironic effect is produced at v. iii. 11–12 when he rejoices in the
glory of their 'two united hearts'. This glory has been the most
meaningful thing in his life, and he can neither repudiate it nor
endure existence without it. Bidden to repent and fly, he refuses to
do either: he will meet his enemies half-way. From the Christian
point of view this behaviour is sinful and deluded, yet it displays
courage and a kind of integrity which earns some of Ford's admiration. Giovanni's speeches at the end of v. iii are, I think, meant to
seem heroic though wrong-headed, like the last speeches of
Coriolanus or Macbeth: Stavig's term, 'role-playing', is too reduc-
tive and perhaps too sophisticated. But it is possible, as already
noted, that the orotund hyperboles of v. iii. 58–62 and v. v. 9–14
are intended to register the beginnings of mental unbalance.

When Giovanni visits Annabella in her chamber (v. v) he
apparently expects, as Vasques does, that they will once more make
love. His bitter opening speech makes it plain that she has refused,
and told him that their affair is over. To Giovanni Annabella's
virtue is the blackest vice: a betrayal which nullifies both the life
and the probable death he has chosen. Only by killing the faithless
sister can he express his anger, frustration, outraged pride and
despair. He can resolve on this, not only because he is wrought up
by tension, danger and incipient madness (46), but because he has
for months lived at odds with religion and conventional morality,

recognizing no law but that of his love. He remains true to the pact
Annabella has broken, and since he can no longer be her lover,
must kill her. Once he is committed to this act some of his anger
falls away and he is free to admire Annabella's beauty for the last
time, to experience some form of love, to weep for the death he is
about to inflict. Meanwhile her role is still defined by repentant
orthodoxy and sisterly love. Each looks back to a lost innocence,
but for Giovanni this is represented by their joyful lovemaking
('our simplicity', 3), whereas Annabella finds it in their presexual
relationship ('Brother, dear brother,' 16). Intimately connected
in birth, love and death, the two are nevertheless living in different
worlds. Despite Annabella's talk of their danger, time stands still
in this room as Ford brings out all the strangeness and pathos of
the situation: the verse moves on with a slow, haunting, sometimes
rather diffuse music, counterpointing death with the language of
ordinary life ('a dining-time'), relaxed speculation ('The schoolmen say . . .'), and love. Asking and dispensing forgiveness, Annabella dies in such an odour of sanctity that Giovanni's valediction—

> Go thou, white in thy soul, to fill a throne
> Of innocence and sanctity in heaven—

takes on almost a choric value. The bed becomes an altar. Her
dying words—'Brother, unkind, unkind'—again invoke the fraternal relationship and reproach Giovanni for violating it, not only
by his present cruelty but by his 'unkind', i.e. unnatural, love. In
the one sense her reproach is poignantly understated; in the other,
it is an accusation which it hardly lies in her mouth to make.

At the close of this scene Giovanni still speaks fairly soberly, but
in v. vi it becomes clear that the shock of having killed his sister
has pushed him over the line between what Kaufmann calls 'auto-
intoxication' and madness. The dismembering, the speeches to
Soranzo ('Look well upon 't; d' ee know it?)' and Florio ('How
much I have deserved to be your son') all have the same crazy
logic. Then in his last few speeches he recaptures lucidity and dies
unrepentant, satisfied with the terms he has made ('Mercy? Why, I
have found it in this justice'), and with no thoughts of after-life
except a wish to be once more delighted by Annabella's beauty.

The orthodox condemnation of the lovers is pronounced by the Cardinal, protector of well-born murderers; his rapacity at v. vi 148–50 shows the Church's justice corrupted in a meaner, more commonplace way than Giovanni's. But since he is an impressively-clad figure suited to the dignity of a Chorus, Ford lets him speak the banal but compassionate closing couplets.

As a piece of theatre '*Tis Pity* has obvious merits: swift and lucid exposition; an action developing through confrontation, conflict, ironic reversal and surprise; plenty of suspense; skilful contrasts of mood from scene to scene, and a shocking *coup de théâtre* in the last. The sub-plots provide some stage excitement and can seldom be heard to creak (IV. ii is an exception). Few Jacobean tragedies outside Shakespeare stand up so well to revival. Certainly the combination of sex, violence, horror and rebellious philosophizing might be expected to make good 'box-office', now as in the seventeenth century, but Ford handles these materials with restraint: even Giovanni's entrance with the bleeding heart is justified by its psychological and symbolic truth. As a tragedy the play succeeds by virtue of the power and insight with which Ford presents the main theme and action in the first, second and fifth acts. His grasp of the tragic possibilities of incest may be contrasted with that shown in Beaumont and Fletcher's *A King and No King*, where it is first sensationally exploited and then magically disappears; or in Massinger's *Unnatural Combat*, where it is wholly and simply evil. Ford has imagined it as a love which offends against religion and a visibly imperfect society, but can still be joyful and tender; as a misconceived, doomed, but not wholly ignoble attempt by two persons to live solely by and for each other. Because Giovanni is the more fully and consistently drawn of these two figures, and because even his last actions (though distorted by madness) express the values with which he began, '*Tis Pity* is his tragedy rather than Annabella's.

He has sometimes been condemned in inappropriate terms. Eliot found the play lacking in significance partly because 'Giovanni is merely selfish and self-willed, . . . almost a monster of egotism'. If any degree of egotism were alien to human nature, the Elizabethan drama would be less meaningful than it is; and other

critics have found Giovanni interesting because of this very
quality. Kaufmann traces, rather fancifully, a deterioration in his
character 'as he grows less and less capable of crediting any other
feelings but his own'. By the time he murders Annabella, he 'is no
longer *with* his sister. He acts unilaterally. . . . His selfishness has
grown perfect, his love become an abstract and self-orienting
thing' (p. 369). Likewise Morris: 'In the last Act Giovanni acts
not *with* but *upon* his sister. His love has become selfish' (p. xxii). I
am not sure that the play is as completely edifying as this account
suggests, or that 'selfishness' in any ordinary sense should be
added to Giovanni's more obvious sins. He believes that their
lovemaking delights Annabella as much as himself (II. i. 13–14, v.
46), and until almost the end he glories in their united hearts. We
do not see him performing acts of kindness and consideration for
Annabella—how many does Romeo perform for Juliet, or Antony
for Cleopatra?—but neither do we see him being callous, unre-
sponsive or mean. Like most passionate lovers he is possessive, but
he demands no more faithfulness than he gives. The only sense in
which he 'acts upon' Annabella is that when, at the height of their
catastrophe, she rejects him and breaks their pact, he kills her. This
is hardly an act of selfish pleasure. It is, of course, arguable that
love which expresses itself in murder no longer deserves its name.
Yet this killing seems an act of love indeed compared with the
sacrifice to Soranzo's vanity which it forestalls.

Egotist or not, Giovanni is reckless and absolute, a true des-
cendant of Tamburlaine and Faustus. His sweet earthly fruition,
his perfect bliss and sole felicity, is the beautiful girl who happens
to be his sister. For the sake of the ideal happiness represented by
their love he defies society, religion, death, damnation and reason.
Within their relationship he demands and gives total loyalty. For a
while the ideal happiness becomes real, and he can tell her:

> I . . . hold myself in being king of thee
> More great, than were I king of all the world.
>
> (II. i. 18–20)

He might easily have added, in the words of a poem published in
the same year with *'Tis Pity*,

> Who is so safe as wee ? where none can doe
> Treason to us, except one of us two.

When God, fate, or the outside world asserts itself and destroys him, he hardly notices it. The world he valued has already been destroyed by the virtue of its other inhabitant.

5. STAGE HISTORY

'*Tis Pity* was still in the Phoenix repertory on 10 August 1639, when it was included in a list of forty-five plays which 'properly & of right belong to the sayd House'. These plays were claimed for the Phoenix by William Beeston, who had succeeded his father as manager and now obtained from the Lord Chamberlain an order forbidding other companies to 'intermedle wth or Act' them.[1] The earliest datable performance was witnessed on 9 September 1661 by Pepys, who thought it 'a simple play and ill acted'. This performance took place at the Salisbury Court theatre, which Beeston had purchased in 1652;[2] but by 1661 he no longer managed his own troupe and was letting the theatre to various companies. The production Pepys saw was probably mounted by the veteran George Jolly and his company, who had spent much of the interregnum touring in Germany.[3] In April 1663 Jolly's troupe began playing at Norwich and continued there for several months.[4] Edward Browne (son of Sir Thomas) paid 1s 6d to see 'Tis pity She is a whore' at the King's Arms, Norwich, in 1662 or 1663,[5] and it is very likely that he too saw Jolly's production. Professor Nicoll suggests that this 'probably undistinguished troupe' was forced to use 'a repertoire of lesser-known or then largely ignored Elizabethan plays'.[6] However this may be (and the evidence is

---

[1] Bentley, I, 330–1.

[2] Bentley, II, 373.

[3] See Leslie Hotson, *The Commonwealth and Restoration Stage* (1928), pp. 167–94; Allardyce Nicoll, *A History of English Drama, 1600–1900*, I (1965), 292, 308–11.

[4] B. M. Wagner, 'George Jolly at Norwich', *Review of English Studies*, VI (1930), 449–52.

[5] Brit. Mus. MS. Sloane 1900, f.63 (Browne's notebook, quoted by Wagner, *loc. cit.*).

[6] Nicoll, I, 310–11.

slender), Jolly's was the last recorded production of *'Tis Pity* for 260 years.[1] As the Restoration developed its own repertory earlier pieces naturally fell out of favour; and the theme of this play precluded any eighteenth-century revival. Even when the Elizabethan dramatists were again greatly esteemed and *'Tis Pity* had been reprinted in several editions, the idea of its being performed was as repulsive to critics as it would have been to the Lord Chamberlain, or to theatre audiences in general. Gifford wrote in 1811 that the play 'carries with it insuperable obstacles to its appearance upon a modern stage'; Hazlitt agreed in 1825 that it 'would no more bear acting, than Lord Byron and Goethé together could have written it'.[2]

The revival of *'Tis Pity* in the theatre began to be conceivable after 6 November 1894, when Maurice Maeterlinck's *Annabella*—a greatly softened adaptation of Ford's play[3]—was produced in Paris at the Théâtre de l'Oeuvre. But it was almost another thirty years before the Phoenix Society gave two 'private' performances of *'Tis Pity* at the Shaftesbury Theatre, London, on 28 and 29 January 1923. In this production the final scene was played without Annabella's heart, and some other, slighter, cuts were made.[4] The main roles were sympathetically played by Ion Swinley and Moyna MacGill, who 'passed over the evil of the blood-relationship between Giovanni and Annabella and insisted

---

[1] The copy of Q described in Rosenbach's 1940 catalogue as marked for 'scenic changes and off-stage noises' (Bentley, III, 464) is now in Mr Robert H. Taylor's collection at Princeton (information from Mr T. V. Lange). No such directions can be found, though at the end of each Act appears the reminder 'Act [i.e. interval] ready' followed by 'strike' or 'knock' (presumably as a signal for music). These indications and the seventeenth-century handwritings employed suggest a Restoration production. Otherwise the prompt notes consist of the usual readying entries and reminders for props ('prouide wine'; 'Giouanni wth a Heart'). The copy in the Newberry Library, Chicago, has also been marked for a seventeenth-century performance.

[2] See below, pp. 134–5; William Hazlitt, 'The Plain Speaker', no. 27, *Works*, ed. P. P. Howe (1930–4), XII, 311.

[3] *Annabella. 'Tis Pity She's a Whore . . . adapté et traduit par* M. M. (Paris, 1895). For the production (by Marcel Schwob) see Sargeaunt, p. 171; Robert Davril, *Le Drame de John Ford* (Paris, 1954), p. 496.

[4] Davril, pp. 499–500.

... upon its aspect as a final barrier to their love'.[1] The select audiences were deeply impressed and reviews were favourable, though the *Times* critic (apparently unaware of the cuts) found the last scene an anticlimax, merely conventional 'theatre'. The same critic cared little for the sub-plots, but both James Agate and Desmond McCarthy found delightful comedy and intense pathos in Harold Scott's performance as Bergetto. Another private performance of *'Tis Pity* was given by the Arts Theatre Club in London on Sunday 30 December 1934, using a two-storey stage.[2] Terence De Marney, as Giovanni, 'seemed to have Hamlet in mind as his model'; Bergetto was again played by Harold Scott. The production was highly realistic, and in the final scene Giovanni brought in 'what appears to be a genuine, and it is certainly a dripping, heart'. The *Times* critic would have preferred less realism and more poetry, but thought the performance 'extremely capable in its kind'.

The first public performance of *'Tis Pity* since the seventeenth century was given by Donald Wolfit and Company on 13 May 1940. This production opened at the Cambridge Arts Theatre and was still in Wolfit's repertory in January 1941, when two matinée performances were given at the Strand Theatre, London.[3] Brother and sister were again very sympathetically presented, as proud and happy lovers thwarted by fate; the audience was alienated only by Giovanni's final 'despairing frenzy'. Wolfit, as Giovanni, was 'excellent in the passages of curt and natural speech without trying to under-act the grand extravagances of the part', and Rosalind

---

[1] *The Times*, 30 January 1923, p. 8. See also reviews published on 3 February in *The Contemporary Theatre* (by James Agate; repr. in his *Brief Chronicles*, 1943) and *The New Statesman* (by Desmond McCarthy). For quotations from these articles see Sargeaunt, pp. 171–3 and Davril, pp. 489–90, 499–500.

[2] See *The Times*, 1 January 1935, p. 12, from which the quotations are taken; also Sargeaunt, p. 173 and Davril, p. 500.

[3] Audrey Williamson writes that after two London performances (she does not mention Cambridge), 'the inevitable Public Informer stepped in and nipped this Jacobean blossom in the bud') *Theatre of Two Decades*, 1951, p. 281). But only two London performances were scheduled, on 18 and 23 January; Wolfit's season of 'Lunchtime Shakespeare' (in which *'Tis Pity* was the only non-Shakespearean item) then closed on 25 January (*Times* theatre columns).

Iden as Annabella was 'all dew and flame'. The penultimate scene, quietly played, was felt to reach high tragedy, though the subsequent appearance of Annabella's skewered heart brought 'slightly horrified smiles'.[1] Its fitness for the twentieth-century stage having thus been established, *'Tis Pity* has fairly often been produced by both amateur and professional companies. A production was mounted by the Nottingham Playhouse in 1955, and another by the A.D.C., at the Cambridge Arts Theatre, in October 1958. In this last production the minor performances were for once the most admired, especially those of Richard Cottrell as Bergetto, Eleanor Bron as Putana, Derek Jacobi as Soranzo and Clive Swift as Vasques.[2]

Sex and violence rather than romantic love were emphasized in David Thompson's production at the Mermaid Theatre, London, in August and September 1961. Thompson staged the play with a bed upon the upper stage and 'with the sensationalism of an X certificate film'.[3] Zena Walker, as Annabella, displayed what one critic called 'a lovely solemn naughtiness' and another 'sly, knowing flirtatiousness', fluttering her eyelashes at both Giovanni and Soranzo. One reviewer of this production questioned whether the play deserved to be taken seriously. Roger Gellert complained that after an interesting beginning, *'Tis Pity*

> ends in a routine Jacobean holocaust of revenge and macabre heroics. We learn nothing of the peculiar strains and stresses of an incestuous relationship, which after the scene of avowal no longer seems to interest Ford except as a springboard for violence. . . . The sub-plotting, almost a caricature of its kind, is of an otiose complexity that defies attention or description.[4]

[1] See *The Times*, 16 May 1940, p. 4 and 20 January 1941, p. 6; also Williamson, pp. 281–2. The *Times* critic of 1941 is indebted not only to T. S. Eliot but to his predecessor of 1923, whose sentences he garbles.

[2] All these performers, then undergraduates, have made careers in the professional theatre. Annabella was played by Margaret Drabble ('too phlegmatic') and Giovanni by Richard Marquand. Elsie Kemp (now Mrs Schmitz) co-directed with Richard Cottrell and has kindly supplied cuttings about this and other productions. For reviews see *Cambridge Daily News*, 15 October, p. 11 and *The Times*, 16 October, p. 4.

[3] *The Times*, 30 August, p. 11.

[4] *New Statesman*, 8 September, p. 320; see also *Spectator*, 15 September, pp. 353–4.

In 1968 John David's Bristol Old Vic production emphasized, according to a programme note, the lovers' 'Contempt for the sordid hypocrisy and sly 'dishonesty of the establishment'.

In the summer of 1972 two productions of '*Tis Pity* were to be found touring Britain simultaneously. One, directed by David Giles, was mounted by the Actors' Company in association with the Cambridge Theatre Company and under the general artistic direction of Richard Cottrell; playing in Victorian costume, Ian McKellen and Felicity Kendal seem to have given an unsympathetic, not wholly satisfying presentation of the lovers.[1] The other, directed by Roland Joffé, was 'an unpretentious, capable, low-budget production'[2] designed for touring by the National Theatre. In this version Nicholas Clay played Giovanni as a sensitive, bewildered, victimized adolescent; Anna Carteret's Annabella seemed a gay irresponsible creature until subdued by the menaces of the Friar; and Putana was transformed into a giggling male tutor (played by James Hayes).

'*Tis Pity* has been translated into French by Georges Pillement as *Dommage qu'elle soit une Prostituée* (Paris, 1925), and was performed in Paris in 1934 (at the Atelier), 1948 (at the Théâtre Verlaine) and 1961 (at the Théâtre de Paris).[3] This last was a sumptuous production by Luchino Visconti, in which the costumes, music and sets (including a backdrop representing the Teatro Farnese at Parma) made more impression than the main performances (by Alain Delon and Romy Schneider). In December 1958 Eugene Van Grona produced the play at the Orpheum Theatre, New York; Christopher Drake as Giovanni was 'moody, aware, determined, and vindictive', while Ursula Stevens played Annabella with 'first the abandon and then the craft and impenitent derision of a voluptuary'.[4] Radio versions were broadcast on

---

[1] This production appeared at the Lyceum Theatre, Edinburgh, in August; subsequently at the New Theatre, Oxford, and at the Cambridge Arts Theatre.

[2] *New Statesman*, 11 August, pp. 203–4; see also *The Times*, 3 August, p. 13.

[3] Davril, p. 500; *New Yorker*, 15 April 1961, pp. 133–4.

[4] *New York Times*, 6 December 1958. This review mentions a New York production of 1925.

the B.B.C. Third Programme in 1962 and on Radio 3 in 1970. Giuseppe Patroni Griffi has directed a film version[1] in which the sub-plots are removed and some difficulties of the main plot solved by imaginative adaptation (see above, p. xlv notes 1 and 3). Some scenes of Griffi's own devising show real insight into Ford's play. Thus after the consummation of their love Giovanni and Annabella, hiding behind a pillar, see Florio pushing from his room the woman with whom he has spent the night. 'Look at our father!' says Annabella delightedly; later the three go arm-in-arm to breakfast. The tender playfulness of guilty love, the contrast of acceptable with unacceptable sins, the domestic harmony masking deadly secrets are all elements transposed from Ford. Though the version of this film released in London on 2 August 1973 was marred by insensitive dubbing, its visual power was still great, and the main performances came through as excellent—in particular, the obsessive playing of Giovanni by Oliver Tobias (see frontispiece).

6. THE TEXT

The first edition of 'Tis Pity, on which all other editions are based, is a quarto of 38 unnumbered leaves (A²B–K⁴) printed by Nicholas Okes for Richard Collins in 1633. The title-page (reproduced on p. 2) occupies A1, followed by 'The Actors Names' on A1ᵛ and 'The Epistle' on A2–A2ᵛ. The text then runs from B1 to K4, with a blank K4ᵛ. In some copies an extra leaf was inserted containing complimentary verses by Thomas Ellice.[2] For the present edition 35 copies of the quarto have been collated,[3] together with the modern editions listed on pp. xv–xvi.

[1] Giovanni, Oliver Tobias; Annabella, Charlotte Rampling; Soranzo, Fabio Testi. See *Observer* and *Sunday Times*, 5 August 1973.

[2] See pp. 4–5; also W. W. Greg, *A Bibliography of the English Printed Drama to the Restoration* (1939–57), II, 632.

[3] I.e. those in the Bodleian Library (Malone 210 (2), 214 (7), 238 (3)), the British Museum (644.b.37, C.12.g.3 (4), 1481.bb.18, Ashley 756), Eton College, Glasgow University, the Guildhall Library, the National Library of Scotland (H.28.e.12, Bute 233), St John's College Cambridge, the Victoria and Albert Museum (D.25.c.32, F.31.m.37), Worcester College Oxford (Plays 3.14, 4.44); and photocopies of those in the university libraries at Chicago, Cornell, Harvard, Haverford, Illinois,

Although the play was never entered in the Stationer's Register, Ford's dedicatory Epistle shows that he authorized its publication; and the appearance of the quarto suggests that it was printed from a fair copy made by Ford's own hand, or at least under his close supervision. The chief evidence for this is a lavish use of italic type which is not characteristic of Okes's printing but which is found in most of Ford's other plays,[1] though these were printed by several different houses. The italicization of stage-directions, speech-headings and quotations (including letters and songs) is normal, and the similar treatment of many proper nouns and their derivatives (*Bononia, Isralite, Promethean*) also follows a fairly widespread practice. But the quarto of *'Tis Pity* frequently, though not consistently, uses italic (often with capitals) for purposes outside these conventions: for titles and other terms denoting particular persons, especially in vocatives (*Signior, Your Grace,* the *Bandetti,* this *Fryars* falshood, *Chardge, Sweet-heart, My Brother,* the rich *Magnifico, Madam Merchant,* a *Gallant hang-man,* my *Hot Hare, This old Damnable hagge*); for abstractions, personifications and antitheses (*Minde . . . Body,* etc., II. v. 14–26; let *My youth* Reuell, III. viii. 17–18; *Busie opinion,* v. iii. 1; *Mercy . . . Iustice,* v. vi. 102); proverbs and other *sententiae*; and other words apparently felt to require emphasis (such as *Oracle,* I. i. 40; *Ocean,* I. i. 64; *naked man,* I. ii. 99; *Maiden-head,* II. i. 10; a *Feeling,* II. vi. 21; *Maides sicknesse,* III. ii. 80; *oh mee,* III. iii. 22; *a place . . . this place,* III. vi. 8, 13; *This disgrace,* IV. iii. 123; *I alone,* v. i. 22; *Now, now,* v. iii. 73). With the single exception of Dekker's *Britannia's Honour* (1628), a City pageant obviously printed from an elaborately marked manuscript, no other play printed by Okes

Indiana, Princeton, Texas and Yale; and in Boston Public Library, the William A. Clark Library at Los Angeles, the Folger Shakespeare Library, the Henry E. Huntington Library, the Newberry Library at Chicago, the New York Public Library, the Pierpont Morgan Library and the Carl H. Pforzheimer Library at New York, and the Robert H. Taylor Collection at Princeton.

[1] Convenient typographical reprints of Ford's quartos may be found in *Materialien zur Kunde des älteren Englischen Dramas,* ed. W. Bang and others, Louvain, XXIII (1908) and n.s. I (1927). A photographic facsimile of *'Tis Pity* (1633) is published by the Scolar Press (Menston, 1969).

in the period 1628–35 shows any of these usages.[1] But they can all be paralleled in the quarto of *Perkin Warbeck* (1634), a play even more lavish of italic than *'Tis Pity*;[2] and again *Perkin Warbeck* is unique in this respect among the plays put forth by its printer, Thomas Purfoot. Of the five other plays which are undoubtedly and wholly by Ford, three show a similar though less abundant use of unconventional italic: *The Lover's Melancholy* (1629, printer unidentified); *Love's Sacrifice* (1633, printed by John Beale); and *The Fancies Chaste and Noble* (1638, printed by Elizabeth Purslowe). Neither Beale nor Elizabeth Purslowe habitually used this kind of 'pointing'.[3] Thus it seems almost a certainty that Ford himself used such marks of emphasis freely, and that they survived to a greater or lesser extent in texts printed from holograph copy or from manuscripts closely reflecting his idiosyncrasies.[4] It accords with this view of the *'Tis Pity* quarto that we find no signs of a working manuscript from the playhouse, such as stage-directions appearing in advance or in the imperative mood, or variations in the forms of speech-prefixes. The play also seems too well printed to have been set from Ford's 'foul papers'. The compositor's only recurrent fault is to have set some two dozen short prose speeches as verse; almost all of these occur in scenes where prose and verse are used alternately, as in I. ii. Verse is set as prose only five times, and in some of these cases the compositor was probably not misreading difficult copy but trying to save space, as will be shown.

---

[1] G. K. Hunter, in 'The Marking of *Sententiae* in Elizabethan Printed Plays, Poems, and Romances', *The Library*, Ser. 5, VI (1951), 171–88, has noted seven other publications of Okes which show 'gnomic pointing', i.e. the marking of *sententiae* by italic or other means; but the latest of these to be printed was *The Duchess of Malfi* (1623).

[2] Cf. especially, in the *Materialien* n.s. I, *'Tis Pity*, lines 122, 919–31; *Perkin Warbeck*, lines 351, 414–33. See also the discussion by Peter Ure in his edition of *Perkin Warbeck* (1968), pp. xviii–xxii.

[3] The other plays printed by Beale between 1631 and 1638 (including Ford's *Broken Heart*) show no unconventional pointing. The only book printed by Elizabeth Purslowe which shows it is her *Certain Learned and Elegant Works of Fulke Greville* (1633), which is very heavily marked and obviously set from a carefully prepared manuscript.

[4] This discussion of Ford's use of italic owes much to unpublished research by Mr N. W. Bawcutt.

Setting was by formes, and in several places the cast-off copy for the inner pages has obviously had to be adjusted to fit the outer pages already set or marked. In two crowded lines of prose (II. ii. 128–30) at the foot of D2, space is saved by the use of ampersand and of the spellings 'bin' and 'fal' for *been* and *fall*, none of which occurs elsewhere in this play; and by the spelling 'wil', used twice in these lines and only once elsewhere. But on F2 copy is 'stretched' by printing a single verse-line (III. iv. 21) as two half-lines. The exigencies of cast-off copy may account for some of the failures to set verse as verse: for example, on E3, where three and a half lines of verse (II. vi. 122–5) are printed as three of prose, the compositor may have had to feed back some type from E4^v, the next outer forme page to be set and a very crowded one. But that he was sometimes slow to recognize the change from prose dialogue to verse is shown by C4, where six verse-lines (II. i. 56–61) are likewise printed as prose. Here the compositor was not pressed for space and could easily have gained a line by closer setting at the entry (57.1–2) which should have marked the switch to verse. On the outer formes, five out of eight 4^v pages show signs either of crowding or of stretching. Thus at the foot of E4^v eight lines of verse (III. ii. 42–9) are printed as six of prose, in the middle of a verse scene with no apparent cause for misreading; while on I4^v two lines of a verse speech (V. v. 39–40) are again printed as four half-lines. Sheets B–E tend to be more closely filled than F–K, as though by the time the casting-off process reached F it was realized that the remaining copy could be fitted to the sheets without undue pressure.

Two skeletons were used, and apart from minor corrections in the early stages[1] their alternation proceeded smoothly until E inner, which was imposed in the outer skeleton; F outer too was imposed in this skeleton, after which the regular exchange of skeletons continued to the end. Thus the press must twice have stood idle while the forme which had just been worked off was

---

[1] '*T'is*' corrected to ''*Tis*' in all four titles of the outer skeleton, at one stage, while B outer was at the press; '*Whoore. .*' corrected to '*Whoore.*' in the 2^v title of the same skeleton, apparently between the printing of B outer and C outer (when the head-title from B1 would have had to be replaced by an ordinary running-title).

washed and stripped and the next forme imposed in the same skeleton. The simplest explanation is that the compositor had fallen so far behind the pressman that by the time he came to impose E inner he found both skeletons prepared for use, and chose the outer, and that the same thing happened when he imposed F outer. This explanation gains some support from the cyclical movement of the types, fourteen of which are so distinctively damaged or malformed that they can be reliably identified. An interval of at least two clear formes usually occurs between appearances of such types, e.g. types from B outer reappear in C inner, but there are three intervals of only one clear forme: a type from $E4^v$ reappears in F3, one from $E3^v$ reappears in F4, and two from FI and $F4^v$ both reappear in $G4^v$. This shows that from the distribution of E outer to the setting of G outer either distribution was very prompt, or the compositor was less comfortably ahead of the press than usual. An alternative explanation for the temporary disappearance of the inner skeleton is that some accident befell the D inner forme after its working-off. Had it been dropped, for example, the skeleton would probably have been out of use until the loosened types had been secured or removed, and the whole cleaned. This theory finds support in the disturbed appearance of the inner skeleton when it returns with F. The titles have been moved round clockwise, that from $D3^v$ appearing on F4 and so on; and two have lost types, '*shee's*' becoming '*shee*' on F2 and "*Tis pitty*' becoming "*Tispitty*' on F4. It may also be worth noting that no types from the D inner setting can be traced elsewhere in the quarto. The inner-skeleton titles kept their new places, but the missing types were restored to both members on I inner.

The only marked feature of the quarto which might suggest the hand of a second compositor is the increase in italic type on sheets H–K. Unconventional italic of the kinds discussed above occurs throughout the play; and from B to G it does so about fifty times, giving an average of once per page. But from H to K it occurs 91 times, giving an average of four times per page, the highest instance being eight times on KI^v. These pages resemble the more heavily-pointed parts of the *Perkin Warbeck* quarto (e.g. BI^v, $B2^v$, $B4^v$, EI, F2, F3). It is possible that with the setting of H outer a new compositor took over who followed the marking of Ford's manuscript more carefully. But it is also possible that the original compositor paid more attention to it after Ford had visited Okes's shop! No one but Ford seems likely to have written the note which follows the text of this play, apologizing for errors of the press (see p. 123 and footnote). One would suppose him to have written it after scrutinizing some sheets already printed; and a man so sensitive to the pointing of his work would surely have noticed if this had not been fully reproduced on sheets B–G, and would have made some effort to set matters right.

Copies of the quarto seen reveal a total of 45 press-corrections. Four copies have unique variants, and formes C inner, D outer, E outer, E inner, I outer and K inner have been found in one state only. Extraordinary trouble seems to have been taken with B outer, for which the press was stopped five times: first to adjust spacing on B3 (at I. ii. 45, preventedvs, I / prevented vs, I); next to restore the upper-case 'I' of 'Innocence' five lines below, which by accident or design had been exchanged for lower-case during the previous correction; then to correct the head- and running-titles; then to correct 'meaned' to 'meane' on B2ᵛ (I. ii. 22); finally to insert a rule below the head-title. Most of the corrections, like these, are unremarkable and might have been made without reference to copy. An exception occurs on G4ᵛ (IV. iii. 12–15). Soranzo is speaking, and in 34 copies the page ends as follows:

> Now I must be the Dad
> To all that gallymaufrey that's stuft
> In thy Corrupted bastard-bearing wombe,
> [catchword]　　　　　　　　　　　　Say,

H1 then continues:

> Shey, must I ?
> 　*Anna.* Beastly man, why 'tis thy fate:
> I sued not to thee. . . .

In the Texas University copy a hitherto unrecorded variant occurs: the catchword 'Say,' becomes 'Why'. 'Why' is undoubtedly the correction, for an earlier stage of printing survives in which obvious misprints are corrected on G outer (all on

G3: migh/might, thy/this, now/now? IV. i. 36–9) while 'Say,'
remains. 'Say,' gives an acceptable reading which has been
adopted by all editors except Gifford, and is perfectly unobjection-
able when seen on G4ᵛ alone. That G outer should have been removed from the press for the sole purpose of changing 'Say,' to
'Why' strongly suggests consultation of copy, or, it is tempting to
suppose, authorial intervention: it fits in well with our previous
hypothesis about Ford's visit to the printing-house that he should
have intervened as G outer was on the press, with G inner either
set or well advanced. 'Why' gives the better reading, for it puts
the question which Annabella immediately answers; Gifford, who
had not noticed the catchword and knew nothing of the Texas
variant, actually emended 'Shey' to 'Why' in preference to 'Say,'
which he took to be a conjectural emendation of Dodsley's. It is
difficult to explain 'Shey', which survived two stages of corrections on H outer (none on H1) and stands in all known copies.[1]

'Tis Pity' was not reprinted until 1744, when Robert Dodsley
included it in his Select Collection of Old Plays. Dodsley sensitively repunctuated the quarto text and made many good emendations, including the brilliant 'ferret' for 'Secret' at IV. iii. 154; more
than half the verbal emendations adopted in the present text are
from his hand.[2] He also made many emendations that were needless, and left the lineation of the quarto virtually intact. This was
corrected in a few places by Isaac Reed in his revised edition of

---

[1] Strangely enough, 'shey' occurs in two other Ford quartos: 'how shey
by that la,' Love's Sacrifice, 416, Materialien, XXIII; 'What's that you
mumble, Gelding, shey,' Fancies, 843, Materialien, n.s. I. In the former
instance Gifford corrected 'shey' to 'say ye', in the second to 'hey?'
Joseph Wright's Dialect Dictionary records 'shay' as a Kentish word
meaning (as noun) a glimmer of light, or (as adjective) weak or pale-
coloured (e.g. of ink); 'shay-brained' means 'foolish'. None of these
meanings fits well in 'Tis Pity', nor has any other word been found which
fits all three cases and could easily be misread as 'shey'.

[2] The following list shows the number of emendations affecting the
sense, verse or staging which each previous editor has contributed to the
present text (verbal emendations, including changes of speech-headings,
are also shown separately in parentheses): Dodsley, 26 (12); Reed, 10;
Weber, 44 (mostly relineations) (3); Gifford, 39 (mostly added stage-
directions) (4); Dyce, 15; Ellis, 1; Walley and Wilson, 1; MacIlwraith,
2 (1); Bawcutt, 5 (1); Sturgess, 2 (1).

the *Old Plays* (1780), and in many more by Henry Weber in the first collected edition of Ford's *Dramatic Works* (1811). Weber was long remembered for the contemptuous treatment of his edition by William Gifford in the *Quarterly Review* (VI, 1811, 462–87) and in the Introduction to Gifford's edition of Ford's *Dramatic Works* (1827).[1] So far as *'Tis Pity* is concerned these attacks are undeserved. Weber's text is better than any other published before the twentieth century: he shows a healthy respect for the quarto and rejects twenty of Dodsley's unnecessary emendations, yet has more genuine improvements to his credit than any other editor of the play, being particularly alert for passages of prose which had previously gone disguised as verse. Gifford restored eleven more quarto readings but at the same time made 23 fresh verbal emendations, few of which now seem justifiable; and he reinstated two of Dodsley's emendations which had been rightly rejected by Weber ('far' for 'for' at I. i. 9; 'conscience' for 'countenance' at V. v. 46). These readings enjoyed a long life, since most of them were retained by Alexander Dyce in his revision of Gifford's edition (1869, reissued 1895) which is still the standard *Complete Works*. Gifford's text was also adopted with or without minor modifications by Havelock Ellis (*John Ford*, Mermaid series, 1888) and the editors of a number of dramatic collections, including Hartley Coleridge (*Dramatic Works of Massinger and Ford* [1840]), H. R. Walley and J. H. Wilson (*Early Seventeenth-Century Plays*, New York, 1930), Esther Cloudman Dunn (*Eight Famous Elizabethan Plays*, Modern Library, New York, 1932; based on Ellis) and G. B. Harrison (*Plays by Webster and Ford*, Everyman's Library, 1933).

The first editor since Gifford to base his text directly on the quarto was S. P. Sherman, in a small volume containing *'Tis Pity* and *The Broken Heart* (Belles-Lettres series, [1915]). Sherman gives an extremely conservative old-spelling text collated with that of the Gifford-Dyce edition. Unfortunately he rejects, not only the

---

[1] Gifford was remarkably successful in imposing his views: the comments made by Dyce in 1869 and Sherman in 1915 on 'the incapacity of Weber' and his 'notoriously defective edition' are clearly not based on first-hand acquaintance with Weber's work.

many needless emendations, but others of the kind which seem to justify an editor's existence: thus he prints 'promise of malice' at IV. i. 78–9, 'Bee thus assur'd' at IV. iii. 122, 'secret' at IV. iii. 154, and 'dispositions' at V. i. 10. The two copies of the quarto which Sherman consulted (at the University of Illinois and Boston Public Library) each contained a high proportion of sheets in uncorrected states, leading him to print 'meaned' at I. ii. 22, 'a curse' at II. ii. 99, and 'tell him' at II. iii. 54; and at V. v. 51 he inexplicably preferred the Boston copy's 'how to woe' to the corrected reading of the Illinois copy, 'how to woo'. His was nevertheless the best edition to have appeared by that date, and remained the best for many years. In 1927 Henry De Vocht included in *John Ford's Dramatic Works* [Part 2] (n.s. I in Bang's *Materialien*, Louvain) a literal and typographical reprint of a British Museum quarto of *'Tis Pity* (644. b. 37). No collation or other apparatus is supplied, and the value of such straightforward reprints has been somewhat lessened by the advent of cheap and rapid photocopying. The text edited by A. K. McIlwraith for the World's Classics volume *Five Stuart Tragedies* (1953) has been printed from a copy of Ellis's Mermaid edition, corrected by De Vocht's reprint (or by a quarto showing similar press variants). A few of Ellis's mistakes (e.g. 'greedy variety', II. v. 42; 'thou' for 'that', v. i. 17; 'what brings you', v. iii. 41) have been reproduced in what is otherwise a useful text. An old-spelling edition of *'Tis Pity* was prepared by Miss Elsie Kemp (now Mrs. Schmitz) at Cambridge University between 1956 and 1959; this has not been published, but the typescript, generously made accessible, has been of benefit to later editors. Two new editions of the play appeared in 1966. One, by Mark Stavig, was an unpretentious contribution to the Crofts Classics series giving no indication of textual procedure. The other, by N. W. Bawcutt in the Regents Renaissance Drama series, was based on a collation of sixteen British copies of the quarto and at once superseded the edition by Sherman. Bawcutt's text is less drastically conservative than Sherman's, and his apparatus is accurate and helpful. Brian Morris's New Mermaid text (1968) restores a few more quarto readings, but otherwise differs from Bawcutt's chiefly in punctuation. A less cautious text, founded on the quarto but containing six new verbal emendations (and some startling misprints) has been edited by Keith Sturgess for the Penguin *John Ford: Three Plays* (1970).

The text of the present edition has been prepared from a photocopy of the quarto in the Folger Shakespeare Library, collated with other copies of the quarto as noted on pp. lxii–lxiii and with the modern editions listed on pp. xv–xvi. Some editorial principles of the Revels Plays are set out in the General Editor's Preface (pp. v–viii). The punctuation of the quarto has been modified where it conflicts with present usage, but no attempt has been made by this means to modernize the style of Ford's sentences. Emendations have been sparingly introduced, the more so as the quarto is comparatively well printed from what must have been a manuscript of high authority: where it makes good sense I have not usually felt entitled to print anything different. This has meant rejecting some ten to fifteen emendations, none of them very important (e.g. at II. ii. 7, II. iv. 24), which the most recent editors accept. In point of verbal readings the present text is closer to the quarto than any other edited text but Sherman's, though rather more freedom has been taken in the case of emendations depending on changes of punctuation. The division into acts is that of the quarto; the formal division into numbered scenes was first made by Weber. Apart from straightforward modernization and the correction of obvious misprints, the collation shows all departures from the quarto. (Forms silently up-dated include *murther*, *burthened* and *vild*.) The collation also records some other emendations which have not been adopted into the text; the editor named in each case is the one by whom the emendation was first introduced.

'TIS PITY SHE'S A WHORE

·TIS
Pitty Shee's a Whore

Acted by the *Queenes* Maiefties Seruants, at *The Phænix* in
Drury-Lane.

LONDON.
Printed by *Nicholas Okes* for *Richard*
Collins, and are to be fold at his fhop
in *Pauls* Church-yard, at the figne
of the three Kings. 1633.

Title page of the 1633 quarto

[THE EPISTLE]

To the truly noble, John, Earl of Peterborough,
Lord Mordaunt, Baron of Turvey.

My Lord,

Where a truth of merit hath a general warrant, there love
is but a debt, acknowledgment a justice. Greatness cannot   5
often claim virtue by inheritance: yet in this yours appears
most eminent, for that you are not more rightly heir to your
fortunes, than glory shall be to your memory. Sweetness of
disposition ennobles a freedom of birth; in both, your lawful
interest adds honour to your own name, and mercy to my   10
presumption. Your noble allowance of these first fruits of my

---

The Epistle] *as running-title to second page of Dedication in Q.*

Epistle] dedicatory letter.

1–2. John Mordaunt (*c.* 1599–1643; Q gives the earlier spelling
Mordant) came of an old Catholic family, disgraced in 1605 by his father's
alleged complicity in the Gunpowder Plot. James I was attracted by
Mordaunt's good looks and wit, remitted his father's fine of £10,000,
created him K.B. in 1616 and took him on the progress to Scotland in
1617. For a short time it seemed that he and not Villiers might succeed
Somerset as reigning favourite. Mordaunt married Elizabeth Howard, an
heiress of strong Puritan opinions, and was converted to Protestantism by
Archbishop Ussher in 1625. Fifth Viscount Mordaunt by his father's
death in 1608, he was created first Earl of Peterborough on 29 February
1628. He raised a regiment for Parliament in 1642 and served under
Essex as General of the Ordnance, but soon afterwards died of consump-
tion. (*D.N.B.; Letter-Book of John Viscount Mordaunt, 1658–1660*, ed.
M. Coate, 1945, pp. ix–x.)

4. *Where . . . warrant*] 'Where there is every reason for believing that
a man has true merit.' *warrant*] conclusive proof, ground for belief
(*O.E.D., sb*[1] 5 b, 8). 'General warrant' seems not to have acquired its legal
meaning of 'warrant for the arrest of unspecified persons' until the reign
of Charles II.

9. *ennobles*] confers higher rank, fame, or refinement upon (*O.E.D.*,
1–4).

freedom of birth] gentle or noble birth (*O.E.D., s.v.* free, *adj* 3).

9–10. *lawful interest*] rightful claim.

11. *noble allowance*] generous acceptance or approval. 'Allow' could
mean anything from 'praise' to 'barely tolerate' (*O.E.D., s.v.* allow 1–3,
allowance 1–4).

3

leisure in the action, emboldens my confidence of your as
noble construction in this presentment; especially since my
service must ever owe particular duty to your favours, by a
particular engagement. The gravity of the subject may easily   15
excuse the lightness of the title: otherwise I had been a severe
judge against mine own guilt. Princes have vouchsafed grace
to trifles, offered from a purity of devotion; your lordship may
likewise please to admit into your good opinion, with these
weak endeavours, the constancy of affection from the sincere   20
lover of your deserts in honour,

JOHN FORD.

11–12. *first fruits of my leisure*] This seems to indicate that '*Tis Pity* was
the earliest piece of writing Ford was willing in 1633 to acknowledge, and
thus the first of his extant independent plays, though other interpretations
are possible: see Introduction, pp. xxxvii–xxxviii. *first fruits*] an offering
to the gods made out of the earliest part of any crop; a payment by the
holder of any feudal or ecclesiastical benefice to his superior, representing
the first year's income. Cf. Congreve, *Love for Love*, Prologue, 23–5.

12. *action*] performance.

13. *construction*] interpretation.

14. *presentment*] (1) 'dramatic performance' (continuing the idea of
'action' from 12); (2) 'dedication' (here the primary sense). (*O.E.D.*, 3, 5.)

15. *particular engagement*] special obligation (cf. IV. i. 55). What obligation Peterborough conferred upon Ford is unknown (but see Introduction,
p. xxxviii).

16. *lightness*] frivolity. For catchpenny titles in this period see Burton,
I, 17. I suspect Ford's title was a catch-phrase: it occurs in [Richard
Head,] *Jackson's Recantation* (1674), p. 20, where it is applied to the beautiful mistress of a highwayman and italicized as though a quotation or
common saying. But the allusion may be to the play itself, which was
revived at the Restoration.

To my Friend, the Author.

With admiration I beheld this Whore
Adorned with beauty, such as might restore
(If ever being as thy Muse hath famed)
Her Giovanni, in his love unblamed. 5
The ready Graces lent their willing aid;
Pallas herself now played the chamber-maid
And helped to put her dressings on: secure
Rest thou, that thy name herein shall endure
To th' end of age; and Annabella be 10
Gloriously fair, even in her infamy.

THOMAS ELLICE.

Verses] *not in all copies of Q.*

To my friend . . . *ELLICE*] Inserted in Brit. Mus. 1481.bb.18 (between A1 and A2) and Huntington (between A2 and B1). The Huntington insert shows slight corrections of typography. Weber was the first modern editor to reprint the verses. For the mode of the compliment, which personifies the play as 'this Whore', cf. the commendatory verses by 'E.G.' (?Edmund Gayton) to Sir Thomas Overbury's *The Wife*: 'When I behold this wife of thine so faire', etc. (*Miscellaneous Works*, ed. Rimbault, 1890, p. 17). Ford too had prefixed verses to *The Wife* (*idem*, pp. 15–16; Dyce, III, 332–3).

2. *admiration*] closer than now to Latin *admirari*, 'wonder'.

4. *famed*] reported; made famous (*O.E.D.*, *vb* 1–3, citing Anthony Stafford, *The Femall Glory*, 1635, 'When we desire to fame some other maid').

6. *Graces*] three daughters of Zeus (also called the Charites), givers of beauty, grace and kindness; generally represented naked and hand-in-hand.

7. *Pallas*] a goddess identified with Athene and Minerva. Besides many other roles Pallas was patron of all artists, 'particularly such as worked in wool, embroidery, painting, and sculpture' (Lemprière's *Classical Dictionary*). Probably no more is intended than a general compliment to Ford's art; but conceivably Ellice means to praise the graces added by the actors, their costumes, etc., in the successful production mentioned both in the 'Epistle' and in the note appended to the play.

12. Thomas Ellice] Nothing is known of this poet; a relative perhaps of 'Master Robert Ellice . . . of Gray's Inn', one of the 'worthily respected friends' to whom Ford dedicated *The Lover's Melancholy*.

The Scene

PARMA

The Actors' Names:

BONAVENTURA, *a friar.*
A Cardinal, *nuncio to the Pope.*   5
SORANZO, *a nobleman.*
FLORIO, *a citizen of Parma.*
DONADO, *another citizen.*
GRIMALDI, *a Roman gentleman.*
GIOVANNI, *son to Florio.*   10
BERGETTO, *nephew to Donado.*
RICHARDETTO, *a supposed physician.* *N's husband*
VASQUES, *servant to Soranzo.*
POGGIO, *servant to Bergetto.*
Banditti.   15
[Officers.
Attendants.]

Women:

ANNABELLA, *daughter to Florio.*
HIPPOLITA, *wife to Richardetto.*   20
PHILOTIS, *his niece.*
PUTANA, *tutress to Annabella.*
[Ladies.]

Scene, Actors' Names] *precede Epistle in* Q.   16–17.] *Gifford; not in* Q.
23.] *Bawcutt; not in* Q.

Actors' Names] Among the *personae* of George Whetstone's *Heptameron of Ciuill Discourses* (1582; reissued 1593 as *Aurelia*) are 'Segnior Soranso, a Gentleman Italion, of wit quick and sharp' and 'Monsier Bargetto [also spelt *Bergetto*] a Frenchman, amourous and light headed' (sig. C1). Poggio (G. F. Poggio Bracciolini, fifteenth-century humanist) and Bonaventura or 'Bonaventure' (Federico Urbinas Bonaventura) are authors frequently quoted by Burton. John Florio would have been known to Ford as the author of *Firste Fruites* (1578; see note to IV. i. 72–3) and of the Italian dictionary *A Worlde of Wordes* (1598), which for *putana* gives 'a whore, a harlot, a strumpet, a queane'. The name *Richardet* occurs in a story by de Rosset which is one of the likeliest sources for *'Tis Pity* (see Introduction, pp. xxvii–xxviii). *Hippolita* recalls two persons of classical mythology, Hippolyta the Amazon queen and Hippolyte the lustful wife of Acastus.

6

'Tis Pity She's a Whore

[Act I]

[I. i]

Enter Friar *and* GIOVANNI.

Fri. Dispute no more in this, for know, young man,
These are no school-points; nice philosophy
May tolerate unlikely arguments,
But Heaven admits no jest; wits that presumed
On wit too much, by striving how to prove   5
There was no God, with foolish grounds of art,
Discovered first the nearest way to Hell;
And filled the world with devilish atheism.
Such questions, youth, are fond; for better 'tis
To bless the sun, than reason why it shines;   10
Yet he thou talk'st of is above the sun—
No more! I may not hear it.
Gio.   Gentle father,
To you I have unclasped my burdened soul,

I. i. Act I] *not in Q;* Actus primus. *Dodsley.*   6. God,] *Dodsley;* God;
Q; God *Dyce.*   art,] *Q;* art *Sherman.*   9. for] *Q;* far *Dodsley.*

I. i. 2. *school-points*] points of academic debate, especially among
'schoolmen', i.e. university theologians (cf. V. v. 30).
nice] fond of making fine distinctions; perhaps also 'wanton' and
'dangerous' (*O.E.D.*, 9 c, 2, 11 a).
4. *admits*] admits of; tolerates.
4–8. *wits . . . atheism*] Cf. *Christes Bloodie Sweat,* sig. C3: '*Schollers*
he saw, how foolishly they stroue, With tearmes of Art and smooth beguil-
ing rimes, To paynt the groseness of vnlawfull loue, And proue the sinnes
that did corrupt the times, Mayntayning vp-start sectes which all with-
stood Truthes precious light'.
6. *art*] scholarship, science.
9. *fond*] futile, foolish.

7

Emptied the storehouse of my thoughts and heart,
Made myself poor of secrets; have not left   15
Another word untold, which hath not spoke
All what I ever durst or think, or know;
And yet is here the comfort I shall have?
Must I not do what all men else may—love?

Fri. Yes, you may love, fair son.

Gio.   Must I not praise   20
That beauty which, if framed anew, the gods
Would make a god of if they had it there,
And kneel to it, as I do kneel to them?

Fri. Why, foolish madman!

Gio.   Shall a peevish sound,
A customary form, from man to man,   25
Of brother and of sister, be a bar
'Twixt my perpetual happiness and me?
Say that we had one father, say one womb
(Curse to my joys!) gave both us life and birth;
Are we not therefore each to other bound   30

---

18. have?] *Dodsley;* haue, *Q.*

---

17. *All what*] all that (accepted contemporary usage).

19. N. W. Bawcutt (*Notes and Queries,* CCXII, 1967, 215) points out the close resemblance of this line to one in the pseudo-Senecan *Octavia,* 'Prohibebor unus facere quod cunctis licet?' (*Seneca's Tragedies,* ed. F. J. Miller, Loeb Classical Library, 1917, vol. II, p. 454, l. 574). The line is spoken by Nero, who clears the way for his marriage to Poppaea by arranging the deaths, first of his mother, then of his wife Octavia.

24. *peevish*] both 'senseless' and 'spiteful' (*O.E.D.,* I, 2).

25. *from man to man*] purely human, without divine sanction; repeated meaninglessly from one man to another.

30–4.] The argument Giovanni uses here in favour of incestuous love had previously been used against it. 'I remember to have read in Saint *Thomas,* in a place where he condemneth marriages of kins-folkes in forbidden degrees, this one reason amongst others: that the love a man beareth to such a woman may be immoderate; for, if the wedlocke, or husband-like affection be sound and perfect, as it ought to be, and also surcharged with that a man oweth to alliance and kindred, there is no doubt, but that surcrease may easily transport a husband beyond the bounds of reason.' Montaigne, 'Of Moderation', trans. Florio (1603); I, 247–8 in *Essayes,* ed. Seccombe (1908).

So much the more by nature ? by the links
Of blood, of reason ? nay, if you will have 't,
Even of religion, to be ever one,
∨ One soul, one flesh, one love, one heart, one *all* ?   ↙
Fri. Have done, unhappy youth, for thou art lost!   35
Gio. Shall then, for that I am her brother born,
My joys be ever banished from her bed ?
No, father; in your eyes I see the change
Of pity and compassion; from your age,
As from a sacred oracle, distils   40
The life of counsel: tell me, holy man,
What cure shall give me ease in these extremes ?   ↳
Fri. Repentance, son, and sorrow for this sin:
For thou hast moved a Majesty above
With thy unrangèd almost blasphemy.   45
Gio. O, do not speak of that, dear confessor.
Fri. Art thou, my son, that miracle of wit
Who once, within these three months, wert esteemed
A wonder of thine age, throughout Bononia ?

45. unrangèd almost] *Dyce;* vn-raunged (almost) *Q;* unranged-almost
Bawcutt.

31-2. *links Of blood*] By this Giovanni means 'affinities of kinship'; but
the phrase expresses the double tie between him and his sister, for the
blood was thought of as the seat or vehicle of passion and sexual appetite ↙
(*O.E.D., sb* 5, 6).

35. *unhappy*] causing misfortune to oneself or others; ill-fated (*O.E.D.,
adj* 1, 2).

40. *distils*] here intransitive.

41. *life of counsel*] essence of wise judgement.

42. *extremes*] straits, hardships.

45. *thy unrangèd almost blasphemy*] Probably 'unranged' means 'un-
disciplined' (*O.E.D., s.v.* range *vb*[1] 1 c) and 'almost' qualifies 'blasphemy'.
But Ford may intend 'unranged' to mean something like 'beyond all limits'
(cf. 'rangeless'), and then 'almost' would qualify this adjective. Q is lavish
with parentheses at this point, seven pairs occurring on the same page
(B1[v]). Whether Giovanni is guilty of blasphemy depends on how strictly
the term is used; it may mean no more than 'impious speech'.

46. *confessor*] stressed on the first syllable until the 19th century.

49. *Bononia*] Latin and early vernacular form of 'Bologna'. Its university had been famous since the 12th century.

How did the university applaud   50
Thy government, behaviour, learning, speech,
Sweetness, and all that could make up a man!
I was proud of my tutelage, and chose
Rather to leave my books than part with thee;
I did so—but the fruits of all my hopes   55
Are lost in thee, as thou art in thyself.
O Giovanni! hast thou left the schools
Of knowledge, to converse with lust and death?
For death waits on thy lust. Look through the world,
And thou shalt see a thousand faces shine   60
More glorious than this idol thou adorest:
Leave her, and take thy choice, 'tis much less sin,
Though in such games as those they lose that win.

Gio. It were more ease to stop the ocean
From floats and ebbs, than to dissuade my vows.   65

Fri. Then I have done, and in thy wilful flames
Already see thy ruin: Heaven is just;
Yet hear my counsel.

Gio.   As a voice of life.

Fri. Hie to thy father's house, there lock thee fast
Alone within thy chamber, then fall down   70
On both thy knees, and grovel on the ground;
Cry to thy heart, wash every word thou utter'st
In tears, and, if 't be possible, of blood;

---

51. *government*] discretion (*O.E.D.*, 2 b).

53. *tutelage*] guardianship.

57. *Giovanni*] Throughout the play this name is pronounced with four syllables.

58. *death*] probably 'spiritual death' (*O.E.D.*, 5); cf. v. i. 36–7.

65. *floats*] floods, risings of the incoming tide. Cf. *Love's Sacrifice*, II. iii (Dyce, II, 48): 'though the float Of infinite desires swell to a tide Too high so soon to ebb'.

vows] desires (*O.E.D.*, sb 4).

68. *voice of life*] 'life-giving voice', or, perhaps, 'voice from Heaven'; cf. IV. iii. 110, also 'oracles of life', *Line of Life*, Dyce, III, 396.

72. *Cry to thy heart*] probably 'call your passions to order' (cf. *Lear*, II. iv. 118–20), but possibly 'call upon your conscience (or understanding)'; *O.E.D.*, cry vb 2, 6–7, heart 5–6, 13.

73. *tears . . . of blood*] tears expressing heartfelt grief; 'it being usuall

Beg Heaven to cleanse the leprosy of lust
That rots thy soul, acknowledge what thou art,   75
A wretch, a worm, a nothing; weep, sigh, pray
Three times a day, and three times every night;
For seven days' space do this, then if thou find'st
No change in thy desires, return to me:
I'll think on remedy. Pray for thyself   80
At home, whilst I pray for thee here—away!
My blessing with thee; we have need to pray.

Gio. All this I'll do, to free me from the rod
Of vengeance; else I'll swear my fate's my God.

Exeunt.

[I. ii]

Enter GRIMALDI *and* VASQUES *ready to fight.*

Vas. Come sir, stand to your tackling, if you prove craven I'll
make you run quickly.

Grim. Thou art no equal match for me.

Vas. Indeed I never went to the wars to bring home news,
nor cannot play the mountebank for a meal's meat, and   5
swear I got my wounds in the field. See you these grey
hairs? they'll not flinch for a bloody nose; wilt thou to
this gear?

I. ii. 1–2.] *so Weber;* Come . . . *Crauen,* | I'le . . . quickly. *Q.*   5–6.
news, nor cannot] *Q;* news. Nor can I *Dodsley;* news; nor I cannot *Gifford.*

---

to call the tears of the greatest sorrow, tears of blood' (Jeremy Taylor,
The Great Exemplar, 1649, pt. I, p. 127).

I. ii. I. *tackling*] weapons (*O.E.D.*, 3). The phrase meant 'stand and
fight'; cf. 'stick to your guns'.

craven] a coward. Reed points out the special use of the term to denote
one who failed to make good his words in a trial at arms.

5. *mountebank*] self-advertising impostor. For the famous Italian
mountebanks see Jonson, *Volpone*, II. ii (*Works*, ed. Herford and Simpson,
1925–52, V, 49 ff. and commentary, IX, 702 ff.).

a meal's meat] food for one meal. Cf. 'To see a scholar crouch and
creep to an illiterate peasant for a meal's meat', Burton, I, 72. Grimaldi
'dines out on' his experiences.

8. *gear*] business (*O.E.D.*, *sb* II c, citing Fletcher and Shirley's *Night
Walker*, 1625, 'You wo' not to this geer of marriage then ?'); also with the
concrete sense of 'fighting-equipment' (*O.E.D.*, *sb* 2).

Grim. Why, slave, think'st thou I'll balance my reputation with
    a cast-suit? Call thy master, he shall know that I dare—   10
Vas. Scold like a cot-quean, that's your profession. Thou
    poor shadow of a soldier, I will make thee know my
    master keeps servants thy betters in quality and per-
    formance; comest thou to fight, or prate?
Grim. Neither, with thee. I am a Roman and a gentleman;   15
    one that have got mine honour with expense of blood.
Vas. You are a lying coward and a fool; fight, or by these hilts
    I'll kill thee. [*Grimaldi draws.*] Brave, my lord! You'll
    fight?
Grim. Provoke me not, for if thou dost—   20
Vas. Have at you!   *They fight; Grimaldi hath the worst.*

           Enter FLORIO, DONADO, SORANZO.

Flo. What mean these sudden broils so near my doors?
    Have you not other places but my house
    To vent the spleen of your disordered bloods?
    Must I be haunted still with such unrest   25
    As not to eat or sleep in peace at home?
    Is this your love, Grimaldi? Fie, 'tis naught.

15–16.] *so Weber;* Neither with thee, / I . . . got / Mine . . . blood. *Q.*
18. S.D.] *this ed.; not in Q.*   18–19. Brave, . . . fight?] *Weber;* —braue
my Lord,—you'le fight. *Q;* brave my lord! You'll fight? *Gifford.*   22.
mean] *Q^b* (meane)*; meaned *Q^a*.

---

10. *cast-suit*] servant or other needy person who might be given cast-off
clothes; cf. *Queen*, 542.
11. *cot-quean*] cottage-wife; hence, ill-mannered or abusive woman (cf.
'fishwife'); applied to men, 'coward, "old woman" ' (cf. John Smith,
Lives of the Berkeleys, *c.* 1625: 'They fell upon him with opprobrious
words, of Coward, Cotquene, Milksopp'). *O.E.D.*, 1–3.
13. *quality*] here both 'birth' and 'character'; the two things were
commonly assumed to go together (cf. I. ii. 38–44).
18. *Brave, my lord!*] Bawcutt, following Gifford, prints without the
comma and paraphrases 'Do you dare to challenge my master?'
22. *sudden*] rash, impetuous, violent (*O.E.D.*, *adj* 2; C. T. Onions,
A Shakespeare Glossary, 1925).
27. *naught*] worthless.

Don. And Vasques, I may tell thee 'tis not well
    To broach these quarrels; you are ever forward
    In seconding contentions.

          Enter above ANNABELLA *and* PUTANA.

Flo.   What's the ground?   30
Sor. That, with your patience, signiors, I'll resolve:
    This gentleman, whom fame reports a soldier—
    For else I know not—rivals me in love
    To Signior Florio's daughter; to whose ears
    He still prefers his suit, to my disgrace,   35
    Thinking the way to recommend himself
    Is to disparage me in his report.
    But know, Grimaldi, though may be thou art
    My equal in thy blood, yet this bewrays
    A lowness in thy mind; which wert thou noble   40
    Thou wouldst as much disdain, as I do thee
    For this unworthiness; and on this ground
    I willed my servant to correct thy tongue,
    Holding a man so base no match for me.
Vas. And had not your sudden coming prevented us, I had   45
    let my gentleman blood under the gills; I should have
    wormed you, sir, for running mad.

---

43. thy] *Sturgess;* this *Q;* his *Dodsley.*   45. had not] *Dodsley;* had *Q.*

---

30. *seconding*] encouraging, 'stirring up'.
ground] cause of dispute.
31. *resolve*] explain (*O.E.D.*, *vb* 11 c, citing this passage).
33. *else*] by other means (*O.E.D.*, 3 a), implying that Soranzo has never seen anything soldierlike in Grimaldi's behaviour.
35. *prefers*] proffers.
39. *bewrays*] reveals.
43. *thy tongue*] I take it that Soranzo is still addressing Grimaldi, and that Q's 'this' was either picked up from 42 or a misreading of 'thy' or 'thie' (cf. the press-correction at IV. i. 37). But 'his' may be right, here and at II. vi. 81.
46. *gills*] flesh under the jaws and ears (*O.E.D.*, *sb*[1] 3 b, quoting Bacon, *Sylva Sylvarum,* 1626: 'Anger . . . maketh both the Cheekes and the Gills Red'). Vasques implies that his kind of medical treatment would have cured Grimaldi's anger.
47. *wormed*] Vasques applies literally and contemptuously Soranzo's

Grim. I'll be revenged, Soranzo.

Vas. On a dish of warm broth to stay your stomach—do,
        honest innocence, do! Spoon-meat is a wholesomer diet   50
        than a Spanish blade.

Grim. Remember this!

Sor.   I fear thee not, Grimaldi.

                                        Exit GRIMALDI.

Flo. My lord Soranzo, this is strange to me,
        Why you should storm, having my word engaged:
        Owing her heart, what need you doubt her ear?   55
        Losers may talk by law of any game.

Vas. Yet the villainy of words, Signior Florio, may be such
        as would make any unspleened dove choleric; blame not
        my lord in this.

Flo. Be you more silent;   60
        I would not for my wealth my daughter's love

52. Remember] *Q* (remember)*;* I'll remember *Sturgess.* 57–9.] *so*
Weber; Yet . . . such, / As . . . Chollerick, / Blame . . . this. *Q.*
57. villainy] *Dodsley;* villaine *Q.*

'correct thy tongue'. To worm a dog was to cut out the 'worm', a small
ligament in its tongue, as a precaution against rabies.

   mad] not only 'insane' and 'foolish', but also 'violently angry' (*O.E.D.*,
adj 5).

   49–50.] Cf. *Lady's Trial*, III. i (Dyce, III, 47), 'Brave man-at-arms, go
turn pander, do; stalk for a mess of warm broth'.

   49. *stay your stomach*] Besides 'quiet your appetite', this has ironical
implications such as 'satisfy (or check) your valour (or pride or anger)';
O.E.D., *s.v.* stay *vb*[1] 20, 29, stomach *sb* 8.

   50. *innocence*] harmless creature (*O.E.D.*, 5).

   Spoon-meat] soft or liquid food, suitable for toothless babies or aged
persons.

   55. *Owing*] owning; perhaps 'If you own . . .'

   56. *Losers may talk*] proverbial: Tilley L458, and cf. *Perkin Warbeck*
II. ii. 95, 'Give losers leave to talk'.

   57. *villainy*] Q probably misreads MS. 'villainie'; though 'villain of
words' (retained by Sherman and Sturgess) might be an elaboration of the
proverbial 'man of words' (Tilley M296).

   58. *unspleened dove*] It was believed that the secretions of both the
spleen and the gall-bladder produced anger, and that pigeons secreted no
gall: see Sir Thomas Browne, *Pseudodoxia Epidemica* (1646), III. iii, and
cf. *Lover's Melancholy*, II. ii (Dyce, I, 44).

Should cause the spilling of one drop of blood.
Vasques, put up, let's end this fray in wine.

    Exeunt [FLORIO, DONADO, SORANZO *and* VASQUES].

Put. How like you this, child? Here's threat'ning, challeng-
 ing, quarrelling and fighting on every side, and all is for 65
 your sake; you had need look to yourself, charge, you'll
 be stol'n away sleeping else shortly.

Ann. But tutress, such a life gives no content
 To me, my thoughts are fixed on other ends;
 Would you would leave me.   70

Put. Leave you? no marvel else; leave me no leaving, charge,
 this is love outright. Indeed I blame you not, you have
 choice fit for the best lady in Italy.

Ann. Pray do not talk so much.

Put. Take the worst with the best, there's Grimaldi the 75
 soldier, a very well-timbered fellow; they say he is a
 Roman, nephew to the Duke Mount Ferratto; they say
 he did good service in the wars against the Millanoys—
 but faith, charge, I do not like him, and be for nothing
 but for being a soldier: one amongst twenty of your 80
 skirmishing captains but have some privy maim or other
 that mars their standing upright. I like him the worse he

71–3.] *so Reed;* Leaue you . . . (Chardge) / This . . . haue / Choyce
. . . *Italy. Q.*

---

 63. *put up*] sheathe your sword.

 69. *ends*] matters; cf. *Tempest*, I. ii. 89.

 71. *no marvel else*] 'I don't wonder [that you should ask]!' *else*] apparently
a colloquial intensive (= 'at all', 'indeed'); not thus recorded by *O.E.D.*,
but cf. *Lady's Trial*, I. i and *Witch of Edmonton*, II. i (Dyce, III, 16–17, 204).

 76. *well-timbered*] well-built.

 79. *and be*] if it be, 'an't be' (cf. II. vi. 13).

 80–1. *one . . . but*] Q's omission of 'not' is here read as a colloquial
acephalous form, like 'Morning' for 'Good-morning' (and cf. II. vi. 19);
though it may be accidental, as at I. ii. 45.

 81. *skirmishing*] includes the sense 'to make flourishes with a weapon'
(*O.E.D., vb* 2).

 privy maim] hidden injury.

 82. *standing upright*] with a sexual double-entendre.

crinkles so much in the hams; though he might serve if
there were no more men, yet he's not the man I would
choose.   85

Ann. Fie, how thou pratest.

Put. As I am a very woman, I like Signior Soranzo well: he
is wise, and what is more, rich; and what is more than
that, kind; and what is more than all this, a nobleman;
such a one, were I the fair Annabella myself, I would   90
wish and pray for. Then he is bountiful; besides he is
handsome, and, by my troth, I think wholesome—and
that's news in a gallant of three and twenty. Liberal, that
I know; loving, that you know; and a man sure, else he
could never ha' purchased such a good name with   95
Hippolita the lusty widow in her husband's lifetime—
and 'twere but for that report, sweetheart, would a were
thine! Commend a man for his qualities, but take a
husband as he is a plain-sufficient, naked man: such a
one is for your bed, and such a one is Signior Soranzo,   100
my life for 't.

---

99. plain-sufficient] *Q;* plain sufficient *Dodsley.*

---

83. *crinkles*] *O.E.D.* cites this passage to illustrate 'crinkle' *vb* 2, 'to
bend shrinkingly or obsequiously with the legs or body; to cringe'. But
in the context of Putana's bawdy, sense 2 b—'to turn aside, to shrink or
recede from one's purpose'—seems equally relevant.

serve] probably with a play on the meaning 'to mount (and impregnate)
the female' (*O.E.D.*, *vb*[1] 52; see also *Shakespeare's Bawdy*).

87. *very*] both 'truthful' and 'real'.

92. *wholesome*] free from (venereal) disease.

93. *gallant*] man of fashion and pleasure; 'ladies' man'; lover (*O.E.D.*,
sb 1, 3).

95. *such a good name*] such favour.

97. *and 'twere*] (and) if it were.

98. *qualities*] accomplishments. 'I had att one time 8 tutors in severall
quallities, languages, musick, dancing, writing, and needlework', Lucy
Hutchinson, *Memoirs of Col. Hutchinson*, ed. Child (1904), p. 33.

99. *plain-sufficient*] Several meanings seem possible: 'plain but ade-
quate'; 'simply (or clearly) sufficient'; 'sufficient for ordinary and obvious
needs'.

Ann. Sure the woman took her morning's draught too soon.

Enter BERGETTO *and* POGGIO.

Put. But look, sweetheart, look what thing comes now:
here's another of your ciphers to fill up the number. O,
brave old ape in a silken coat! Observe.   105

Ber. Didst thou think, Poggio, that I would spoil my new
clothes, and leave my dinner to fight?

Pog. No sir, I did not take you for so arrant a baby.

Ber. I am wiser than so: for I hope, Poggio, thou never
heard'st of an elder brother that was a coxcomb, didst,   110
Poggio?

Pog. Never indeed sir, as long as they had either land or
money left them to inherit.

Ber. Is it possible, Poggio? O monstrous! Why, I'll undertake, with a handful of silver, to buy a headful of wit   115
at any time. But sirrah, I have another purchase in
hand, I shall have the wench mine uncle says; I will but
wash my face, and shift socks, and then have at her
i'faith!—Mark my pace, Poggio.   [*Walks affectedly.*]

103–5.] *so Weber;* But . . . now: / Here's . . . number: / Oh . . .
obserue. *Q.*   106–7.] *so Dodsley;* Did'st . . . my / New . . . fight.
Q.   109–11.] *so Reed;* I am . . . thou / Neuer . . . Coxcomb, /
Did'st *Poggio? Q.*   119. S.D.] *Sturgess.*

---

102. *morning's draught*] drink of ale, wine or spirits taken early or at
mid-morning; cf. *Merry Wives,* II. ii. 133.

104. *ciphers*] noughts; hence, nonentities. *O.E.D.* (*sb* 1, 2) quotes
Henry Smith, *Sermons* (1622): 'You are . . . like cyphers, which supply
a place, but signifie nothing'.

105. *brave*] finely dressed.

ape in a silken coat] proverbial metaphor for an unworthy person dis-
playing wealth or finery: see Tilley, A262–3, D452, and cf. *Lover's
Melancholy,* II. ii (Dyce, 1, 46).

110. *coxcomb*] simpleton (from the shape of the professional fool's
headdress).

115. *buy . . . wit*] with a meaning unintended by Bergetto, 'purchase wisdom by bitter experience'; cf. 'Bought wit is dear' and related
proverbs (Tilley, W545–6, W556, W567).

118. *shift socks*] change my stockings (or light shoes).

119. *Mark my pace*] Watch how I walk.

Pog. Sir, I have seen an ass and a mule trot the Spanish   120
pavin with a better grace, I know not how often.

Exeunt [BERGETTO *and* POGGIO].

Ann. This idiot haunts me too.

Put. Ay, ay, he needs no description. The rich magnifico
that is below with your father, charge, Signior Donado
his uncle, for that he means to make this his cousin a   125
golden calf, thinks that you will be a right Israelite, and
fall down to him presently: but I hope I have tutored
you better. They say a fool's bauble is a lady's playfellow; yet you having wealth enough, you need not cast
upon the dearth of flesh at any rate: hang him, innocent!   130

Enter GIOVANNI.

Ann. But see, Putana, see; what blessed shape
Of some celestial creature now appears?
What man is he, that with such sad aspect

120–1.] *so Q; aside Weber.*   130. flesh at] *Q;* flesh, at *Dodsley.*
130.1.] *so Q;* Giovanni *passes over the Stage Gifford.*

121. *pavin*] a stately dance (also 'pavan', 'pavane').
125. *cousin*] used of relatives generally, and of intimates.
126. *golden calf*] wealthy simpleton; cf. *Line of Life*, Dyce, III, 404. For
the related 'golden ass' see T. Overbury, *Miscellaneous Works* (1890),
pp. 53–4; Tilley, A349, A352, A360; Burton, I, 66. See also Exodus XXXII.
127. *presently*] immediately.
128–9. *a fool's bauble . . . playfellow*] variant, with a sexual innuendo,
of the proverb 'Fools and little dogs are ladies' playfellows' (Tilley F528);
cf. *Queen*, 826–9. *bauble*] stick with a carved head, carried by the professional fool as an emblem of office. For the innuendo cf. *Romeo and
Juliet*, II. iv. 88–9: 'this drivelling love is like a great natural that runs
lolling up and down to hide his bauble in a hole' (*et. seq.*).
129–30. *you need . . . flesh*] 'You need not be influenced by the shortage
of men.' *cast upon*] reckon on, base your calculations on (*O.E.D.*, cast *vb*
38 b, where this passage is cited).
130. *at any rate*] probably modifies 'cast'—'whatever price men are
fetching in terms of dowry demanded'—but may refer back to 'you'—'you
at least need not worry about such matters'.
innocent] simpleton, idiot.
131–5.] See Introduction, pp. xxviii, xliv–xlv.

           Walks careless of himself?
Put.   Where?
Ann.   Look below.
Put. O, 'tis your brother, sweet—
Ann.   Ha!
Put.   'Tis your brother.   135
Ann. Sure 'tis not he: this is some woeful thing
           Wrapped up in grief, some shadow of a man.
           Alas, he beats his breast, and wipes his eyes
           Drowned all in tears; methinks I hear him sigh.
           Let's down, Putana, and partake the cause;   140
           I know my brother, in the love he bears me,
           Will not deny me partage in his sadness.
           My soul is full of heaviness and fear.

                         Exeunt [ANNABELLA *and* PUTANA].

Gio. Lost, I am lost; my fates have doomed my death;
           The more I strive, I love, the more I love,   145
           The less I hope; I see my ruin, certain.
           What judgment or endeavours could apply
           To my incurable and restless wounds
           I throughly have examined, but in vain.
           O that it were not in religion sin   150
           To make our love a god, and worship it!

---

134. Look below] *Q;* Look, below *Dodsley.*   143.1. *Exeunt* ... PUTANA]
Weber (Exeunt from the Balcony); Exit Q.

---

   140. *partake*] be informed of.
   142. *partage*] a share. The line has some dramatic irony.
   143.1/144.] Editors from Gifford to Ellis, thinking in terms of 19th-
century staging and not wishing the exchange of incestuous vows to take
place in the street, mark a change of scene here to 'A Hall in Florio's
House', and alter the S.D. at 130.1 to get Giovanni off-stage while the
change of scene takes place.
   144–6.] These lines simultaneously express Giovanni's recognition that
his love is damnable and his fear that its frustration must cause his death.
   150–1.] Cf. *Christes Bloodie Sweat,* sig. F3: 'Loue is no god, as some of
wicked times (Led with the dreaming dotage of their folly) Haue set him
foorth in their lasciuious rimes, Bewitch'd with errors, and conceits
vnholy: It is a raging blood affections blind, Which boiles both in the
body and the mind'.

I have even wearied Heaven with prayers, dried up
The spring of my continual tears, even starved
My veins with daily fasts; what wit or art
Could counsel, I have practised: but alas,   155
I find all these but dreams, and old men's tales
To fright unsteady youth; I'm still the same.
Or I must speak, or burst; 'tis not, I know,
My lust, but 'tis my fate that leads me on.
Keep fear and low faint-hearted shame with slaves!   160
I'll tell her that I love her, though my heart
Were rated at the price of that attempt.
Oh me! she comes.

Enter ANNABELLA *and* PUTANA.

Ann.   Brother!
Gio. [*Aside*]   If such a thing
As courage dwell in men, ye heavenly powers,
Now double all that virtue in my tongue.   165
Ann. Why brother, will you not speak to me?
Gio. Yes; how d'ee, sister?
Ann.   Howsoever I am,
Methinks you are not well.
Put. Bless us, why are you so sad, sir?
Gio. Let me entreat you leave us awhile, Putana,—   170
Sister, I would be private with you.
Ann. Withdraw, Putana.

163. *Aside*] *Gifford.*   166–8.] *so this ed.;* Why . . . me? | Yes . . .
Sister? | Howsoeuer . . . well.   *Q;* Why, brother, | Will . . . sister? |
Howe'er . . . well. *Gifford.*   167. Howsoever] *Q;* Howsoe'er *Weber;*
Howe'er *Gifford;* However *McIlwraith.*

152–3. *dried up . . . tears*] From the context these seem to be the
penitential tears called for by the Friar; though love too finds relief in
tears, and dries up the 'radical moisture' of the body (Burton, III, 153–4,
172–3).

154. *art*] medical lore (cf. II. iii. 40).

160. *Keep*] keep company (*O.E.D.*, *vb* 45). 'Let fear . . . dwell with
slaves.'

Put. I will. [*Aside*] If this were any other company for her,
    I should think my absence an office of some credit; but
    I will leave them together.   *Exit.* 175

Gio. Come sister, lend your hand, let's walk together.
    I hope you need not blush to walk with me;
    Here's none but you and I.

Ann. How's this?

Gio. Faith, I mean no harm.   180

Ann. Harm?

Gio. No, good faith; how is 't with 'ee?

Ann. [*Aside*] I trust he be not frantic. [*To him*] I am very
    well, brother.

Gio. Trust me, but I am sick; I fear so sick   185
    'Twill cost my life.

Ann. Mercy forbid it! 'tis not so, I hope.

Gio. I think you love me, sister.

Ann. Yes, you know I do.

Gio. I know 't, indeed.—Y' are very fair.   190

Ann. Nay, then I see you have a merry sickness.

Gio. That's as it proves. The poets feign, I read,
    That Juno for her forehead did exceed
    All other goddesses; but I durst swear
    Your forehead exceeds hers, as hers did theirs.   195

---

173. I will] *so Weber; on separate line in Q. Aside*] *Weber.*   178–82.] *so
Q;* Here's ... this? / 'Faith ... good faith: / How ... frantic— *Weber.*
180. Faith] *Q;* I'faith *Gifford.*   183–4.] *so Bawcutt;* I ... franticke— /
I ... brother. *Q.*   183. *Aside*] *Gifford* (*Q has long dash*).   188–190.]
so Q; I think ... I do. / I know it ... fair. *Weber;* I think ... you know /
I do ... fair *Dyce.*   192. The] *Dodsley;* they *Q.*

---

174. *an office . . . credit*] ironically, 'a post of honour'; also 'a good
turn deserving some reward'. For *credit* as 'right to some return' cf.
2 *Henry IV*, v. i. 46. Cf. also below, IV. iii. 102.

    183. *frantic*] mad.

    192. *proves*] turns out.

    The poets] Q's 'they', rejected by all editors, may conceivably be a
demonstrative adjective (*O.E.D.*, 5).

    193. *Juno*] Jupiter's sister, who became his mistress and afterwards his
wife.

Ann. Troth, this is pretty!

Gio.   Such a pair of stars
     As are thine eyes would, like Promethean fire,
     If gently glanced, give life to senseless stones.

Ann. Fie upon 'ee!

Gio. The lily and the rose, most sweetly strange,   200
     Upon your dimpled cheeks do strive for change.
     Such lips would tempt a saint; such hands as those
     Would make an anchorite lascivious.

Ann. D'ee mock me, or flatter me?

Gio. If you would see a beauty more exact   205
     Than art can counterfeit or nature frame,
     Look in your glass, and there behold your own.

Ann. O, you are a trim youth.

Gio. Here!   *Offers his dagger to her.*

Ann.   What to do?

Gio.   And here's my breast, strike home!
     Rip up my bosom, there thou shalt behold   210
     A heart in which is writ the truth I speak.
     Why stand 'ee?

Ann.   Are you earnest?

Gio.   Yes, most earnest;
     You cannot love—

Ann.   Whom?

Gio.   Me. My tortured soul
     Hath felt affliction in the heat of death.

212–3.] *so Dyce;* Why . . . earnest? / Yes most earnest. / You . . .
Whom? / Me . . . soule *Q.*   213. love—] *this ed.;* love? *Q;* love.
Dodsley.

197–8. *Promethean . . . stones*] Prometheus made the first man and
woman from clay, and gave them life by means of fire stolen from Heaven.

200–1.] Cf. *Christies Bloodie Sweat*, sig. B3ᵛ: 'His face in which the
Rose did with the lilly, Striue curiously for chaunge in little space'.

201. *change*] mutual interchange; cf. 'the change of words' (= conversation), *Much Ado*, IV. i. 183.

203. *anchorite*] religious recluse, hermit.

208. *trim*] fine, 'nice' (*O.E.D.*, *adj* 3).

214. *affliction . . . death*] suffering of mortal intensity (*O.E.D.*, *s.v.* heat
sb 11).

            O Annabella, I am quite undone: 215
            The love of thee, my sister, and the view
          ⌈ Of thy immortal beauty hath untuned
          ⌊ All harmony both of my rest and life.
            Why d'ee not strike?
Ann.   Forbid it, my just fears;
            If this be true, 'twere fitter I were dead.   220
Gio. True, Annabella? 'tis no time to jest:
            I have too long suppressed the hidden flames
            That almost have consumed me; I have spent
            Many a silent night in sighs and groans,
            Ran over all my thoughts, despised my fate,   225
            Reasoned against the reasons of my love,
            Done all that smoothed-cheek Virtue could advise,
            But found all bootless: 'tis my destiny
            That you must either love, or I must die.
Ann. Comes this in sadness from you?
Gio.   Let some mischief   230
            Befall me soon, if I dissemble aught.
Ann. You are my brother, Giovanni.
Gio.   You
            My sister, Annabella; I know this;

217. hath] *Q;* have *Dodsley.*   221. True, Annabella?] *Dodsley;* True
Annabella; *Q.*   227. smoothed-cheek] *Q;* smooth-cheek'd *Dodsley.*
232. brother,] *Dodsley;* brother *Q.*   233. sister,] *Dodsley;* Sister *Q.*

---

   225. *despised my fate*] attempted to disregard (or defy) my destiny
(*O.E.D., s.v.* despise *vb* 3 b, despite *sb* 5 c).
   227. *smoothed-cheek*] smooth-faced; clean-shaven (cf. 'starv'd-gut star-
gazer', *Queen*, 131–2). Virtue is personified either as a youth whose beard-
less face and fresh untroubled looks betoken inexperience (cf. 'ill-aduis'd
By young, and smooth-fac'd Councell', Quarles, *Esther*, 1621), or as a
spruce gentleman with ingratiating manners and a plausible tongue. See
O.E.D. s.v. smooth *adj* 1 b, 6, 14, *vb* 1, 3; smoothed 1–2; smooth-faced
1–2; and cf. 'smooth-boots' and 'smug' *adj.*
   230. *sadness*] seriousness.
   231. *dissemble*] pretend.
   232–3. *brother, . . . sister,*] Q regularly omits commas before vocatives. To omit them in a modernized text has the effect of widening the
question from one of relationship to one of identity, a reading not borne
out by the immediate context.

And could afford you instance why to love
So much the more for this; to which intent   235
Wise Nature first in your creation meant
To make you mine: else 't had been sin and foul
To share one beauty to a double soul.
Nearness in birth or blood doth but persuade
A nearer nearness in affection.   240
I have asked counsel of the holy Church,
Who tells me I may love you, and 'tis just
That since I may, I should; and will, yes will:
Must I now live, or die?

Ann.   Live; thou hast won
The field, and never fought; what thou hast urged,   245
My captive heart had long ago resolved.
I blush to tell thee—but I'll tell thee now—
For every sigh that thou hast spent for me,
I have sighed ten; for every tear shed twenty:
And not so much for that I loved, as that   250
I durst not say I loved; nor scarcely think it.

---

239. birth or] *Q;* birth and *Weber.*

---

234. *afford you instance*] show you reason or cause.
236–8.] In Neoplatonic theory love results from a congenital affinity of souls which should ideally reveal itself in physical likeness. In his *Hymne in Honovr of Beavtie* (1596) Spenser advises ladies 'That likest to your selues ye them [your lovers] select, The which your forms first sourse may sympathize, And with like beauties parts be inly deckt' (190–3); adding that none should be linked in love 'But those whom heauen did at first ordaine, And made out of one mould the more t' agree' (204–7). Elsewhere he compares the lovers kindling each other's beauty to a pair of mirrors (176–82). But Spenser distinguishes between 'gentle Loue' and 'that foule blot, that hellish fierbrand, Disloiall lust' (169–70). (*Spenser's Minor Poems*, ed. E. de Selincourt, Oxford, 1910.)
239. *persuade*] induce; recommend (*O.E.D.*, 5–7).
246. *resolved*] settled (*O.E.D.*, *vb* 13 d); but the verb is a rich one, with implications not only of firmly deciding and choosing (*O.E.D.*, 13) but also of passing from discord into harmony, relaxing, dissolving, and even disintegrating (*O.E.D.*, 4–5, 21–2). This second group of meanings is enforced not by syntax but by context, and by the softly-flowing sound of this line coming after violently broken ones.

Gio. Let not this music be a dream, ye gods,
            For pity's sake I beg 'ee!
Ann.   On my knees,   *She kneels.*
            Brother, even by our mother's dust, I charge you,
            Do not betray me to your mirth or hate: 255
            Love me, or kill me, brother.
Gio.   On my knees,   *He kneels.*
            Sister, even by my mother's dust I charge you,
            Do not betray me to your mirth or hate:
            Love me, or kill me, sister.
Ann. You mean good sooth then?
Gio.   In good troth I do,   260
            And so do you I hope: say, I'm in earnest.
Ann. I'll swear 't, and I.
Gio.   And I, and by this kiss—

                                        Kisses her.

            Once more; yet once more; now let's rise—by this,
            I would not change this minute for Elysium.
            What must we now do?
Ann.   What you will.
Gio.   Come then;   265
            After so many tears as we have wept,
            Let's learn to court in smiles, to kiss and sleep.

                                        Exeunt.

262. swear 't, and] *Sherman;* swear 't and *Q;* swear it, and *Dodsley;* swear
it, *Gifford.*

260. *mean good sooth*] are really speaking the truth. 'Mean' seems to have
its sense of 'say', not recorded transitively after 1494 though intransitive
examples continue to 1625 (*O.E.D.*, *vb*[1] 6). The sense of 'intend' is also
probably present.
261–2.] Giovanni's 'say,' demands a reply, but it is unlikely that he is
telling Annabella to repeat the phrase 'I'm in earnest' (which no editor
prints in quotation-marks). 'I'm in earnest' refers to Giovanni himself,
removes any lingering suspicion (260) that this has been an elaborate joke,
and encourages Annabella to do the same. Her 'I'll swear 't' may refer
back to his last words ('I really believe you are in earnest') or forward
('and I swear I am too'). On this latter reading Q's syntax would be
slightly unusual, but there is no difficulty of grammar, sense or metre,
and Gifford's simplifying emendation seems unnecessary.

[I. iii]

Enter FLORIO *and* DONADO.

Flo. Signior Donado, you have said enough,
　　　I understand you, but would have you know
　　　I will not force my daughter 'gainst her will.
　　　You see I have but two, a son and her;
　　　And he is so devoted to his book,   5
　　　As I must tell you true, I doubt his health:
　　　Should he miscarry, all my hopes rely
　　　Upon my girl. As for worldly fortune,
　　　I am, I thank my stars, blessed with enough;
　　　My care is how to match her to her liking;   10
　　　I would not have her marry wealth, but love,
　　　And if she like your nephew, let him have her:
　　　Here's all that I can say.

Don.   Sir, you say well,
　　　Like a true father, and for my part, I,
　　　If the young folks can like—'twixt you and me—   15
　　　Will promise to assure my nephew presently
　　　Three thousand florins yearly during life,
　　　And after I am dead, my whole estate.

Flo. 'Tis a fair proffer, sir; meantime your nephew
　　　Shall have free passage to commence his suit: 20
　　　If he can thrive, he shall have my consent.
　　　So for this time I'll leave you, signior.   *Exit.*

Don.   Well,
　　　Here's hope yet, if my nephew would have wit;
　　　But he is such another dunce, I fear
　　　He'll never win the wench. When I was young   25

I. iii. 7. *miscarry*] come to harm.

8. *girl*] Unlike Shakespeare, Ford makes this a disyllable ('girrel');
cf. II. i. 78.

24. *such another dunce*] such a (perfect) dunce: cf. *Lover's Melancholy*,
III. i (Dyce, I, 50).

I could have done 't i'faith, and so shall he
If he will learn of me; and in good time
He comes himself.

Enter BERGETTO *and* POGGIO.

How now, Bergetto, whither away so fast?

Ber. O uncle, I have heard the strangest news that ever came   30
out of the mint—have I not, Poggio?

Pog. Yes indeed, sir.

Don. What news, Bergetto?

Ber. Why, look ye uncle, my barber told me just now that
there is a fellow come to town, who undertakes to make   35
a mill go without the mortal help of any water or wind,
only with sandbags! And this fellow hath a strange horse,
a most excellent beast I'll assure you uncle, my barber
says, whose head, to the wonder of all Christian people,
stands just behind where his tail is—is 't not true,   40
Poggio?

Pog. So the barber swore forsooth.

I. iii. 29. How] *Weber; Pog.* How *Q.*

---

26. *I could have done 't*] meaning probably 'I used to be able to do it',
as at II. i. 79.

27. *in good time*] just at the right moment.

30–1. *news . . . mint*] 'New out of the mint' was proverbial (Tilley
M985), and Bergetto's phrase suggests manufactured novelties (*O.E.D.*,
s.v. news 1, mint *sb*[1] 3).

34. *my barber*] To pass on news and gossip was a recognized part of the
barber's trade: see *Fancies*, v. ii (Dyce, II, 312); Jonson, *Staple of News*,
I. ii. 20–1, I. v. 9 (*Works*, ed. Herford and Simpson, VI, 286, 293).

36. *mill*] not necessarily a corn-mill; the general industrial sense was
established (*O.E.D.*, *sb*[1] 3–4).

37. *with sandbags*] Apparently one of many projects for 'perpetual
motion'. A wheel can be driven by sand falling into compartments at its
rim, but the work done will not equal that needed to raise the sand into
position.

38–41. *a strange horse . . . tail is*] 'For a long time "The Wonderful
Horse, With His Head Where His Tail Ought To Be" was a popular
side-show at fairs. Those who paid their money to see the wonder do not
seem to have resented the trick, but to have persuaded their friends to see
it too' (*Oxford Dictionary of Nursery Rhymes*, ed. I. and P. Opie, 1955,
pp. 379–80). Its tail was tied to the manger.

Don. And you are running thither?

Ber. Ay forsooth uncle.

Don. Wilt thou be a fool still? Come sir, you shall not go; 45
you have more mind of a puppet-play than on the business I told ye. Why, thou great baby, wou't never have
wit? wou't make thyself a May-game to all the world?

Pog. Answer for yourself, master.

Ber. Why uncle, should I sit at home still, and not go abroad 50
to see fashions like other gallants?

Don. To see hobby-horses! What wise talk I pray had you
with Annabella, when you were at Signior Florio's
house?

Ber. O, the wench: Ud's sa'me, uncle, I tickled her with a 55
rare speech, that I made her almost burst her belly with
laughing.

Don. Nay I think so, and what speech was 't?

Ber. What did I say, Poggio?

Pog. Forsooth, my master said that he loved her almost as 60
well as he loved parmasent, and swore—I'll be sworn for
him—that she wanted but such a nose as his was, to be
as pretty a young woman as any was in Parma.

Don. O gross!

Ber. Nay uncle, then she asked me whether my father had any 65

---

43. thither] *Gifford;* hither *Q.*

---

46. *have more mind of*] think more about; have more liking for (*O.E.D.*,
mind *sb*[1] 7, 13 d–e).

48. *May-game*] source of mirth, laughing-stock (*O.E.D.*, 3). One May
Day entertainment was the morris dance, in which both Fool and Hobby-
horse performed.

51. *see fashions*] see life, see what's going on; cf. *Don Quixote*, p. 774,
where 'gad Abroad to see Fashions' means visiting the town by night.

52. *hobby-horses*] performers costumed as horses in the morris dance
and other popular entertainments; see *Witch of Edmonton*, II. i, v. iv
(Dyce, III, 198–200, 232–4). Here contemptuous, as in *Much Ado*, III. ii. 65.

55. *Ud's sa' me*] God save me.

56–7. *burst . . . laughing*] cf. 'break the rim of his belly with laughing',
Burton, I, 55.

61. *parmasent*] Parmesan (cheese).

more children than myself; and I said, 'No, 'twere better
he should have had his brains knocked out first'.

Don. This is intolerable.

Ber. Then said she, 'Will Signior Donado your uncle leave
you all his wealth?'   70

Don. Ha! that was good, did she harp upon that string?

Ber. Did she harp upon that string, ay that she did. I
answered, 'Leave me all his wealth? Why, woman, he
hath no other wit, if he had he should hear on 't to his
everlasting glory and confusion; I know,' quoth I, 'I am   75
his white boy, and will not be gulled'; and with that she
fell into a great smile, and went away. Nay, I did fit her.

Don. Ah sirrah, then I see there is no changing of nature;
well, Bergetto, I fear thou wilt be a very ass still.

Ber. I should be sorry for that, uncle.   80

Don. Come, come you home with me; since you are no better
a speaker, I'll have you write to her after some courtly
manner, and enclose some rich jewel in the letter.

Ber. Ay marry, that will be excellent.

Don. Peace, innocent!   85
Once in my time I'll set my wits to school:
If all fail, 'tis but the fortune of a fool.

Ber. Poggio, 'twill do Poggio!   *Exeunt.*

74. wit] *Q;* will *Dodsley.*   78–9.] *so Weber;* Ah ... nature, / Well ...
still. *Q.*

---

74. *wit*] thought.
76. *white boy*] fair-haired boy; hence, favourite.
77. *fit*] fitly answer, cope with.

Act II

Enter GIOVANNI *and* ANNABELLA, *as from their chamber.*

Gio. Come Annabella, no more sister now
    But love, a name more gracious; do not blush,
    Beauty's sweet wonder, but be proud, to know
    That yielding thou hast conquered, and inflamed
    A heart whose tribute is thy brother's life.   5
Ann. And mine is his; O, how these stol'n contents
    Would print a modest crimson on my cheeks,
    Had any but my heart's delight prevailed!
Gio. I marvel why the chaster of your sex
    Should think this pretty toy called maidenhead   10
    So strange a loss, when being lost, 'tis nothing,
    And you are still the same.
Ann.   'Tis well for you;
    Now you can talk.
Gio.   Music as well consists

II. i. Act II] *Actus Secundus. Q.*

II. i. 0.1. as from their chamber] a balcony entrance; the conversation among persons on different levels at 56–75 would cause no difficulty.
    6. *contents*] pleasures.
    10. *toy*] (quaint or amusing) trifle.
    12. *well for you*] 'all right for you'.
    13–14. *Music . . . playing*] Applied simply to music this saying (not found elsewhere) may mean either 'A good ear is as necessary to a performer as expert technique' or something analogous to 'Beauty is in the eye of the beholder'. In this context it means 'The woman's part in the sexual act is equal to the man's, though more passive, and her organ enjoys what it receives'. Musical metaphors for sex are very numerous; cf. also 'Like punishment and equal pain both key and keyhole do sustain', Tilley P637.

In th' ear, as in the playing.

Ann.   O, y' are wanton!
Tell on 't, y' are best, do.

Gio.   Thou wilt chide me, then?   15
Kiss me, so; thus hung Jove on Leda's neck,
And sucked divine ambrosia from her lips.
I envy not the mightiest man alive,
But hold myself in being king of thee
More great, than were I king of all the world.   20
But I shall lose you, sweetheart.

Ann.   But you shall not.

Gio. You must be married, mistress.

Ann.   Yes, to whom?

Gio. Someone must have you.

Ann.   You must.

Gio.   Nay, some other.

Ann. Now prithee do not speak so without jesting;
You'll make me weep in earnest.

Gio.   What, you will not!   25
But tell me, sweet, canst thou be dared to swear
That thou wilt live to me, and to no other?

Ann. By both our loves I dare; for didst thou know,

15. then?] *this ed.;* then. *Q.*   24. so without jesting;] *this ed.;* so, without iesting *Q;* so, without jesting. *Dodsley;* so; without jesting *Gifford.*

---

16. *Jove on Leda's neck*] Jupiter in the form of a swan took refuge in
Leda's bosom and thus seduced her.

17. *ambrosia*] the sweet and scented food of the gods, which made those
who ate it immortal.

23. *have*] The sexual meaning (see *Shakespeare's Bawdy*) is probably
present.

24.] Annabella's last two speeches have been playful, on the assumption
that Giovanni is 'jesting'. To take 'without jesting' as modifying the
following clause obscures the sequence of responses and creates tautology,
'without jesting . . . in earnest'.

25. *What, you will not!*] Will you really (weep)? Cf. II. iv. 40. Here,
half-disbelieving, half-soothing.

26. *be dared*] be bold enough; accept this challenge.

27. *live to me*] devote yourself to me (*O.E.D.*, *vb*[1] 4 c). Here as at
III. vi. 38 it seems to be total loyalty, not just physical 'faithfulness', that
is demanded.

My Giovanni, how all suitors seem
To my eyes hateful, thou wouldst trust me then.   30
Gio. Enough, I take thy word; sweet, we must part:
Remember what thou vow'st; keep well my heart.
Ann. Will you begone?
Gio. I must.
Ann. When to return?   35
Gio. Soon.
Ann. Look you do.
Gio. Farewell.   *Exit.*
Ann. Go where thou wilt, in mind I'll keep thee here,
And where thou art, I know I shall be there.   40
Guardian!

Enter PUTANA.

Put. Child, how is 't child? Well, thank Heaven, ha?
Ann. O guardian, what a paradise of joy
Have I passed over!
Put. Nay, what a paradise of joy have you passed under! Why,   45
now I commend thee, charge; fear nothing, sweetheart,
what though he be your brother? Your brother's a man
I hope, and I say still, if a young wench feel the fit upon
her, let her take anybody, father or brother, all is one.
Ann. I would not have it known for all the world.   50
Put. Nor I indeed, for the speech of the people; else 'twere
nothing.

33–8.] *so Dodsley;* Will . . . must. / When . . . Soone. / Looke . . . Farewell.
Q; Will . . . return? / Soon . . . Farewell. *Weber;* Will . . . gone? / I must. /
When . . . Farewell. *Dyce.*   38. *Exit] so Q; Dyce places after 40.*   45.
Nay . . . under] *so Dodsley; as one line of verse in Q.*

---

37. *Look you do*] Mind you do.
44. *passed over*] passed through ('paradise' in 43 probably keeps some of
its meaning 'garden', though this is lost in 45).
45–9.] In *A Line of Life* (1620) Ford wrote of flattering dependants: 'A
folly is committed: how slight are they ready to prove it, how sedulous to
slighten, how damnably disposed to make it nothing! insomuch as those
vipers of humanity are fitly to be termed the man's whore and the woman's
knave' (Dyce, III, 404).
48. *fit*] (sexual) impulse, mood; cf. *Lady's Trial*, III, i (Dyce, III, 45).
51. *for*] because of (*O.E.D., prep* 21).

Flo. (*Within*) Daughter Annabella!

Ann. O me, my father!—Here, sir!—Reach my work.

Flo. (*Within*) What are you doing?

Ann.   So, let him come now.   55

> *Enter* FLORIO, RICHARDETTO *like a Doctor of Physic,*
> *and* PHILOTIS *with a lute in her hand.*

Flo. So hard at work, that's well! You lose no time.
Look, I have brought you company: here's one,
A learned doctor, lately come from Padua,
Much skilled in physic; and for that I see
You have of late been sickly, I entreated   60
This reverend man to visit you some time.

Ann. Y' are very welcome, sir.

Rich.   I thank you, mistress;
Loud fame in large report hath spoke your praise
As well for virtue as perfection:
For which I have been bold to bring with me   65
A kinswoman of mine, a maid, for song
And music, one perhaps will give content:
Please you to know her?

Ann.   They are parts I love,
And she for them most welcome.

Phil.   Thank you, lady.

56–61.] *so Weber; as prose in Q.*   61. reverend] *Reed;* reuerent *Q.*
68. her?] *Dodsley;* her. *Q.*

---

54. *Reach my work*] Hand me my embroidery or sewing.

58. *from Padua*] presumably from the university.

63. *large*] full and free.

64. *perfection*] either of form and beauty, or of accomplishments
(*O.E.D.*, 3, 6). The praise of Annabella and the seemingly innocent conversation which follows (in which four persons out of five have something
to hide) is full of echoes of Annabella's sexual initiation; thus 'virtue' has
an ironical effect here, and 'perfection' may recall 'Women receive perfection by men' (Tilley W718).

68. *parts*] talents; the context activates another meaning, 'sexual organs'
(*O.E.D.*, *sb* 12, 3).

Flo. Sir, now you know my house, pray make not strange;   70
       And if you find my daughter need your art,
       I'll be your paymaster.
Rich.   Sir, what I am
       She shall command.
Flo.   You shall bind me to you.—
       Daughter, I must have conference with you
       About some matters that concerns us both.—   75
       Good master doctor, please you but walk in,
       We'll crave a little of your cousin's cunning;
       I think my girl hath not quite forgot
       To touch an instrument, she could have done 't;
       We'll hear them both.   80
Rich.   I'll wait upon you, sir.   *Exeunt.*

[II. ii]

          Enter SORANZO *in his study, reading a book.*

Sor. 'Love's measure is extreme, the comfort pain,
       The life unrest, and the reward disdain.'
       What's here? Look 't o'er again: 'tis so, so writes
       This smooth licentious poet in his rhymes.

72–3. Sir . . . command] *so Weber; one line in Q.*   75. concerns] *Q;*
concern *Weber.*

II. ii. 1. Sor.] *Ellis; not in Q;* [Reads] *Dyce.*

---

 70. *make not strange*] don't stand upon ceremony.
 73. *bind me to you*] i.e. by ties of gratitude.
 77. *cunning*] skill.
 78. *girl*] a disyllable (cf. I. iii. 8).
 79. *touch*] play; also 'handle' and 'excite' (*O.E.D.*, vb 9, 22, 12).
 instrument] with the unintentional innuendo of 'penis'; cf. T. Heywood,
A Woman Killed with Kindness, ed. van Fossen, 1961, xvi, 20–1; *Shrew,*
III. i. 61–5.
 she could have done 't] she was able to do it.

 II. ii. 1. *Love's . . . extreme*] Love is inordinate.
 4. *licentious*] probably a reference to Sannazaro's reputation as a love
poet.
 his rhymes] perhaps the *Rime* (collected 1540), though the lines have not
been identified.

But Sannazar, thou liest, for had thy bosom   5
Felt such oppression as is laid on mine,
Thou wouldst have kissed the rod that made the smart.
To work then, happy Muse, and contradict
What Sannazar hath in his envy writ: [*Writes.*]
'Love's measure is the mean, sweet his annoys,   10
His pleasures life, and his reward all joys.'
Had Annabella lived when Sannazar
Did in his brief encomium celebrate
Venice, that queen of cities, he had left
That verse which gained him such a sum of gold,   15
And for one only look from Annabell
Had writ of her, and her diviner cheeks.
O, how my thoughts are—

Vas. (*Within*) Pray forbear, in rules of civility, let me give
     notice on 't: I shall be taxed of my neglect of duty and   20
     service.

Sor. What rude intrusion interrupts my peace?
     Can I be nowhere private?

Vas. (*Within*) Troth, you wrong your modesty.

Sor. What's the matter, Vasques, who is 't?   25

Enter HIPPOLITA *and* VASQUES.

7. the smart] *Q;* thee smart *Dodsley.*   9. S.D.] *Gifford.*   11. pleasures]
Q; pleasure's *Dodsley.*

---

5. *Sannazar*] Iacopo Sannazaro (1455–1530), Neapolitan pastoral poet;
best known for his *Arcadia* (1501–4), a romance in prose and verse which
had passed through sixty editions by 1600.

7. *the smart*] 'Thee' could be spelt 'the' but is so spelt only once elsewhere in Q (at v. vi. 100).

10. *Love's . . . mean*] Love's standard is the true one (cf. the 'golden
mean').

annoys] troubles.

11. *life*] a favourite word of Ford's, often approximating to 'Heaven'
(*O.E.D.*, 2; cf. I. i. 68, IV. iii. 110).

13. *encomium*] eulogy. For the encomium on Venice see Appendix II.

20. *taxed of*] blamed for.

22–3.] Cf. *Lover's Melancholy*, IV. iii (Dyce, I, 84); both passages recall
Hieronimo's famous entry in Kyd's *Spanish Tragedy* (ed. Edwards,
1959), II. v. 1.

Hip. 'Tis I:

Do you know me now? Look, perjured man, on her
Whom thou and thy distracted lust have wronged.
Thy sensual rage of blood hath made my youth
A scorn to men and angels; and shall I   30
Be now a foil to thy unsated change?
Thou know'st, false wanton, when my modest fame
Stood free from stain or scandal, all the charms
Of Hell or sorcery could not prevail
Against the honour of my chaster bosom.   35
Thine eyes did plead in tears, thy tongue in oaths
Such and so many, that a heart of steel
Would have been wrought to pity, as was mine:
And shall the conquest of my lawful bed,
My husband's death urged on by his disgrace,   40
My loss of womanhood, be ill-rewarded
With hatred and contempt? No, know Soranzo,
I have a spirit doth as much distaste
The slavery of fearing thee, as thou
Dost loathe the memory of what hath passed.   45

Sor. Nay, dear Hippolita—

Hip.   Call me not dear,
Nor think with supple words to smooth the grossness
Of my abuses: 'tis not your new mistress,
Your goodly Madam Merchant, shall triumph

---

28. *distracted*] drawn first in one direction, then another; cf. 'my weake
facultie, and distracted studies' (W. Austin, *Certain Meditations*, 1635,
cited by *O.E.D.*, distracted, 3).
    29. *sensual rage of blood*] violence of sexual passion (cf. I. i. 32 and note).
    31. *foil*] contrast (to heighten enjoyment elsewhere); cf. *Line of Life*,
Dyce, III, 383, 'in some, . . . reason is . . . not the directress, but the
foil to their passions'.
    40. *urged on*] hastened.
    41. *womanhood*] womanly modesty; position of an honourable woman.
    43. *distaste*] dislike.
    49. *Madam Merchant*] Florio's wealth has apparently been gained by
trade, so that Hippolita can claim noble birth as an advantage over
Annabella (51).
    49–50. *triumph On my dejection*] exult in my overthrow. 'Triumph' needs

                On my dejection; tell her thus from me,   50
                My birth was nobler, and by much more free.
Sor. You are too violent.
Hip.   You are too double
                In your dissimulation; seest thou this,
                This habit, these black mourning weeds of care?
                'Tis thou art cause of this, and hast divorced   55
                My husband from his life and me from him,
                And made me widow in my widowhood.
Sor. Will you yet hear?
Hip.   More of thy perjuries?
                Thy soul is drowned too deeply in those sins,
                Thou need'st not add to th' number.
Sor.   Then I'll leave you;   60
                You are past all rules of sense.
Hip.   And thou of grace.
Vas. Fie mistress, you are not near the limits of reason: if my

58. thy] *Q^b;* the *Q^a.*

---

to be stressed on the second syllable, as at IV. iii. 64 (but not at v. vi. 11).
    51. *free*] honourable (cf. 'The Epistle', 9).
    55-7.] Soranzo's intrigue with Hippolita was known to Richardetto
(above, 40; II. iii. 7 ff.), so that she and her husband were estranged before
his supposed death. Thus she has been doubly divorced (= 'separated',
O.E.D., 4) or doubly widowed (first metaphorically and then literally).
Alternatively, 57 may mean 'and made me doubly a widow by yourself
casting me off'; cf. Byron, *Don Juan*, I, clxxxv.
    61.] 'Sense' and 'grace' have many meanings, but Soranzo apparently
tells Hippolita that she is beyond reason, to which she replies that he is
beyond divine forgiveness; if she is deranged in her wits, he is deranged
in his soul. For a similar antithesis cf. *Pilgrimage of Perfection* (1531,
cited by *O.E.D.*, rule *sb* 10): 'it discerneth or iudgeth . . . by the rules
of grace, ferre aboue all naturall reason'.   *rules*] principles, standards;
regular workings, as in 'the rules of friendship as of love', *Lady's Trial*,
v. ii (Dyce, III, 89), and 'rules of zeale' (*Christes Bloodie Sweat*, sig. H1).
grace] primarily 'divine forgiveness', but cf. *Cymbeline*, I. i. 135: '*Cym.*
Past grace? obedience? *Imo.* Past hope, and in despair; that way, past
grace', where 'past grace' first means 'without virtue or seemliness' and
then 'beyond the reach of God's mercy'.
    62. *limits of reason*] boundaries of reasonable speech and behaviour.

lord had a resolution as noble as virtue itself, you take the
course to unedge it all. Sir, I beseech you do not perplex
her, griefs, alas, will have a vent; I dare undertake Madam   65
Hippolita will now freely hear you.

Sor. Talk to a woman frantic! Are these the fruits of your
    love?

Hip. They are the fruits of thy untruth, false man!
    Didst thou not swear, whilst yet my husband lived,   70
    That thou wouldst wish no happiness on earth
    More than to call me wife? Didst thou not vow
    When he should die to marry me? For which
    The devil in my blood, and thy protests,
    Caused me to counsel him to undertake   75
    A voyage to Ligorne—for that we heard
    His brother there was dead, and left a daughter
    Young and unfriended, who with much ado
    I wished him to bring hither: he did so,
    And went; and as thou know'st, died on the way.   80
    Unhappy man to buy his death so dear
    With my advice! yet thou for whom I did it
    Forget'st thy vows, and leav'st me to my shame.

Sor. Who could help this?

Hip.   Who? Perjured man, thou couldst,
    If thou hadst faith or love.

Sor.   You are deceived: 85
    The vows I made, if you remember well,
    Were wicked and unlawful, 'twere more sin
    To keep them than to break them; as for me,
    I cannot mask my penitence. Think thou

---

63. *resolution*] firm purpose (Vasques seems to hint that Soranzo had intended some reparation).

64. *unedge*] make blunt, discourage.
perplex] perhaps 'vex' (*O.E.D.*, *vb* I b).

67. *frantic*] mad.

76. *voyage*] here, a land journey.

Ligorne] (pronounced 'Ligórn') Livorno, then known to Italians as Legorno, often anglicized as Leghorn. This large seaport is less than 100 miles from the inland town of Parma, but the journey would be through dangerous mountain districts; cf. v. iv. 3–4

How much thou hast digressed from honest shame   90
In bringing of a gentleman to death
Who was thy husband; such a one as he,
So noble in his quality, condition,
Learning, behaviour, entertainment, love,
As Parma could not show a braver man.   95

Vas. You do not well, this was not your promise.

Sor. I care not, let her know her monstrous life.
Ere I'll be servile to so black a sin
I'll be a corse. Woman, come here no more,
Learn to repent and die; for by my honour   100
I hate thee and thy lust; you have been too foul.   [*Exit.*]

Vas. This part has been scurvily played.

Hip. How foolishly this beast contemns his fate,
And shuns the use of that which I more scorn
Than I once loved, his love; but let him go,   105
My vengeance shall give comfort to his woe.

She offers to go away.

Vas. Mistress, mistress, Madam Hippolita; pray, a word or
two.

Hip. With me, sir?

Vas. With you if you please.   110

Hip. What is 't?

Vas. I know you are infinitely moved now, and you think

---

98. I'll] *Q;* I *Dodsley.*   99. a corse] *Q^b* (Coarse)*; a Curse *Q^a;* accurs'd
Bawcutt conj. Schmitz.   100. *Exit*] *Dodsley; not in Q.*   102.] *so Q;*
aside Gifford.   105. loved,] *Weber;* lou'd *Q;* lov'd; *Reed.*   106. his]
Q; this *Schmitz.*   107–8.] *so Weber;* Mistresse . . . Hippolita, / Pray . . .
two. *Q.*   107. mistress, Madam] *Q^b;* Mistresse Madam *Q^a.*

---

90. *digressed from honest shame*] deviated from honour and modesty.
94. *entertainment*] hospitality (cf. *Timon,* I. ii. 176).
95. *braver*] finer.
99. *corse*] corps. But Mrs Schmitz conjectures that MS. 'accurst' was
misread or misremembered into Q^a's 'a Curse', which was corrected to
'a Coarse' as the easiest way of making sense.
103. *contemns his fate*] 'Treats with contemptuous disregard his
approaching doom' seems the likeliest meaning; cf. I. ii. 225.
106. *his woe*] the woe caused by him; cf. *Romeo and Juliet,* II. iii. 46, 'I
have forgot that name, and that name's woe'.

you have cause: some I confess you have, but sure not
so much as you imagine.

Hip. Indeed!   115

Vas. O you were miserably bitter, which you followed even
to the last syllable; faith, you were somewhat too shrewd.
By my life, you could not have took my lord in a worse
time since I first knew him; tomorrow you shall find
him a new man.   120

Hip. Well, I shall wait his leisure.

Vas. Fie, this is not a hearty patience, it comes sourly from
you; troth, let me persuade you for once.

Hip. [*Aside*] I have it, and it shall be so; thanks, opportunity!
[*To him*] Persuade me to what?   125

Vas. Visit him in some milder temper; O, if you could but
master a little your female spleen, how might you win
him!

Hip. He will never love me. Vasques, thou hast been a too
trusty servant to such a master, and I believe thy   130
reward in the end will fall out like mine.

Vas. So perhaps too.

Hip. Resolve thyself it will. Had I one so true, so truly
honest, so secret to my counsels, as thou hast been to
him and his, I should think it a slight acquittance, not   135
only to make him master of all I have, but even of
myself.

Vas. O, you are a noble gentlewoman!

Hip. Wou't thou feed always upon hopes? Well, I know
thou art wise, and seest the reward of an old servant   140
daily what it is.

Vas. Beggary and neglect.

Hip. True; but Vasques, wert thou mine, and wouldst be

124. *Aside*] Dodsley; Q prints perswade ... what? *on separate line between*
long dashes.

---

116. *followed*] kept up.
117. *shrewd*] abusive.
133. *Resolve thyself*] make up your mind (that).

        private to me and my designs, I here protest myself, and
        all what I can else call mine, should be at thy dispose.   145
Vas. [*Aside*] Work you that way, old mole ? then I have the
        wind of you. [*To her*] I were not worthy of it, by any
        desert that could lie within my compass; if I could—
Hip. What then ?
Vas. I should then hope to live in these my old years with   150
        rest and security.
Hip. Give me thy hand, now promise but thy silence,
        And help to bring to pass a plot I have;
        And here in sight of Heaven, that being done,
        I make thee lord of me and mine estate.   155
Vas. Come, you are merry; this is such a happiness that I
        can neither think or believe.
Hip. Promise thy secrecy, and 'tis confirmed.
Vas. Then here I call our good genii for witnesses, whatsoever
        your designs are, or against whomsoever, I will not only   160
        be a special actor therein, but never disclose it till it be
        effected.
Hip. I take thy word, and with that, thee for mine;
        Come then, let's more confer of this anon.
        On this delicious bane my thoughts shall banquet: 165
        Revenge shall sweeten what my griefs have tasted.   *Exeunt.*

---

146. *Aside*] Dodsley; *Q has long dash after* you.   148. lie within] *Dyce;*
lye - - - - within *Q;*   156-7.] *so Weber;* Come . . . merry, / This . . . can /
Neither . . . beleeue. *Q.*   159. for witnesses] *Dodsley;* foe-witnesses *Q.*

---

    145. *all what*] all that (cf. I. i. 17).
    dispose] disposal.
    146-7. *Work you . . . wind of you*] a mixed metaphor which probably
conflates two phrases from *Hamlet*: 'Well said, old mole! canst work i' th'
earth so fast ?' (I. v. 162) and 'Why do you go about to recover the wind
of me . . . ?' (III. ii. 337-9). *have the wind of you*] pick up your scent;
guess your intention.
    159. *good genii*] tutelary spirits, 'guardian angels'. 'They are . . .
appointed by those higher Powers to keep men from their nativity, and to
protect or punish them, as they see cause; and are called *boni* and *mali*
Genii by the Romans . . . . As Anthony Rusca contends, . . . every
man hath a good and a bad Angel attending of him in particular all his life
long.' (Burton, I, 207, 226.) Cf. v. i. 31.

[II. iii]

Enter RICHARDETTO *and* PHILOTIS.

Rich. Thou seest, my lovely niece, these strange mishaps,
     How all my fortunes turn to my disgrace,
     Wherein I am but as a looker-on,
     Whiles others act my shame, and I am silent.

Phil. But uncle, wherein can this borrowed shape   5
     Give you content?

Rich.   I'll tell thee, gentle niece:
     Thy wanton aunt in her lascivious riots
     Lives now secure, thinks I am surely dead
     In my late journey to Ligorne for you—
     As I have caused it to be rumoured out;   10
     Now would I see with what an impudence
     She gives scope to her loose adultery,
     And how the common voice allows hereof;
     Thus far I have prevailed.

Phil.   Alas, I fear
     You mean some strange revenge.

Rich.   O, be not troubled;   15
     Your ignorance shall plead for you in all.
     But to our business: what, you learnt for certain
     How Signior Florio means to give his daughter
     In marriage to Soranzo?

Phil.   Yes, for certain.

Rich. But how find you young Annabella's love   20
     Inclined to him?

Phil.   For aught I could perceive,
     She neither fancies him or any else.

Rich. There's mystery in that which time must show.
     She used you kindly?

II. iii. 4. *act*] bring about (*O.E.D.*, *vb* 2).
     5. *borrowed shape*] disguise; cf. *Broken Heart*, II. iii, III. i (Dyce, I, 251, 255).
     8. *secure*] relaxed, unsuspecting.
     13. *the common voice*] public opinion.
     allows] judges.
     24. *used you*] behaved towards you.

Phil.   Yes.

Rich.   And craved your company?

Phil. Often.

Rich.   'Tis well, it goes as I could wish;   25
I am the doctor now, and as for you,
None knows you; if all fail not we shall thrive.
But who comes here?

Enter GRIMALDI.

I know him, 'tis Grimaldi:
A Roman and a soldier, near allied
Unto the Duke of Montferrato; one   30
Attending on the Nuncio of the Pope
That now resides in Parma, by which means
He hopes to get the love of Annabella.

Grim. Save you, sir.

Rich.   And you, sir.

Grim.   I have heard
Of your approvèd skill, which through the city   35
Is freely talked of, and would crave your aid.

Rich. For what, sir?

Grim.   Marry sir, for this—
But I would speak in private.

Rich.   Leave us, cousin.

                                            Exit PHILOTIS.

Grim. I love fair Annabella, and would know
Whether in arts there may not be receipts   40
To move affection.

II. iii. 28. *Enter* GRIMALDI] *so Q; Gifford places after 33.*   35. approvèd]
Dyce; approu'd *Q.*   40. arts] *Q* (Arts); art *Dyce.*

---

34. *Save you*] God save you.

40. *arts*] (medical) studies and skills; cf. 'arts-man' (i.e. physician),
Lover's Melancholy, III. i, v. i (Dyce, I, 69, 99).

40–1. *receipts To move affection*] recipes to arouse love. Burton (III,
149–53) discusses love-philtres chiefly of a magical kind, but magic and
medicine were not yet clearly distinguished: cf. 'medicines to make me
love him', *I Henry IV*, II. ii. 20–1.

Rich.   Sir, perhaps there may,
    But these will nothing profit you.
Grim.   Not me?
Rich. Unless I be mistook, you are a man
    Greatly in favour with the Cardinal.
Grim. What of that?
Rich.   In duty to his grace,   45
    I will be bold to tell you, if you seek
    To marry Florio's daughter, you must first
    Remove a bar 'twixt you and her.
Grim.   Who's that?
Rich. Soranzo is the man that hath her heart,
    And while he lives, be sure you cannot speed.   50
Grim. Soranzo—what, mine enemy, is 't he?
Rich. Is he your enemy?
Grim. The man I hate worse than confusion!
    I'll kill him straight.
Rich.   Nay, then take mine advice,
    Even for his grace's sake the Cardinal: 55
    I'll find a time when he and she do meet,
    Of which I'll give you notice, and to be sure
    He shall not 'scape you, I'll provide a poison
    To dip your rapier's point in, if he had
    As many heads as Hydra had, he dies.   60
Grim. But shall I trust thee, doctor?
Rich.   As yourself,
    Doubt not in aught. [*Aside*] Thus shall the fates decree,
    By me Soranzo falls, that ruined me.   *Exeunt.*

52–4.] *so this ed.;* Is . . . Enemy? / The . . . hate, / Worse then Confusion; /
I'le . . . streight. / Nay . . . aduice, *Q;* Is . . . hate, / Worse . . . straight. / Nay
. . . advice, *Reed.*   54. kill] *Q*^{b}*;* tell *Q*^{a}*;* to *Ellis* (*conj. Gifford*).   62.
Aside] *Bawcutt; Exit* GRIM. *Gifford.*   63. By me] *Q;* By thee *Sturgess.*
ruined] *Q*^{b}*;* min'd *Q*^{a}.

---

50. *speed*] succeed.
    60. *Hydra*] a monster usually described with nine heads, sometimes with
fifty or a hundred; as each head was cut off two more grew in its place.
Hercules killed it by sealing off the wounds with fire.

[II. iv]

Enter DONADO, BERGETTO *and* POGGIO.

Don. Well sir, I must be content to be both your secretary
and your messenger myself: I cannot tell what this letter
may work, but as sure as I am alive, if thou come once to
talk with her, I fear thou wou't mar whatsoever I make.

Ber. You make, uncle? Why, am not I big enough to carry   5
mine own letter, I pray?

Don. Ay, ay, carry a fool's head o' thy own; why thou dunce,
wouldst thou write a letter, and carry it thyself?

Ber. Yes, that I would, and read it to her with my own
mouth; for you must think, if she will not believe me   10
myself when she hears me speak, she will not believe
another's handwriting. O, you think I am a blockhead,
uncle! No sir, Poggio knows I have indited a letter myself, so I have.

Pog. Yes truly, sir, I have it in my pocket.   15

Don. A sweet one no doubt, pray let's see 't.

Ber. I cannot read my own hand very well, Poggio; read it,
Poggio.

Don. Begin.

Pog. (Reads) 'Most dainty and honey-sweet mistress, I could   20
call you fair, and lie as fast as any that loves you, but my
uncle being the elder man I leave it to him, as more fit
for his age, and the colour of his beard; I am wise enough
to tell you I can board where I see occasion, or if you
like my uncle's wit better than mine, you shall marry   25

II. iv. 5. Why,] *Dyce;* why *Q.*   17–18.] *so Gifford;* I . . . *Poggio,* / Reade
it *Poggio. Q.*   20. (*Reads*)] *Poggio* reades. *Q (centred in own line).*
24. board] *Q;* bourd *Weber (conj. Reed).*

II. iv. 8. *wouldst . . . carry it thyself*] an old 'noodle tale', probably
of folk origin, included in the *Facetie* (Venice, 1581) of M. L. Domenichi;
see *The Facetiae of Poggio and other Medieval Story-tellers,* trans. E.
Storer (Broadway Translations, n.d.), p. 68.
24. *board*] engage closely (in conversation or embraces). Cf. *Shrew,*
I. ii. 93–4, 'I will board her, though she chide as loud As thunder'.
occasion] a favourable opportunity.

me; if you like mine better than his, I will marry you
in spite of your teeth; so commending my best parts to
you, I rest

> Yours upwards and downwards, or you may choose,
>   Bergetto.'   30

Ber. Ah, ha! here's stuff, uncle!

Don. Here's stuff indeed to shame us all; pray whose advice
did you take in this learned letter?

Pog. None, upon my word, but mine own.

Ber. And mine, uncle, believe it, nobody's else; 'twas mine   35
own brain, I thank a good wit for 't.

Don. Get you home sir, and look you keep within doors till I
return.

Ber. How! that were a jest indeed; I scorn it i'faith.

Don. What, you do not!   40

Ber. Judge me, but I do now.

Pog. Indeed sir, 'tis very unhealthy.

Don. Well sir, if I hear any of your apish running to motions
and fopperies till I come back, you were as good no;
look to 't.   *Exit.* 45

Ber. Poggio, shall 's steal to see this horse with the head in 's
tail?

Pog. Ay, but you must take heed of whipping.

Ber. Dost take me for a child, Poggio? Come, honest Poggio.

> *Exeunt.*

32–3.] *so Weber;* Here's . . . all, / Pray . . . Letter? *Q.*   44. no] *Q;* not
Dodsley.   49.] *so Weber;* Dost . . . *Poggio,* / Come honest *Poggio. Q.*

---

27. *in spite of your teeth*] despite your opposition.

parts] qualities; cf. II. i. 68 and note.

43. *motions*] puppet-shows. In Shakespeare's day a constant succession
of these shows could be seen in Fleet Street. Ben Jonson introduces one
into *Bartholomew Fair* (ed. Horsman, 1960), v. iii–iv, with Cokes showing
the same unsophisticated pleasure as Bergetto.

44. *fopperies*] follies.

you were as good no] 'you'll regret it' (where *as good* is meiosis for
'much better'). Cf. 'yf thou doest thou were as good no', *Wealth and Health*
(1557, ed. Greg 1907, 658); 'Call her again, and thou wert better no',
Henry Porter, *Two Angry Women of Abington* (1599), II. i (p. 121 in *Nero
and Other Plays* [1888]).

[II. v]

Enter Friar *and* GIOVANNI.

Fri. Peace! thou hast told a tale whose every word
  Threatens eternal slaughter to the soul;
  I'm sorry I have heard it: would mine ears
  Had been one minute deaf, before the hour
  That thou camest to me! O young man cast away,   5
  By the religious number of mine order,
  I day and night have waked my aged eyes
  Above my strength, to weep on thy behalf;
  But Heaven is angry, and be thou resolved,
  Thou art a man remarked to taste a mischief;   10
  Look for 't; though it come late, it will come sure.

Gio. Father, in this you are uncharitable;
  What I have done, I'll prove both fit and good.
  It is a principle, which you have taught
  When I was yet your scholar, that the frame   15
  And composition of the mind doth follow
  The frame and composition of body;

II. v. 2. the] *Q; thy Reed.* 5. man cast away] *this ed.; man* cast-away
Q; man, castaway *Dyce;* man castaway *Bawcutt.* 6. number] *Q;*
founder *conj. Gifford.* 8. my] *Dodsley;* thy *Q.* 15. frame] *Dodsley;*
Fame *Q.* 17. of] *Q;* of the *Gifford.*

II. v. 2. *the soul*] Reed's emendation is attractive: 'thy' may have been
spelt 'thie' in MS., or the long-tailed 'h' of a secretary hand may have been
misread. Cf. I. ii. 43, II. ii. 58 (where an identical error is corrected at the
press), III. vii. 24, IV. i. 37.

 5. *cast away*] lost; damned.

 6. *number*] company, body; cf. 'the honoured number' (patricians),
Coriolanus, III. i. 72.

 10. *remarked*] marked out.

 14–26. In Q the main terms of Giovanni's argument (*Minde, Body,
Bodies, Beauty,* etc.) are emphasized by capitals and italic, as Ford probably
intended: see Introduction, pp. lxiii–lxiv.

 14–19. *It is . . . virtue*] Cf. *Honour Triumphant* (1606): 'If the temperature of the mind follow the temperature of the body,—text it is,—then,
without controversy, as the outward shape is more singular, so the inward
virtues must be more exquisite' (Dyce, III, 359).

 16, 17. *composition*] pronounced first with four syllables, then with five;
cf. 'marriage' below, 40–1.

So where the body's furniture is beauty,
The mind's must needs be virtue; which allowed,
Virtue itself is reason but refined,   20
And love the quintessence of that; this proves
My sister's beauty, being rarely fair,
Is rarely virtuous; chiefly in her love,
And chiefly in that love, her love to me.
If hers to me, then so is mine to her;   25
Since in like causes are effects alike.

Fri. O ignorance in knowledge! Long ago,
How often have I warned thee this before!
Indeed, if we were sure there were no Deity,
Nor Heaven nor Hell, then to be led alone   30
By Nature's light—as were philosophers
Of elder times—might instance some defence.
But 'tis not so: then madman, thou wilt find
That Nature is in Heaven's positions blind.

Gio. Your age o'errules you: had you youth like mine,   35
You'd make her love your Heaven, and her divine.

Fri. Nay, then I see th' art too far sold to Hell;
It lies not in the compass of my prayers
To call thee back; yet let me counsel thee:
Persuade thy sister to some marriage.   40

Gio. Marriage? Why, that's to damn her; that's to prove
Her greedy of variety of lust.

Fri. O fearful! If thou wilt not, give me leave
To shrive her; lest she should die unabsolved.

Gio. At your best leisure, father; then she'll tell you   45
How dearly she doth prize my matchless love;

---

18. *where . . . beauty*] where the body is 'furnished', i.e. adorned, with beauty.

21. *quintessence*] purest or most perfect manifestation (of virtue, as virtue is of reason). The word is stressed on the first syllable, with perhaps a secondary stress on the third; cf. *Fame's Memorial*, Dyce III, 289, 311.

28. *warned*] forbidden (*O.E.D.*, *vb*[2] 2).

32. *instance*] prove.

34. *in Heaven's positions*] to what Heaven affirms. A 'position' is a statement or tenet, usually in some syllogistic argument like Giovanni's.

Then you will know what pity 'twere we two
Should have been sundered from each other's arms.
View well her face, and in that little round
You may observe a world of variety: 50
For colour, lips, for sweet perfumes, her breath;
For jewels, eyes; for threads of purest gold,
Hair; for delicious choice of flowers, cheeks;
Wonder in every portion of that throne.
Hear her but speak, and you will swear the spheres   55
Make music to the citizens in Heaven;
But father, what is else for pleasure framed
Lest I offend your ears shall go unnamed.

Fri. The more I hear, I pity thee the more,
That one so excellent should give those parts   60
All to a second death. What I can do

---

50. world of] *Q;* world's *Gifford.*   51. colour] *Q;* coral *Dodsley.*
54. throne] *Q;* form *Dodsley.*

49–50.] Ford seems to be recalling another argument from *Honour Triumphant*, i.e. that in contemplating the beloved person we are led to contemplate God's universe, of which she is the microcosm. 'Being overcome with the affection of some excellently deserving beauty, with admiration of the singular perfection thereof, with what curious workmanship it is framed, with what glory of majesty it is endowed, it is an immediate occasion to bring them in serious conceit of weighing the wonders of the heavens in compacting such admirable quintessence in so precious a form, by which they will deeply revolve the dignity of God in that mould, and truly acknowledge the weakness of their own nature in comparison of beauty' (Dyce, III, 368–9).

54. *throne*] Possibly a secretary-hand 'fforme' has been misread, but Ford associates thrones with heavenly power and beauty. In *The Sun's Darling*, III. iii (Dyce, III, 139), Summer addresses the Sun as 'Life of my love! throne where my glories sit!' Cf. also the description in *Love's Sacrifice*, I. ii (Dyce, II, 21–2) of 'the court, Where, like so many stars, on several thrones Beauty and greatness shine in proper orbs; Sweet matter for my meditation'.

55–6. *spheres Make music*] The concentric heavenly spheres of Ptolemaic cosmology were said to make as they revolved a divine music, expressing their perfect harmony and inaudible to mortals (cf. *Merchant*, v. i. 60–5).

61. *a second death*] damnation. 'But the fearful, and unbelieving, and the abominable, and murderers, and whoremongers, . . . shall have their part in the lake which burneth with fire and brimstone: which is the second death' (Revelation, XXI. 8; see also XX, *passim*).

Is but to pray; and yet I could advise thee,
Wouldst thou be ruled.

Gio.   In what?

Fri.   Why, leave her yet:
The throne of Mercy is above your trespass;
Yet time is left you both—

Gio.   To embrace each other,   65
Else let all time be struck quite out of number;
She is like me, and I like her resolved.

Fri. No more, I'll visit her; this grieves me most,
Things being thus, a pair of souls are lost.   *Exeunt.*

[II. vi]

Enter FLORIO, DONADO, ANNABELLA, PUTANA.

Flo. Where's Giovanni?

Ann.   Newly walked abroad,
And, as I heard him say, gone to the friar,
His reverend tutor.

Flo.   That's a blessed man,
A man made up of holiness; I hope
He'll teach him how to gain another world.   5

Don. Fair gentlewoman, here's a letter sent
To you from my young cousin; I dare swear
He loves you in his soul: would you could hear
Sometimes, what I see daily, sighs and tears,
As if his breast were prison to his heart!   10

Flo. Receive it, Annabella.

Ann.   Alas, good man!   [*Takes the letter.*]

Don. What's that she said?

Put. And please you, sir, she said 'Alas, good man!' [*Aside to*

II. vi. 3. reverend] *Dodsley;* reuerent *Q.*   11. S.D.] *Gifford.*   13, 17,
20. *Aside*] *this ed.*

66. *number*] order, sequence (*O.E.D.*, *sb* 13, *vb* 5 b).

II. vi. 13. *And please*] if it please.

Don.] Truly, I do commend him to her every night before
her first sleep, because I would have her dream of him;   15
and she hearkens to that most religiously.

Don. [*Aside to Put.*] Say'st so? Godamercy Putana, there's
something for thee, and prithee do what thou canst on his
behalf; sha'not be lost labour, take my word for 't.

Put. [*Aside to Don.*] Thank you most heartily, sir; now I have   20
a feeling of your mind, let me alone to work.

Ann. Guardian!

Put. Did you call?

Ann. Keep this letter.

Don. Signior Florio, in any case bid her read it instantly.   25

Flo. Keep it, for what? Pray read it me here right.

Ann. I shall, sir.   *She reads.*

Don. How d'ee find her inclined, signior?

Flo. Troth sir, I know not how; not all so well
    As I could wish.   30

Ann. Sir, I am bound to rest your cousin's debtor.
    The jewel I'll return; for if he love,
    I'll count that love a jewel.

Don.   Mark you that?
    Nay, keep them both, sweet maid.

Ann.   You must excuse me,
    Indeed I will not keep it.

Flo.   Where's the ring,   35
    That which your mother in her will bequeathed,
    And charged you on her blessing not to give 't
    To any but your husband? Send back that.

Ann. I have it not.

Flo.   Ha! have it not, where is 't?

Ann. My brother in the morning took it from me,   40

---

17. *Godamercy*] well done; many thanks.
21. *feeling*] appreciation, understanding (*O.E.D., sb* 6), with a play on
the satisfying tangibility of the evidence; italicized in Q.
mind] views, intentions.
25. *in any case*] at all events.
26. *here right*] on the spot, at once.

Said he would wear 't today.

Flo.   Well, what do you say
To young Bergetto's love? Are you content
To match with him? Speak.

Don.   There's the point indeed.

Ann. [*Aside*] What shall I do? I must say something now.

Flo. What say, why d'ee not speak?

Ann.   Sir, with your leave,   45
Please you to give me freedom?

Flo.   Yes, you have 't.

Ann. Signior Donado, if your nephew mean
To raise his better fortunes in his match,
The hope of me will hinder such a hope.
Sir, if you love him, as I know you do,   50
Find one more worthy of his choice than me:
In short, I'm sure I sha'not be his wife.

Don. Why, here's plain dealing; I commend thee for 't,
And all the worst I wish thee, is Heaven bless thee!
Your father yet and I will still be friends,   55
Shall we not, Signior Florio?

Flo.   Yes, why not?
Look, here your cousin comes.

Enter BERGETTO *and* POGGIO.

Don. [*Aside*] O coxcomb, what doth he make here?

Ber. Where's my uncle, sirs?

Don. What's the news now?   60

Ber. Save you, uncle, save you; you must not think I come for
nothing, masters; and how, and how is 't? What, you
have read my letter? Ah, there I—tickled you i'faith!

44. *Aside*] *Gifford.*   46. freedom?] *Gifford;* freedome. *Q.* have 't] *this
ed.;* haue *Q;* have it *Gifford.*   58.   *Aside*] *Dyce.*

45. *What say*] what do you say (cf. *Queen,* 3664).
46. *have 't*] Q's 'haue' is presumably a misreading of 'hau't', a form which
appears in Q at I. i. 32; cf. 'stald' for 'seal'd', *Lady's Trial,* line 229
(*Materialien,* n.s. I).
58. *doth he make*] is he doing.

Pog. [*Aside to Ber.*] But 'twere better you had tickled her in
    another place.   65

Ber. Sirrah sweetheart, I'll tell thee a good jest, and riddle
    what 'tis.

Ann. You say you'd tell me.

Ber. As I was walking just now in the street, I met a swagger-
    ing fellow would needs take the wall of me; and because 70
    he did thrust me, I very valiantly called him rogue. He
    hereupon bade me draw; I told him I had more wit than
    so; but when he saw that I would not, he did so maul
    me with the hilts of his rapier, that my head sung whilst
    my feet capered in the kennel.   75

Don. [*Aside*] Was ever the like ass seen?

Ann. And what did you all this while?

Ber. Laugh at him for a gull, till I see the blood run about
    mine ears, and then I could not choose but find in my
    heart to cry; till a fellow with a broad beard—they say he 80
    is a new-come doctor—called me into this house, and
    gave me a plaster—look you, here 'tis; and sir, there was
    a young wench washed my face and hands most ex-
    cellently, i'faith I shall love her as long as I live for 't—
    did she not, Poggio?   85

Pog. Yes, and kissed him too.

Ber. Why la now, you think I tell a lie, uncle, I warrant.

Don. Would he that beat thy blood out of thy head, had

64. *Aside to Ber.*] *Dyce.*   76. *Aside*] *Dyce.*   81. this] *Q;* his *Gifford.*

---

66. *Sirrah sweetheart*] a less uncouth combination than it now sounds;
'sirrah' could be addressed to women, usually facetiously (*O.E.D.*, *s.v.*
sirrah, 1 b, 2).
    riddle] guess.
    70. *take the wall of me*] Streets were narrow, there was no special paving
for pedestrians, and mud and filth drained into a central gutter or 'kennel';
so the best and most honourable place to walk was by the wall. To yield
this place was a courtesy, to take it by forcing another man towards the
kennel was to claim superiority and often led to disputes, sometimes to
death (see *Diary of Samuel Pepys*, ed. Latham and Matthews, 1, 1970,
p. 46, n. 4).
    75. *kennel*] See preceding note.
    78. *gull*] fool, dupe.

beaten some wit into it! for I fear thou never wilt have
any.   90

Ber. O uncle, but there was a wench would have done a man's
heart good to have looked on her; by this light, she had a
face methinks worth twenty of you, Mistress Annabella.

Don. [*Aside*] Was ever such a fool born?

Ann. I am glad she liked you, sir.   95

Ber. Are you so? by my troth, I thank you forsooth.

Flo. Sure 'twas the doctor's niece, that was last day with us
here.

Ber. 'Twas she, 'twas she!

Don. How do you know that, simplicity?   100

Ber. Why, does not he say so? If I should have said no, I
should have given him the lie, uncle, and so have
deserved a dry-beating again; I'll none of that.

Flo. A very modest, well-behaved young maid as I have
seen.   105

Don. Is she indeed?

Flo. Indeed she is, if I have any judgment.

Don. Well sir, now you are free, you need not care for send-
ing letters now: you are dismissed, your mistress here
will none of you.   110

Ber. No? why, what care I for that; I can have wenches
enough in Parma for half-a-crown apiece, cannot I,
Poggio?

Pog. I'll warrant you sir.

Don. Signior Florio,   115
       I thank you for your free recourse you gave
       For my admittance; and to you, fair maid,

94. *Aside*] *Dyce.*   104–7.] *so Gifford;* A very ... seene. / Is shee indeed? /
Indeed / Shee ... Iudgement. *Q;* A very ... maid, / As ... Indeed /
She ... judgment. *Weber.*   104. maid as] *Q;* maid, as *Dodsley.*   109.
letters now:] *Gifford;* letters, now *Q.*   115–19.] *so Dyce; as prose in Q.*

---

95. *liked*] probably 'pleased' (*O.E.D.*, *vb*¹ 1).

100. *simplicity*] simpleton (cf. 'innocence', I. ii. 50).

103. *dry-beating*] properly, a beating that does not draw blood; sometimes, a severe beating (*O.E.D.*, dry *adj* 12).

116. *recourse*] access.

That jewel I will give you 'gainst your marriage.
Come, will you go sir ?

Ber. Ay, marry will I. Mistress, farewell mistress; I'll come   120
again tomorrow; farewell mistress.

Exeunt DONADO, BERGETTO *and* POGGIO.

Enter GIOVANNI.

Flo. Son, where have you been ? what, alone, alone, still, still ?
I would not have it so, you must forsake
This over-bookish humour. Well, your sister
Hath shook the fool off.

Gio.   'Twas no match for her.   125

Flo. 'Twas not indeed, I meant it nothing less;
Soranzo is the man I only like:
Look on him, Annabella! Come, 'tis supper-time,
And it grows late.   *Exit.*

Gio. Whose jewel's that ?   130

Ann. Some sweetheart's.

Gio.   So I think.

Ann.   A lusty youth,
Signior Donado, gave it me to wear
Against my marriage.

Gio.   But you shall not wear it:
Send it him back again.

122–5.] *so Weber; as prose in* Q.   122. still, still ?] Q; still ? *Gifford*.
131–3. A lusty . . . again.] *so Gifford;* A lusty . . . me / To . . . Marriage, /
But . . . againe. Q.

---

118. *'gainst*] in anticipation of (i.e., as a wedding-present given in
advance).

122. *alone, alone, still, still ?*] If dittography has occurred it is perhaps
more likely that the compositor repeated 'alone,' than that he first erro-
neously set 'still,' and then correctly 'still ?'.

still] always. Though Giovanni has not been so completely alone as
Florio thinks, he does have solitary habits, which were considered both a
symptom and a cause of morbid mental states (see Burton, *passim*).

124. *humour*] habit of life, 'attitude'.

126. *meant . . . less*] did not intend it at all.

127. *the man I only like*] probably 'the man I prefer above all others', but
possibly 'the only man of them I like' (*O.E.D.*, only *adv* 3, 1 c).

Ann.   What, you are jealous?

Gio. That you shall know anon, at better leisure;   135
    Welcome, sweet night! the evening crowns the day. *Exeunt.*

---

134. *jealous*] suspiciously vigilant; Giovanni's reply seems to play on
another sense, 'ardently amorous' (*O.E.D.*, 2; not recorded later than
1555).

136. *the evening crowns the day*] Cf. 'evenings crown the days', *Hero and
Leander* (Chapman's continuation, 1598), III. 10, and later forms in
Tilley E190.

crowns] both 'completes' and 'rewards', as in *finis coronat opus* and its
English derivatives (Tilley E116).

Act III

Enter BERGETTO *and* POGGIO.

Ber. Does my uncle think to make me a baby still? No,
Poggio, he shall know I have a sconce now.

Pog. Ay, let him not bob you off like an ape with an apple.

Ber. 'Sfoot, I will have the wench, if he were ten uncles, in
despite of his nose, Poggio.   5

Pog. Hold him to the grindstone, and give not a jot of ground;
she hath in a manner promised you already.

Ber. True, Poggio, and her uncle the doctor swore I should
marry her.

Pog. He swore, I remember.   10

Ber. And I will have her, that's more; didst see the codpiece-
point she gave me, and the box of marmalade?

III. i. Act III] *Actus Tertius.* Q.   6–9.] *so Weber;* Hold ... ground, /
Shee ... already. / True ... Doctor / Swore ... her. Q.   8. *Ber.*]
Dodsley; Pog. Q.

III. i. 2. *sconce*] head, brain.

3. *bob you off*] put you off by a fraud (*O.E.D.*, bob *vb* 1 b).

like an ape with an apple] Cf. 'a toy to mock an ape', i.e. a petty
device to distract or cheat, *Oxford Dictionary of English Proverbs* (1970),
T456. The meaning here may be sexual: apes were thought of as lustful
(cf. *Othello*, III. iii. 407), and apples as antaphrodisiacs: cf. 'He that's
cooled with an apple and heated with an egg, over me shall never spread
his leg' (Tilley A293).

4. *'Sfoot*] by God's foot.

11–12. *codpiece-point*] lace, probably ornamental, for tying the codpiece.
This was a bag-like compartment in front of tight-fitting breeches, to
accommodate the male organs; it was often exaggerated or decorated.
But by 1633 codpieces had been utterly out of fashion for at least thirty
years (C. W. and P. Cunnington, *English Costume in the 16th Century*,
1954, p. 118).

12. *box*] pot, jar.

marmalade] fruit preserve of any kind, e.g. of plums, quinces (Burton,
II, 29) or dates (*O.E.D.*).

Pog. Very well, and kissed you, that my chops watered at
    the sight on 't; there's no way but to clap up a marriage
    in hugger mugger.   15
Ber. I will do 't, for I tell thee Poggio, I begin to grow
    valiant methinks, and my courage begins to rise.
Pog. Should you be afraid of your uncle?
Ber. Hang him, old doting rascal, no: I say I will have her.
Pog. Lose no time, then.   20
Ber. I will beget a race of wise men and constables, that shall
    cart whores at their own charges, and break the Duke's
    peace ere I have done myself. Come away!   *Exeunt.*

[III. ii]

        Enter FLORIO, GIOVANNI, SORANZO, ANNABELLA,
                    PUTANA *and* VASQUES.

Flo. My lord Soranzo, though I must confess
    The proffers that are made me have been great
    In marriage of my daughter, yet the hope
    Of your still rising honours have prevailed
    Above all other jointures: here she is,   5
    She knows my mind, speak for yourself to her;
    And hear you, daughter, see you use him nobly.

22–3. charges, . . . done] *Q;* charges . . . done, *Gifford.*

---

14. *clap up*] hastily arrange.
15. *in hugger mugger*] secretly.
17. *courage begins to rise*] with a play on the meaning for 'courage' of
'sexual desire' (*O.E.D.*, *sb* 3 e; cf.*Queen*, 1865) and a concrete implication
in 'rise'.
22. *cart whores*] a punishment: 'more to calme their pride, Instead of
Coaches they in Carts doe ride', Dekker, *2 Honest Whore*, v. ii. 437–8
(*Dramatic Works*, ed. Bowers, Cambridge, 1953–61, II, 217).
    at their own charges] at their own expense; possibly with the implication
'on their own account' (cf. *Lear*, IV. vi. 160–3).
23. *ere I have done myself*] before I have finished breaking it myself.

III. ii. 5. *jointures*] unions; cf. 'sympathise in jointure with thy courage',
Fame's Memorial (Dyce, III, 287).

For any private speech I'll give you time;
Come, son, and you the rest, let them alone,
Agree as they may.

Sor.   I thank you, sir.   10
Gio. [*Aside to Ann.*] Sister, be not all woman: think on me.
Sor. Vasques!
Vas. My lord?
Sor. Attend me without.

          Exeunt omnes, manent SORANZO *and* ANNABELLA.
Ann.   Sir, what's your will with me?
Sor. Do you not know what I should tell you?
Ann.   Yes,   15
You'll say you love me.
Sor.   And I'll swear it, too;
Will you believe it?
Ann.   'Tis not point of faith.

          Enter GIOVANNI *above.*

Sor. Have you not will to love?
Ann.   Not you.
Sor.   Whom then?
Ann. That's as the Fates infer.
Gio. [*Aside*] Of those I'm regent now.
Sor.   What mean you, sweet?   20
Ann. To live and die a maid.
Sor.   O, that's unfit.

III. ii. 9. son, and you the rest,] *Bawcutt;* sonne and you, the rest *Q;* son;
and you the rest, *Weber;* son, and you the rest; *Gifford.*   10. Agree]
Q; Agree they *Gifford.*   11. *Aside to Ann.*] *Dodsley.*   14. manent]
this ed.; manet Q.   14–15. Sir . . . you?] *so Q;* Sir . . . know / What
. . . you? *Weber.*   15–17. Yes . . . believe it] *so this ed.;* Yes . . . mee. /
And . . . beleeue it *Q.*   20. *Aside*] *Dyce (so for all Gio.'s speeches to 64).*

    10. *Agree as they may*] Gifford's emendation regularizes the metre, but
is not necessary for sense or grammar.
    11. *all woman*] altogether a woman, i.e. inconstant.
    15. *should tell*] may be about to tell (*O.E.D.*, s.v. shall, 22 d).
    17. *point of faith*] an essential doctrine.
    19. *infer*] bring about (*O.E.D.*, I).

Gio. [*Aside*] Here's one can say that's but a woman's note.
Sor. Did you but see my heart, then would you swear—
Ann. That you were dead.
Gio. [*Aside*]   That's true, or somewhat near it.
Sor. See you these true love's tears?
Ann.   No.
Gio. [*Aside*]   Now she winks.   25
Sor. They plead to you for grace.
Ann.   Yet nothing speak.
Sor. O, grant my suit!
Ann.   What is 't?
Sor.   To let me live—
Ann. Take it.
Sor.   —still yours.
Ann.   That is not mine to give.
Gio. [*Aside*] One such another word would kill his hopes.
Sor. Mistress, to leave those fruitless strifes of wit,   30
    I know I have loved you long, and loved you truly;
    Not hope of what you have, but what you are
    Have drawn me on: then let me not in vain
    Still feel the rigour of your chaste disdain.
    I'm sick, and sick to th' heart.
Ann.   Help, aqua-vitae!   35
Sor. What mean you?
Ann.   Why, I thought you had been sick!
Sor. Do you mock my love?
Gio. [*Aside*]   There, sir, she was too nimble.
Sor. [*Aside*] 'Tis plain, she laughs at me!—These scornful
    taunts
    Neither become your modesty, or years.

31. I know] *Q;* Know *Dodsley.*   33. Have] *Q;* Hath *Gifford.*   38–
49.] *so Reed; as prose in Q.*   38. *Aside*] *Gifford.*

---

  22. *note*] either 'tune' or 'characteristic' (*O.E.D.*, *sb*[1] 3, 4, 7); cf. 'the
right describing note to know a Poet by', Sidney, *Defence of Poesie*, ed.
Feuillerat (1923), p. 11.
  25. *winks*] closes both eyes.
  35. *aqua-vitae*] spirits.
  37. *nimble*] quick-witted.

Ann. You are no looking-glass, or if you were   40
    I'd dress my language by you.
Gio. [*Aside*]   I'm confirmed.
Ann. To put you out of doubt, my lord, methinks
    Your common sense should make you understand
    That if I loved you, or desired your love,
    Some way I should have given you better taste;   45
    But since you are a nobleman, and one
    I would not wish should spend his youth in hopes,
    Let me advise you here to forbear your suit,
    And think I wish you well, I tell you this.
Sor. Is 't you speak this?
Ann.   Yes, I myself: yet know—   50
    Thus far I give you comfort—if mine eyes
    Could have picked out a man, amongst all those
    That sued to me, to make a husband of,
    You should have been that man; let this suffice.
    Be noble in your secrecy, and wise.   55
Gio. [*Aside*] Why, now I see she loves me.
Ann.   One word more:
    As ever virtue lived within your mind,
    As ever noble courses were your guide,
    As ever you would have me know you loved me,
    Let not my father know hereof by you: 60
    If I hereafter find that I must marry,
    It shall be you or none.
Sor.   I take that promise.
Ann. O, O my head!
Sor.   What's the matter, not well?
Ann. O, I begin to sicken!

48. you here] *Q;* you *Gifford.*

---

41. *dress*] arrange, put right.
45. *better taste*] a better sample.
51-4.] *if mine eyes . . . that man*] Probably these lines and 61-2 should
be read as conveying further contempt under the guise of a compliment:
Soranzo is the fittest of all Annabella's suitors to be made, first a con-
venience, then a cuckold of.

Gio. [*Aside*]   Heaven forbid!   *Exit from above.*
Sor. Help, help, within there, ho!   65
    Look to your daughter, Signior Florio.

Enter FLORIO, GIOVANNI, PUTANA.

Flo. Hold her up, she swoons.
Gio. Sister, how d'ee?
Ann.   Sick, brother, are you there?
Flo. Convey her to her bed instantly, whilst I send for a
    physician; quickly, I say.   70
Put. Alas, poor child!   *Exeunt, manet* SORANZO.

Enter VASQUES.

Vas. My lord.
Sor. Oh Vasques, now I doubly am undone,
    Both in my present and my future hopes:
    She plainly told me that she could not love,   75
    And thereupon soon sickened, and I fear
    Her life's in danger.
Vas. [*Aside*] By'r Lady sir, and so is yours, if you knew all.
    [*Aloud*] 'Las, sir, I am sorry for that; may be 'tis but the
    maid's sickness, an overflux of youth—and then, sir,   80
    there is no such present remedy as present marriage. But
    hath she given you an absolute denial?
Sor. She hath and she hath not; I'm full of grief,
    But what she said I'll tell thee as we go.   *Exeunt.*

[III. iii]

Enter GIOVANNI *and* PUTANA.

65-7.] *so Q;* Help ... daughter, / Signior ... swoons. *Walley.*   66.
Look] *Gifford; Gio.* Looke *Q, Weber (who moves 66.1 to precede this line).*
78. *Aside*] *Gifford* (*Q has long dash after* all *in* 79).

---

80. *maid's sickness*] an anaemic disease affecting young women at
puberty, also called 'green sickness' from the greenish pallor it gives; now
termed 'chlorosis'.
    81–2. *present*] immediate.

Put. O sir, we are all undone, quite undone, utterly undone,
      and shamed forever; your sister, O your sister!

Gio. What of her? For Heaven's sake speak, how does she?

Put. O that ever I was born to see this day!

Gio. She is not dead, ha, is she?   5

Put. Dead! no, she is quick; 'tis worse, she is with child.
      You know what you have done, Heaven forgive 'ee! 'tis
      too late to repent, now Heaven help us!

Gio. With child? How dost thou know 't?

Put. How do I know 't? Am I at these years ignorant what   10
      the meanings of qualms and water-pangs be? of chang-
      ing of colours, queasiness of stomachs, pukings, and
      another thing that I could name? Do not, for her and
      your credit's sake, spend the time in asking how and
      which way 'tis so: she is quick, upon my word, if you let   15
      a physician see her water y' are undone.

Gio. But in what case is she?

Put. Prettily amended: 'twas but a fit, which I soon espied,
      and she must look for often henceforward.

Gio. Commend me to her, bid her take no care;   20
      Let not the doctor visit her, I charge you,
      Make some excuse till I return—O me,
      I have a world of business in my head!
      Do not discomfort her.—
      How do this news perplex me! If my father   25

III. iii. 1–2.] *so Weber;* Oh . . . vtterly vndone, / And . . . oh your sister. *Q.*
6–8.] *so Weber;* Dead . . . childe, / You . . . forgiue 'ee, / 'Tis . . . vs. *Q.*
8. repent, now] *Q;* repent now, *Gifford.*   24–6.] *so Gifford;* Doe . . .
mee! / If . . . well, *Q.*   25. do this] *Q;* does this *Dodsley;* do these *Weber.*

III. iii. 6. *quick*] both 'alive' and 'pregnant'.

11. *water-pangs*] frequent impulse to urinate.

13. *another thing*] Menstruation has ceased.

18. *prettily amended*] pretty well better.

20. *take no care*] not to worry.

24. *discomfort*] discourage, distress.

25. *How do this news*] For *this* as a plural form see *O.E.D. s.v.* these,
Illustration of Forms, γ; Kyd, *Spanish Tragedy*, ed. Edwards (1959),
II. v. 22 and note.

Come to her, tell him she's recovered well,
Say 'twas but some ill diet: d'ee hear, woman,
Look you to 't.

Put. I will, sir.   *Exeunt.*

[III. iv]

Enter FLORIO *and* RICHARDETTO.

Flo. And how d'ee find her, sir?
Rich.   Indifferent well:
I see no danger, scarce perceive she's sick,
But that she told me she had lately eaten
Melons, and as she thought, those disagreed
With her young stomach.
Flo.   Did you give her aught?   5
Rich. An easy surfeit-water, nothing else.
You need not doubt her health; I rather think
Her sickness is a fullness of her blood—
You understand me?
Flo.   I do; you counsel well,
And once within these few days will so order 't   10

III. iv. 10. will] *Q;* we'll *conj. this ed.*

III. iv. 1. *Indifferent*] tolerably.
5. *young stomach*] unintentionally suggestive of pregnancy, through phrases like 'with young' and 'young bones'; cf. Marston, *Malcontent*, II. ii.
6. *easy*] mild.
surfeit-water] medicinal drink to correct any kind of excess.
8. *fullness*] superabundance or richness. Blood was thought of as the seat of sexual appetite (especially in women, as opposed to 'seed' in men); cf. *Hamlet*, III. iv. 69; Webster, *White Devil*, ed. Brown (1960), V. vi. 240. 'Fullness of blood' indicated readiness for sexual intercourse. Burton uses the phrase in discussing the dangers of sexual abstinence, seen by some authorities as a cause of melancholy, the 'falling-sickness', and other afflictions (II, 39; see also I, 269–70). Richardetto's words are true in a different way from that intended; cf. IV. iii. 8 and note.
10. *once*] some time (*O.E.D.*, 5).

   She shall be married, ere she know the time.
Rich. Yet let not haste, sir, make unworthy choice,
   That were dishonour.
Flo.   Master doctor, no,
   I will not do so neither; in plain words,
   My lord Soranzo is the man I mean.   15
Rich. A noble and a virtuous gentleman.
Flo. As any is in Parma. Not far hence
   Dwells Father Bonaventure, a grave friar,
   Once tutor to my son; now at his cell
   I'll have 'em married.
Rich.   You have plotted wisely.   20
Flo. I'll send one straight to speak with him tonight.
Rich. Soranzo's wise, he will delay no time.
Flo. It shall be so.

     Enter Friar *and* GIOVANNI.

Fri.   Good peace be here and love!
Flo. Welcome, religious friar, you are one
   That still bring blessing to the place you come to.   25
Gio. Sir, with what speed I could, I did my best
   To draw this holy man from forth his cell
   To visit my sick sister, that with words
   Of ghostly comfort in this time of need
   He might absolve her, whether she live or die.   30
Flo. 'Twas well done, Giovanni, thou herein
   Hast showed a Christian's care, a brother's love.
   Come, father, I'll conduct you to her chamber,
   And one thing would entreat you.
Fri.   Say on, sir.

21.] *so Weber;* I'le ... straight / To ... to night. *Q.*

---

 11. *she shall be married*] Florio's prescription is orthodox. 'Virgins must be provided for in season, to prevent many diseases . . . 'tis good to get them husbands betimes, . . . to prevent other gross inconveniences, and for a thing that I know besides' (Burton, III, 273).
 29. *ghostly*] spiritual.

Flo. I have a father's dear impression,   35
    And wish, before I fall into my grave,
    That I might see her married, as 'tis fit;
    A word from you, grave man, will win her more
    Than all our best persuasions.
Fri.   Gentle sir,
    All this I'll say, that Heaven may prosper her.   40

                                                        Exeunt.

[III. v]

                        Enter GRIMALDI.

Grim. Now if the doctor keep his word, Soranzo,
    Twenty to one you miss your bride. I know
    'Tis an unnoble act, and not becomes
    A soldier's valour; but in terms of love,
    Where merit cannot sway, policy must.   5
    I am resolved, if this physician
    Play not on both hands, then Soranzo falls.

                        Enter RICHARDETTO.

Rich. You are come as I could wish: this very night
    Soranzo, 'tis ordained, must be affied
    To Annabella; and for aught I know,   10
    Married.

III. v. 6. resolved,] *Q;* resolv'd; *Sherman.*   8–11. You . . . Married] *so
Reed; as prose in Q.*

---

35. *impression*] Bawcutt comments 'the meaning is not clear', but glosses
from *O.E.D.*, 7, ' "notion" or "idea" (of the sort that fathers usually
have)'. But the meaning may be 'imprinted likeness' (*O.E.D.*, 2); thus
Thomas Heywood refers to a bastard who 'had . . . an impression of the
fathers face, by which the adulterer might easily bee knowne' (*Gunaikeion*,
1624, p. 168). Florio's speech might then be paraphrased: 'I bear the
imprinted likeness of my own dear father, and before I die I should wish
to see my own child married (and ready to transmit the likeness to another
generation)'.

III. v. 4. *terms*] circumstances (*O.E.D.*, *sb* 10).
5. *policy*] sagacity, cunning.
7. *Play not on both hands*] is not deceiving me (*O.E.D.*, *sb* hand 40).
9. *affied*] betrothed.

Grim.   How!

Rich.   Yet your patience:
The place, 'tis Friar Bonaventure's cell.
Now I would wish you to bestow this night
In watching thereabouts; 'tis but a night;
If you miss now! Tomorrow I'll know all.   15

Grim. Have you the poison?

Rich.   Here 'tis in this box,
Doubt nothing, this will do 't; in any case,
As you respect your life, be quick and sure.

Grim. I'll speed him.

Rich.   Do; away, for 'tis not safe
You should be seen much here; ever my love.   20

Grim. And mine to you.   *Exit.*

Rich. So, if this hit, I'll laugh and hug revenge;
And they that now dream of a wedding-feast
May chance to mourn the lusty bridegroom's ruin.
But to my other business: niece Philotis!   25

Enter PHILOTIS.

Phil. Uncle?

Rich.   My lovely niece, you have bethought 'ee?

Phil. Yes, and as you counselled,
Fashioned my heart to love him, but he swears
He will tonight be married; for he fears

---

15. now! Tomorrow] *Weber;* now, to morrow *Q.*   26–7.] *so Q;* Uncle. /
My lovely niece, / You . . . counsell'd, *Gifford.*

15.] Q's punctuation makes poor sense. Dyce interprets 'It is but a
night lost; for if you miss now, I shall have the whole tomorrow, and shall
then be enabled to give you fresh instructions'. But Richardetto's object is
to convince Grimaldi that all may be lost unless he acts at once.
    19. *speed*] despatch, destroy.
    22. *hit*] succeed.
    hug] delight in, cherish (*O.E.D., vb* 1 b–d).
    28. *Fashioned*] adapted, managed; in contexts like this passing easily
into 'perverted' or 'counterfeited' (cf. 'fashion a carriage to rob love from
any', *Much Ado,* I. iii. 25–6). The word masks some uncertainty in Ford's
handling of this character.

His uncle else, if he should know the drift,   30
Will hinder all, and call his coz to shrift.

Rich. Tonight? why, best of all; but let me see,
Ay—ha—yes,—so it shall be: in disguise
We'll early to the friar's, I have thought on 't.

        Enter BERGETTO *and* POGGIO.

Phil. Uncle, he comes!

Rich.   Welcome, my worthy coz.   35

Ber. Lass, pretty lass, come buss lass; [*Kisses her.*] aha,
Poggio!

Phil. There's hope of this yet.

Rich. You shall have time enough, withdraw a little,
We must confer at large.   40

Ber. Have you not sweetmeats, or dainty devices for me?

Phil. You shall enough, sweetheart.

Ber. Sweetheart! mark that, Poggio; by my troth I cannot
choose but kiss thee once more for that word 'sweetheart'.
[*Kisses her.*] Poggio, I have a monstrous swelling about   45
my stomach, whatsoever the matter be.

Pog. You shall have physic for 't, sir.

Rich. Time runs apace.

Ber. Time's a blockhead! [*Kisses her.*]

---

33. Ay] *Dodsley; I Q.*   36. S.D.] *Weber.*   38. *Phil.*] *Q; Rich. Gifford
(who marks as aside); Pog. Schmitz.*   42. shall enough] *Q;* shall [have]
enough *Gifford.*   45. S.D.] *this ed.*   49. S.D.] *this ed.*

---

   30. *drift*] intention.

   31. *call . . . to shrift*] call to account *coz*] 'cousin'.

   32. *best of all*] all the better (cf. *Don Quixote*, p. 240, 'What care I,
quoth he, tho' they be Blacks? Best of all: 'tis but loading a ship with
'em . . .').

   36. *buss*] kiss.

   38.] This I take to be a mildly encouraging remark—'He's coming on!'
—consistent with 42. But if Q's S.P. is rejected the speech should go to
Poggio rather than Richardetto.

   40. *at large*] either 'fully' or 'as a body, in general'. 'This is not the time
for a *tête-à-tête.*'

   41. *devices*] contrivances, like the 'codpiece-point' (III. i. 11–12).

   42. *You shall enough*] A word or words may have dropped out; but
enough occurs in many elliptical constructions, though *O.E.D.* gives no
exact parallel.

Rich. Be ruled: when we have done what's fit to do,   50
 Then you may kiss your fill, and bed her too.   *Exeunt.*

[III. vi]

Enter the Friar *in his study, sitting in a chair,* ANNABELLA *kneeling and whispering to him, a table before them and wax lights; she weeps, and wrings her hands.*

Fri. I am glad to see this penance; for believe me,
 You have unripped a soul so foul and guilty,
 As I must tell you true, I marvel how
 The earth hath borne you up; but weep, weep on,
 These tears may do you good; weep faster yet,   5
 Whiles I do read a lecture.
Ann.   Wretched creature!

III. vi.] *Weber adds '*The Friar's *Cell'; Gifford adds '*FLORIO'S *House'.* o.i. *in his study*] om. *Weber;* ANNABELLA'S *Chamber Gifford.*

III. vi. o.i. in his study] It is uncertain where Ford meant this impressive scene to be located. The Friar has been led to Annabella's chamber (III. iv. 33) at a moment when she is thought to be at death's door (ii. 76–7, iv. 30). But her sickness soon passes (iii. 18, iv. 2), so that Florio can plan to have her married at the Friar's cell, 'within these few days' or even 'now' (iv. 10–11, 19–20). 'Now' is ambiguous, but Richardetto, though he is on-stage when the Friar is led to Annabella's chamber, expects her to be betrothed if not actually married at the cell 'this very night' (v. 8–12). The present scene-heading, together with the Friar's authoritative behaviour at vi. 43–7, suggests Ford was thinking of the cell as the location for Annabella's confession and the betrothal which follows immediately after. But 'below' (vi. 44) rather suggests that we are still in Annabella's chamber, with Soranzo waiting downstairs.

1 ff.] The Friar's part in this scene has many echoes of the penitential poem *Christes Bloodie Sweat* (1613), by 'I.F.', who was almost certainly Ford himself (see Introduction, p. xxi). For the description of Hell, where the parallel is closest, an anterior source may be Nashe's *Pierce Penilesse* (*Works*, ed. McKerrow, revd. Wilson, Oxford, 1966, I, 218). For the main parallels see M. Joan Sargeaunt, 'Writings ascribed to John Ford', *Review of English Studies*, x (1934), 168–9.

6. *read a lecture*] give an exposition (of Annabella's sins); deliver a reprimand. Cf. *Christes Bloodie Sweat*, sig. G4: 'Guilt reades a lecture of her [the soul's] foule misdeeds, And bids her looke vpon this streame of red'.

Fri. Ay, you are wretched, miserably wretched,
Almost condemned alive. There is a place—
List, daughter!—in a black and hollow vault,
Where day is never seen; there shines no sun,   10
But flaming horror of consuming fires;
A lightless sulphur, choked with smoky fogs
Of an infected darkness: in this place
Dwell many thousand thousand sundry sorts
Of never-dying deaths: there damnèd souls   15
Roar without pity, there are gluttons fed
With toads and adders; there is burning oil
Poured down the drunkard's throat, the usurer
Is forced to sup whole draughts of molten gold;
There is the murderer forever stabbed,   20
Yet can he never die; there lies the wanton
On racks of burning steel, whiles in his soul
He feels the torment of his raging lust.
Ann. Mercy, O mercy!
Fri.   There stands these wretched things
Who have dreamt out whole years in lawless sheets   25
And secret incests, cursing one another.
Then you will wish each kiss your brother gave
Had been a dagger's point; then you shall hear
How he will cry, 'O, would my wicked sister
Had first been damned, when she did yield to lust!'   30
But soft, methinks I see repentance work
New motions in your heart; say, how is 't with you?

---

24. stands] *Q;* stand *Reed.*

---

11. *horror*] literally 'bristling'; here suggesting a surface jagged with
flame, or the flame's flickering motion. Cf. Chapman, 'Such fresh horror
as you see driven through the wrinkled waves' (cited by *Webster's New
International Dictionary*), and Milton, *Nativity Ode,* 172.

13. *infected*] poisoned, filled with corruption.

24. *stands . . . things*] acceptable Elizabethan grammar; see Clark and
Glover, Preface to *The Cambridge Shakespeare* (1863–6), sect. B.

32. *motions*] stirrings, impulses; a closely-related usage denotes the
working of God in the human soul (*O.E.D., sb* 9).

Ann. Is there no way left to redeem my miseries?

Fri. There is, despair not: Heaven is merciful,
  And offers grace even now. 'Tis thus agreed,   35
  First, for your honour's safety that you marry
  The Lord Soranzo; next, to save your soul,
  Leave off this life, and henceforth live to him.

Ann. Ay me!

Fri.   Sigh not, I know the baits of sin
  Are hard to leave; O, 'tis a death to do 't.   40
  Remember what must come! are you content?

Ann. I am.

Fri.   I like it well, we'll take the time.
  Who's near us there?

Enter FLORIO, GIOVANNI.

Flo.   Did you call, father?

Fri. Is Lord Soranzo come?

Flo.   He stays below.

Fri. Have you acquainted him at full?

Flo.   I have,   45
  And he is overjoyed.

Fri.   And so are we;
  Bid him come near.

Gio. [*Aside*]   My sister weeping, ha!
  I fear this friar's falsehood. [*To them*] I will call him. *Exit.*

Flo. Daughter, are you resolved?

Ann.   Father, I am.

Enter GIOVANNI, SORANZO *and* VASQUES.

45–6. I have . . . overjoyed] *so Weber; as one line in Q.*   46–7. And so . . .
near] *so Weber; as one line in Q.*   47. *Aside*] *Gifford.*   47–8. My sister
. . . him] *so Weber; My . . . falsehood, / I . . . him. Q.*

---

38. *live to*] devote yourself to.

39–40.] Cf. *Christes Bloodie Sweat*, sig. D2: 'Yet O, tis hard to leaue the
baites of pleasure'.

42. *the time*] the favourable moment (*O.E.D.*, *sb* 16, and cf. Tilley,
T312, 'Take time when time comes').

Flo. My lord Soranzo, here   50
    Give me your hand; for that I give you this.

                        [*Joins their hands.*]

Sor. Lady, say you so too?
Ann.   I do, and vow
    To live with you and yours.
Fri.   Timely resolved:
    My blessing rest on both! More to be done,
    You may perform it on the morning sun.   *Exeunt.*   55

[III. vii]

    Enter GRIMALDI *with his rapier drawn, and a dark lantern.*

Grim. 'Tis early night as yet, and yet too soon
    To finish such a work; here I will lie
    To listen who comes next.   *He lies down.*

51. hand;] *Reed;* hand, Q.   51.1.] *Gifford.*   52–3. I . . . yours] *so*
Weber; as one line in Q.

---

51. *Give me your hand*] What follows is to be taken as a formal betrothal,
of a kind practised in England at this period, in which each party gives a
legally binding promise to marry the other. Soranzo does not in fact give
any promise, but Ford was not concerned to be factually accurate: cf. the
'stage marriage' in *Perkin Warbeck*, II. iii. 86–90, or the last scene of *Love's
Sacrifice*, in which two short sentences suffice to install Roselli as reigning
duke and marry him to Fiormonda (Dyce, II, 106–7).
    for that] Probably 'in exchange for that hand of yours'; but perhaps 'in
order that', or 'since'.
    54–5. *More . . . sun*] Unless Ford has been unusually careless this
does not refer to the marriage ceremony, which does not take place for
'some two days' or more (III. viii. 3); in any case betrothal would be
pointless if marriage were to follow within hours. Conceivably the Friar
means the drawing-up of settlements; but Ford's main intention is to end
the scene with a remark to the effect that enough has been done for one
night.

    III. vii. 0.1. *dark lantern*] a lantern which could be kept burning while
its light was concealed by a slide or shutter. One used by Guy Fawkes is
now in the Ashmolean Museum; see also *Pickwick Papers*, ch. xxxix.
    2–3. *lie To listen*] Grimaldi puts his ear to the ground to detect a distant
footfall; cf. *1 Henry IV*, II. ii. 30–2.

Enter BERGETTO *and* PHILOTIS *disguised, and after*
RICHARDETTO *and* POGGIO.

Ber. We are almost at the place I hope, sweetheart.
Grim. [*Aside*] I hear them near, and heard one say   5
    'sweetheart';
    'Tis he: now guide my hand, some angry Justice,
    Home to his bosom. [*Aloud*] Now have at you, sir!
                           Strikes Bergetto and exit.
Ber. O help, help, here's a stitch fallen in my guts; O for a
    flesh-tailor quickly!—Poggio!
Phil. What ails my love?   10
Ber. I am sure I cannot piss forward and backward, and yet
    I am wet before and behind; lights, lights, ho lights!
Phil. Alas, some villain here has slain my love!
Rich. O, Heaven forbid it! Raise up the next neighbours   14
    Instantly, Poggio, and bring lights.   *Exit* POGGIO.
    How is 't, Bergetto? slain? It cannot be;
    Are you sure y' are hurt?
Ber. O, my belly seethes like a porridge-pot; some cold water,
    I shall boil over else. My whole body is in a sweat, that
    you may wring my shirt; feel here—why, Poggio!   20

Enter POGGIO *with* Officers, *and lights and halberts.*

Pog. Here; alas, how do you?
Rich. Give me a light—what's here? all blood! O sirs,
    Signior Donado's nephew now is slain!

III. vii. 5. *Aside*] Dyce.   8–9.] *so Weber;* Oh ... gutts, / Oh for ...
Poggio. *Q.*   16–17.] *so Gifford;* How ... slaine? / It ... hurt? *Q.*

---

6. *some angry Justice*] Cf. *Lear*, IV. ii. 78–9, which in the Folio reads
'This shewes you are above You Justices' (in the Quarto 'Justisers').
Earlier lines of the same scene provide a gloss: 'If that the heavens do not
their visible spirits Send quickly down to tame these vile offences' (46–7).
    8. *here's a stitch fallen*] a stitch has burst (*O.E.D.*, fall *vb* 26 c); hence the
call for a 'flesh-tailor'.
    14. *next*] nearest.
    20.1 halberts] the usual weapons of a watch or civic guard, combining
spear with battle-axe.

Follow the murderer with all the haste
Up to the city, he cannot be far hence;   25
Follow, I beseech you.

Off.   Follow, follow, follow!

                          Exeunt Officers.

Rich. Tear off thy linen, coz, to stop his wounds;
Be of good comfort, man.

Ber. Is all this mine own blood? nay then, goodnight with
me; Poggio, commend me to my uncle, dost hear? Bid   30
him for my sake make much of this wench—O, I am
going the wrong way sure, my belly aches so—O, farewell, Poggio—O——O——   *Dies.*

Phil. O, he is dead!

Pog.   How! dead?

Rich.   He's dead indeed.

'Tis now too late to weep; let's have him home,   35
And with what speed we may find out the murderer.

Pog. O my master, my master, my master!   *Exeunt.*

[III. viii]

Enter VASQUES *and* HIPPOLITA.

Hip. Betrothed?

Vas. I saw it.

Hip. And when's the marriage-day?

Vas.   Some two days hence.

Hip. Two days? Why man, I would but wish two hours

24. the haste] *Q;* despatch *Morris.*

---

24. *the haste*] Easier emendations than Morris's might be 'your haste'
(y^r misread as y^e); 'thy haste' (see note to II. v. 2); or 'thou hast' (conjec-
tured by Dr R. Southall). 'Thou' or 'thy' would be addressed to the chief
officer, and 'all thou hast' would mean 'all the men you have with you'.
Or a line may have dropped out after 'haste'; or Ford may have imperfectly
revised the sentence.

32. *going the wrong way*] dying; cf. *Queen*, 910-11.

To send him to his last and lasting sleep;   5
And Vasques, thou shalt see, I'll do it bravely.

Vas. I do not doubt your wisdom, nor, I trust, you my
secrecy: I am infinitely yours.

Hip. I will be thine in spite of my disgrace.
So soon? O wicked man, I durst be sworn   10
He'd laugh to see me weep.

Vas. And that's a villainous fault in him.

Hip. No, let him laugh; I'm armed in my resolves,
Be thou still true.

Vas. I should get little by treachery against so hopeful a   15
preferment as I am like to climb to.

Hip. Even to my bosom, Vasques; let my youth
Revel in these new pleasures. If we thrive,
He now hath but a pair of days to live.   *Exeunt.*

[III. ix]

Enter FLORIO, DONADO, RICHARDETTO, POGGIO *and* Officers.

Flo. 'Tis bootless now to show yourself a child,
Signior Donado; what is done, is done;
Spend not the time in tears, but seek for justice.

Rich. I must confess, somewhat I was in fault,
That had not first acquainted you what love   5
Passed 'twixt him and my niece; but as I live,
His fortune grieves me as it were mine own.

Don. Alas, poor creature, he meant no man harm,
That I am sure of.

Flo.   I believe that too;

III. viii. 7–8.] *so Weber;* I doe . . . secresie, / I am . . . yours. *Q.*

III. viii. 17. *my youth*] probably 'a contemptuous reference to Soranzo'
(Bawcutt, and see I. ii. 93); but possibly a reference to herself, as at II. ii.
29, in real or pretended anticipation of her new life with Vasques.

III. ix. 1. *bootless*] useless.

But stay, my masters, are you sure you saw   10
The murderer pass here?

Off. And it please you sir, we are sure we saw a ruffian, with
a naked weapon in his hand all bloody, get into my lord
Cardinal's grace's gate, that we are sure of; but for fear
of his grace, bless us! [*They cross themselves.*] we durst go   15
no further.

Don. Know you what manner of man he was?

Off. Yes, sure I know the man, they say a is a soldier; he that
loved your daughter, sir, an 't please ye, 'twas he for
certain.   20

Flo. Grimaldi, on my life!

Off.   Ay, ay, the same.

Rich. The Cardinal is noble, he no doubt
Will give true justice.

Don. Knock someone at the gate.

Pog. I'll knock, sir.   *Poggio knocks.* 25

Servant (*Within*). What would 'ee?

Flo. We require speech with the lord Cardinal
About some present business; pray inform
His grace that we are here.

Enter Cardinal *and* GRIMALDI.

Car. Why, how now, friends! what saucy mates are you   30
That know nor duty nor civility?
Are we a person fit to be your host?
Or is our house become your common inn,
To beat our doors at pleasure? What such haste
Is yours, as that it cannot wait fit times?   35
Are you the masters of this commonwealth,
And know no more discretion? O, your news

III. ix. 15. S.D.] *this ed.*

---

30. *saucy mates*] impudent fellows ('mates' here implies low social
status).

36. *masters . . . commonwealth*] magistrates of this community.

          Is here before you, you have lost a nephew,
          Donado, last night by Grimaldi slain:
          Is that your business ? Well sir, we have knowledge   40
              on 't;
          Let that suffice.
Grim.   In presence of your grace,
          In thought I never meant Bergetto harm;
          But Florio, you can tell, with how much scorn
          Soranzo backed with his confederates
          Hath often wronged me: I to be revenged—   45
          For that I could not win him else to fight—
          Had thought by way of ambush to have killed him,
          But was unluckily therein mistook;
          Else he had felt what late Bergetto did.
          And though my fault to him were merely chance,   50
          Yet humbly I submit me to your grace,   [*Kneeling*.]
          To do with me as you please.
Car.   Rise up, Grimaldi.   [*He rises*.]
          You citizens of Parma, if you seek
          For justice: know, as Nuncio from the Pope,
          For this offence I here receive Grimaldi   55
          Into his Holiness' protection.
          He is no common man, but nobly born;
          Of princes' blood, though you, sir Florio,
          Thought him too mean a husband for your daughter.
          If more you seek for, you must go to Rome,   60
          For he shall thither; learn more wit, for shame.
          Bury your dead.—Away, Grimaldi; leave 'em.
                              Exeunt Cardinal *and* GRIMALDI.
Don. Is this a churchman's voice? Dwells Justice here?

51-2. S.D.'s] *Gifford*.

_____

    46. *else*] by other means (cf. I. ii. 33).
    50. *were*] was (for the frequent anomalous use of 'be' and 'were' in such
clauses see Abbott, sect. 301).
    59. *mean*] of low birth or rank, or poor.

Flo. Justice is fled to Heaven and comes no nearer.
    Soranzo, was 't for him? O impudence!   65
    Had he the face to speak it, and not blush?
    Come, come Donado, there's no help in this,
    When cardinals think murder's not amiss;
    Great men may do their wills, we must obey,
    But Heaven will judge them for 't another day.   *Exeunt.*

68. amiss;] *Gifford;* amisse, *Q; amiss. Dodsley.*

---

64. *Justice . . . Heaven*] Astraea, goddess of justice, dwelt among men
during the golden age, but was driven away by the murderous crimes of
the iron age and placed in the heavens as the constellation Virgo.

Act IV

A banquet. Hautboys. Enter the Friar, GIOVANNI, ANNABELLA,
PHILOTIS, SORANZO, DONADO, FLORIO, RICHARDETTO,
PUTANA *and* VASQUES.

Fri. These holy rites performed, now take your times,
    To spend the remnant of the day in feast;
    Such fit repasts are pleasing to the saints
    Who are your guests, though not with mortal eyes
    To be beheld. Long prosper in this day,   5
    You happy couple, to each other's joy!
Sor. Father, your prayer is heard: the hand of goodness
    Hath been a shield for me against my death;
    And, more to bless me, hath enriched my life
    With this most precious jewel—such a prize,   10
    As earth hath not another like to this.

IV. i. Act IV] *Actus Quartus. Q.*

IV. i. 0.1. a banquet] This could mean a full-scale feast, light refresh-
ments, or simply wine (*O.E.D.*, *sb*[1]). It may be the ceremonial wine-
drinking which traditionally followed a wedding, though this usually took
place in the church (*Shakespeare's England*, II, 147).

Hautboys] Oboes.

3–4. *saints Who are your guests*] 'Saints' probably refers, not just to
canonized persons, but to members of the 'communion of saints'—a
mystical body which includes the faithful on earth, souls in Purgatory and
Heaven, and, according to St Thomas Aquinas, the angels (*Catholic
Encyclopaedia*, 1907–12, *s.v.* Communion of Saints). It is consistent with
Catholic doctrine that members of this spiritual family who are not
corporeally present may share in the rejoicing which follows a sacrament
of marriage.

5. *Long . . . day*] May this day prove fortunate, and may you prosper
long in marriage.

Cheer up, my love; and gentlemen, my friends,
Rejoice with me in mirth: this day we'll crown
With lusty cups to Annabella's health.

Gio. O, torture! were the marriage yet undone,   *Aside.* 15
Ere I'd endure this sight, to see my love
Clipped by another, I would dare confusion,
And stand the horror of ten thousand deaths.

Vas. Are you not well, sir?

Gio.   Prithee fellow, wait,
I need not thy officious diligence.   20

Flo. Signior Donado, come, you must forget
Your late mishaps, and drown your cares in wine.

Sor. Vasques!

Vas.   My lord?

Sor.   Reach me that weighty bowl.
Here, brother Giovanni, here's to you;
Your turn comes next, though now a bachelor: 25
Here's to your sister's happiness and mine!

                    [*Drinks, and offers him the bowl.*]

Gio. I cannot drink.

Sor.   What?

Gio.   'Twill indeed offend me.

Ann. Pray, do not urge him if he be not willing.

                                        Hautboys.

Flo. How now, what noise is this?

Vas. O sir, I had forgot to tell you: certain young maidens of 30
Parma, in honour to Madam Annabella's marriage, have
sent their loves to her in a masque, for which they humbly
crave your patience and silence.

26.1] *Gifford.*   28.1] *so Gifford; after 35 in* Q.

---

17. *Clipped*] embraced.
confusion] destruction; damnation.
27. *offend me*] Both 'displease my feelings' and 'cause me physical pain
or harm' (*O.E.D.*, 6–7). Giovanni intends Soranzo to understand the
words in the second sense: he is not picking a quarrel but pleading indis-
position.

Sor. We are much bound to them, so much the more
    As it comes unexpected; guide them in.   35

Enter HIPPOLITA *and* Ladies *in white robes* [*all masked*], *with
    garlands of willows. Music, and a dance.*

Sor. Thanks, lovely virgins; now might we but know
    To whom we have been beholding for this love,
    We shall acknowledge it.
Hip.   Yes, you shall know: [*Unmasks.*]
    What think you now?
Omnes.   Hippolita!
Hip.   'Tis she,
    Be not amazed; nor blush, young lovely bride,   40
    I come not to defraud you of your man.
    [*To Sor.*] 'Tis now no time to reckon up the talk
    What Parma long hath rumoured of us both:
    Let rash report run on; the breath that vents it
    Will, like a bubble, break itself at last.   45
    [*To Ann.*] But now to you, sweet creature; lend 's your hand.
    Perhaps it hath been said that I would claim
    Some interest in Soranzo, now your lord;
    What I have right to do, his soul knows best:
    But in my duty to your noble worth,   50
    Sweet Annabella, and my care of you,
    Here take, Soranzo, take this hand from me.
    I'll once more join what by the holy Church
    Is finished and allowed: have I done well?
Sor. You have too much engaged us.
Hip.   One thing more: 55

34–5.] *so Gifford; as prose in Q.*   35.1. *all masked*] *Gifford.*   35.2.]
Q adds 'Dance' on right of measure.   37. this] *Q*ᵇ; thy *Q*ᵃ.   38. S.D.]
Weber.   42. *To Sor.*] *this ed.*   46. *To Ann.*] *this ed.*

37. *love*] act of kindness (*O.E.D.*, *sb.* I c).
54. *allowed*] approved.
55. *engaged us*] obliged us, placed us in your debt (apparently not
ironical; cf. 63–4).

That you may know my single charity,
Freely I here remit all interest
I e'er could claim, and give you back your vows;
And to confirm 't—reach me a cup of wine—
My lord Soranzo, in this draught I drink   60
Long rest t'ee! [*Aside to Vas.*] Look to it, Vasques.

Vas. [*Aside to Hip.*] Fear nothing.

> *He gives her a poisoned cup; she drinks.*

Sor. Hippolita, I thank you, and will pledge
This happy union as another life:
Wine there!   65

Vas. You shall have none, neither shall you pledge her.

Hip. How!

Vas. Know now, mistress she-devil, your own mischievous
treachery hath killed you; I must not marry you.

Hip. Villain!   70

Omnes. What's the matter?

Vas. Foolish woman, thou art now like a firebrand, that hath
kindled others and burnt thyself. *Troppo sperar, inganna,*
thy vain hope hath deceived thee; thou art but dead; if
thou hast any grace, pray.   75

---

59. confirm 't—reach ... wine—] *Gifford;* confirm't, reach ... wine *Q.*
61. *Aside to Vas.*] *Weber* (*Q has long dash after* 't'ee' *and places* 'looke ...
Vasques' on right of measure).   62. *Aside to Hip.*] *Dyce.*   68–9.] *so
Weber;* Know . . . treachery / Hath . . . marry you. *Q.*   73. *inganna*]
Weber; niganna Q.

---

56. *single charity*] sincere love (*O.E.D.*, single, *adj* 14).
57. *remit*] renounce.
interest] concern (in Soranzo; with some sense of 'stake, share').
64. *union*] accordance, agreement.
72–3. *thou . . . thyself*] Cf. 'He is like a brand af [*sic*] fire, kyndeleth
others, and burneth hym selfe', *Florio his Firste Fruites* (1578), f. 34 (facsimile ed. A. del Re, Formosa, 1936). This section of John Florio's phrase-
book gives Italian proverbs and their English translations; three of
Vasques's sayings appear on two facing pages (see next note, and note at
IV. iii. 167–8).
73. Troppo sperar, inganna] 'Too much hoping, deceiueth' (Florio,
f. 33ᵛ). Cf. Tilley H608.
74. *but dead*] as good as dead (cf. *2 Henry VI*, III. ii. 387).

Hip. Monster!

Vas. Die in charity, for shame!—This thing of malice, this
woman, had privately corrupted me with promise of
marriage, under this politic reconciliation to poison my
lord, whiles she might laugh at his confusion on his   80
marriage-day. I promised her fair, but I knew what my
reward should have been; and would willingly have
spared her life, but that I was acquainted with the danger
of her disposition—and now have fitted her a just payment in her own coin. There she is, she hath yet ——   85
and end thy days in peace, vile woman; as for life there's
no hope, think not on 't.

Omnes. Wonderful justice!

Rich.   Heaven, thou art righteous. // ——

Hip. O, 'tis true,
    I feel my minute coming; had that slave   90
    Kept promise—O, my torment!—thou this hour
    Hadst died, Soranzo.—Heat above hell-fire!—
    Yet ere I pass away—cruel, cruel flames!—
    Take here my curse amongst you: may thy bed
    Of marriage be a rack unto thy heart—   95
    Burn, blood, and boil in vengeance; O my heart,
    My flame's intolerable!—May'st thou live
    To father bastards, may her womb bring forth
    Monsters, and die together in your sins

77. Die ... shame] *as separate line in Q.*   79. marriage] *Dodsley;* malice
Q.   95–6. heart— / Burn, ... vengeance;] *this ed.;* heart, / Burne ...
Vengeance— *Q.*

---

79. *marriage*] Q's 'malice' has obviously been picked up from 77.
politic] craftily contrived.

85. Q's dashes may represent words missing or indecipherable in MS.
(e.g. 'a minute to live; repent'). Alternatively, as Bawcutt suggests, 'yet'
may be an error for 'it', or, less plausibly, for 'that'.

90. *minute*] appointed moment (*O.E.D., sb*[1] 1 c).

96. *Burn . . . vengeance*] Q seems mispunctuated here: it is much
easier to take this phrase as addressed to her own blood, seething with
poison (cf. III. vii. 18), than as part of her rhetorical curse.

my heart] It is unlike Ford to end two consecutive lines with the same
word; conceivably he wrote 'my heat'.

Hated, scorned and unpitied!— O — O —   *Dies.* 100

Flo. Was e'er so vile a creature?

Rich.   Here's the end
Of lust and pride.

Ann.   It is a fearful sight.

Sor. Vasques, I know thee now a trusty servant,
And never will forget thee. Come, my love,
We'll home, and thank the Heavens for this escape.   105
Father and friends, we must break up this mirth;
It is too sad a feast.

Don.   Bear hence the body.

Fri. [*Aside to Gio.*] Here's an ominous change;
Mark this, my Giovanni, and take heed!
I fear the event: that marriage seldom's good,   110
Where the bride-banquet so begins in blood.   *Exeunt.*

[IV. ii]

Enter RICHARDETTO *and* PHILOTIS.

Rich. My wretched wife, more wretched in her shame
Than in her wrongs to me, hath paid too soon
The forfeit of her modesty and life.
And I am sure, my niece, though vengeance hover,
Keeping aloof yet from Soranzo's fall,   5
Yet he will fall, and sink with his own weight.
I need not—now my heart persuades me so—
To further his confusion: there is One
Above begins to work, for, as I hear,
Debates already 'twixt his wife and him   10
Thicken and run to head; she, as 'tis said,

---

108. *Aside to Gio.*] *Gifford.*

---

110. *event*] outcome.

IV. ii. 8. *confusion*] destruction.
11. *thicken*] multiply.
run to head] increase in violence; draw to a crisis (*O.E.D.*, head *sb* 31).
As Morris remarks, the phrase as a whole suggests a boil about to burst.

Slightens his love, and he abandons hers;
Much talk I hear. Since things go thus, my niece,
In tender love and pity of your youth,
My counsel is that you should free your years   15
From hazard of these woes, by flying hence
To fair Cremona, there to vow your soul
In holiness a holy votaress;
Leave me to see the end of these extremes.
All human worldly courses are uneven;   20
No life is blessed but the way to Heaven.

Phil. Uncle, shall I resolve to be a nun?

Rich. Ay, gentle niece, and in your hourly prayers
Remember me, your poor unhappy uncle.
Hie to Cremona now, as fortune leads,   25
Your home your cloister, your best friends your beads;
Your chaste and single life shall crown your birth:
Who dies a virgin lives a saint on earth.

Phil. Then farewell world, and worldly thoughts adieu!
Welcome, chaste vows, myself I yield to you.   30

Exeunt.

[IV. iii]

Enter SORANZO *unbraced, and* ANNABELLA *dragged in.*

Sor. Come strumpet, famous whore, were every drop
Of blood that runs in thy adulterous veins
A life, this sword—dost see 't?—should in one blow

IV. ii. 28. lives] *Dodsley;* liue *Q.*

12. *slightens*] slights, treats with indifference.
abandons] renounces, ceases to hold (*O.E.D., vb* 7).
18. *votaress*] nun.
19. *extremes*] desperate actions or sufferings.
20. *uneven*] rugged and difficult; perhaps also 'unjust' (cf. *Romeo and Juliet*, IV. i. 5, 'Uneven is the course; I like it not').
27. *crown*] complete, fulfil.

IV. iii. 0.1. unbraced] with part of clothing unfastened or removed (here probably with doublet unbuttoned).

                Confound them all; harlot, rare, notable harlot,
                That with thy brazen face maintain'st thy sin,   5
                Was there no man in Parma to be bawd
                To your loose cunning whoredom else but I?
                Must your hot itch and plurisy of lust,
                The heyday of your luxury, be fed
                Up to a surfeit, and could none but I   10
                Be picked out to be cloak to your close tricks,
                Your belly-sports? Now I must be the dad
                To all that gallimaufry that's stuffed
                In thy corrupted bastard-bearing womb?
                Why must I?
Ann.   Beastly man, why, 'tis thy fate: 15
                I sued not to thee, for, but that I thought
                Your over-loving lordship would have run
                Mad on denial, had ye lent me time,
                I would have told 'ee in what case I was;
                But you would needs be doing.
Sor.   Whore of whores!   20

---

iv. iii. 13. that's] *Q; that is Reed.*   15. Why] *Q^b catchword; Say, Q^a*
catchword; Shey, Q (15).

---

   4. *Confound*] destroy.
   5. *maintain'st*] perseveres in; defends (*O.E.D.*, 1–2, 14).
   6. *bawd*] brothel-keeper or pander.
   8. *plurisy*] superabundance (*O.E.D.*, s.v. pleurisy 2). This usage results
from interpreting 'pleurisy' (inflammation of the *pleura*, lungs) as though
derived from *plus, pluris*. Ford uses the word to mean an excess of blood
(*Lover's Melancholy*, I, ii), or of the lustful element in a woman's blood
(*Fancies*, IV. i), or of both together (*Broken Heart*, IV. ii; see Dyce, I, 22,
293, II, 287, also *Queen*, 1187). Quartos of all plays give the form 'plurisie'.
   9. *heyday*] excitement.
   luxury] lecherousness.
   11. *close*] both 'secret' and 'physically close'.
   tricks] stratagems; games; techniques (cf. v. v. 1–3).
   13. *gallimaufry*] confused jumble; its use here is perhaps influenced by
'fry', i.e. progeny.
   15. *Why*] See Introduction, pp. lxvii–lxviii.
   19. *case*] state.
   20. *would needs be doing*] had to be acting, could not wait; with an insulting under-sense of *do* as 'copulate' (cf. *Queen*, 600–1, 997–1010, 2967;
Love's Sacrifice, I. ii; *Fancies*, I. ii, II. i; Dyce, II, 21, 237, 262).

          Darest thou tell me this?
Ann.   O yes, why not?
          You were deceived in me: 'twas not for love
          I chose you, but for honour; yet know this,
          Would you be patient yet, and hide your shame,
          I'd see whether I could love you.
Sor.   Excellent quean!   25
          Why, art thou not with child?
Ann.   What needs all this,
          When 'tis superfluous? I confess I am.
Sor. Tell me by whom.
Ann.   Soft, sir, 'twas not in my bargain.
          Yet somewhat, sir, to stay your longing stomach
          I'm content t' acquaint you with: the man,   30
          The more than man that got this sprightly boy—
          For 'tis a boy, that for your glory, sir,
          Your heir shall be a son—
Sor.   Damnable monster!
Ann. Nay, and you will not hear, I'll speak no more.
Sor. Yes, speak, and speak thy last.
Ann.   A match, a match: 35
          This noble creature was in every part
          So angel-like, so glorious, that a woman,
          Who had not been but human as was I,
          Would have kneeled to him, and have begged for love.
          You, why you are not worthy once to name   40
          His name without true worship, or indeed,
          Unless you kneeled, to hear another name him.
Sor. What was he called?
Ann.   We are not come to that:
          Let it suffice, that you shall have the glory

28. Soft, sir] *Q;* Soft, *Gifford.*   32. boy, that for your] *McIlwraith;* Boy
that for *Q;* boy, therefore *Dodsley;* boy, and therefore *Reed;* boy; that's
for your *Bawcutt.*

---

25. *quean*] promiscuous woman, prostitute.
29. *stay your longing stomach*] appease your appetite (for information).
34. *and*] if.
35. *match*] bargain.

To father what so brave a father got.   45
In brief, had not this chance fall'n out as 't doth,
I never had been troubled with a thought
That you had been a creature; but for marriage,
I scarce dream yet of that.
Sor. Tell me his name!
Ann.   Alas, alas, there's all;   50
Will you believe?
Sor.   What?
Ann.   You shall never know.
Sor. How!
Ann.   Never: if you do, let me be cursed.
Sor. Not know it, strumpet! I'll rip up thy heart
And find it there.
Ann.   Do, do.
Sor.   And with my teeth
Tear the prodigious lecher joint by joint.   55
Ann. Ha, ha, ha, the man's merry.
Sor.   Dost thou laugh?
Come whore, tell me your lover, or by truth
I'll hew thy flesh to shreds: who is 't?
Ann. '*Che morte più dolce che morire per amore?*'   *Sings.*

50-1. Alas . . . believe] *so Q; as one line Weber.*   52. Never . . . cursed]
so Bawcutt; Neuer, / If . . . curst *Q;* Never; if / You . . . curs'd *Gifford.*
59. *più*] *Weber; pluis Q.*

---

45. *To father*] to play the part of father to.
brave] handsome, splendid.
48. *a creature*] created, in existence.
48-9. *but for . . . of that*] Obscure. Perhaps 'except that we have been
married, your existence means almost nothing to me'; or 'as for our really
being married, I can still hardly imagine such a thing'. See also Introduction, p. xlv, n. 3.
55. *prodigious*] monstrous.
59. Che . . . amore] This sentence occurs in *Florio his Firste Fruites*
(1578), ch. iv ('Amorous talke'), f. 13ᵛ, and means 'What death is sweeter
than to die for love?' It is offered as a useful phrase for the Englishman
learning Italian, and occurs during a model conversation; Annabella's
next speech is based on the reply. Ford probably took both sentences from
Florio (cf. IV. i. 72-3, IV. iii. 167-8). Possibly Florio himself is quoting, but
the words do not fit any ordinary Italian metre.

Sor. Thus will I pull thy hair, and thus I'll drag   60
    Thy lust-belepered body through the dust.
    Yet tell his name.

Ann. *'Morendo in gratia a lui, morirei senza dolore.'*   *Sings.*

Sor. Dost thou triumph? The treasure of the earth
    Shall not redeem thee, were there kneeling kings   65
    Did beg thy life, or angels did come down
    To plead in tears, yet should not all prevail
    Against my rage: dost thou not tremble yet?

Ann. At what? to die? No, be a gallant hangman,
    I dare thee to the worst, strike, and strike home;   70
    I leave revenge behind, and thou shalt feel 't.

Sor. Yet tell me ere thou diest, and tell me truly,
    Knows thy old father this?

Ann.   No, by my life.

Sor. Wilt thou confess, and I will spare thy life?

Ann. My life! I will not buy my life so dear.   75

Sor. I will not slack my vengeance.

Enter VASQUES.

Vas.   What d'ee mean, sir?

63. *a lui*] *this ed.; Lei Q; Dei Weber; dee Gifford.*   *morirei] Bawcutt;*
morire Q^a; morirere Q^b.   71. I leave] Q^b; leaue Q^a.   76.] *Gifford adds*
S.D. *'Draws his sword' after* 'vengeance'.

---

63. Morendo . . . dolore] 'Dying in favour with him, I would die
without pain.' The reply Florio gives for the question in 59 is '*Si morendo
in gratia á lei, morirei volentieri, ma altrimenti non voglio*' (translated as
'Yea, dying in her fauor, I would dye gladly, but otherwise I wyl not').
Ford has apparently adapted these words to make a rhyming line to
match 59. One cannot be sure what he intended this line to mean, or
how much of Q's false Italian originated with Ford, how much with the
compositor. The reading '*a lui*' (suggested independently by Mr. D. Reidy
and Dr. C. Roaf) implies that Ford changed Florio's pronoun to make it
refer to the absent Giovanni. Bawcutt's emendation '*morirei*' seems confirmed by Florio; Q's two attempts at this word suggest consultation of
difficult copy.

64. *triumph*] exult; stressed on the second syllable, as at II. ii. 49.

76. *slack*] either 'leave undone, forgo' (*O.E.D., vb* 1, and cf. *Lover's*
Melancholy, I. ii, Dyce, I, 24) or 'delay' (*O.E.D., vb* 5).

Sor. Forbear, Vasques, such a damnèd whore
Deserves no pity.

Vas.   Now the gods forfend!
And would you be her executioner, and kill her in your
rage too? O, 'twere most unmanlike! She is your wife;   80
what faults hath been done by her before she married
you, were not against you; alas poor lady, what hath she
committed, which any lady in Italy in the like case
would not? Sir, you must be ruled by your reason, and
not by your fury, that were unhuman and beastly.   85

Sor. She shall not live.

Vas. Come, she must. You would have her confess the
authors of her present misfortunes, I warrant 'ee; 'tis an
unconscionable demand, and she should lose the estima-
tion that I, for my part, hold of her worth, if she had   90
done it: why sir, you ought not of all men living to know
it. Good sir, be reconciled; alas, good gentlewoman!

Ann. Pish, do not beg for me, I prize my life
As nothing; if the man will needs be mad,
Why let him take it.

Sor.   Vasques, hear'st thou this?   95

Vas. Yes, and commend her for it: in this she shows the
nobleness of a gallant spirit, and beshrew my heart but
it becomes her rarely. [*Aside to Sor.*] Sir, in any case
smother your revenge; leave the scenting-out your
wrongs to me; be ruled, as you respect your honour, or   100

---

81. hath] *Q;* have *Gifford.*   88. authors] *Q;* author *Dyce.*   98–101.
S.D.'s] *Weber* (*Q* has long dashes).   100. ruled,] *Reed;* rul'd *Q.*

---

81. *what faults hath been done*] acceptable contemporary usage (Abbott,
sect. 334), though the compositor may have picked up 'hath' from 82.

82–4. *what hath . . . would not*] meant as an ironical truth: cf. 'a
chaste wife, or a mother that never stept awry, are wonders, wonders in
Italy', *Love's Sacrifice*, I. ii (Dyce, II, 19). Vasques is a Spaniard.

88. *authors*] persons responsible; begetters, fathers (*O.E.D.*, 1–2). The
plural may be meant to include accomplices such as Putana, or illogically
to insinuate that Annabella has had more lovers than one.

97. *beshrew*] curse.

97–8. *but it becomes*] if it does not become.

you mar all. [*Aloud*] Sir, if ever my service were of any
credit with you, be not so violent in your distractions:
you are married now; what a triumph might the report
of this give to other neglected suitors! 'Tis as manlike to   √
bear extremities, as godlike to forgive.   105

Sor. O Vasques, Vasques, in this piece of flesh,
This faithless face of hers, had I laid up
The treasure of my heart!—Hadst thou been virtuous,
Fair, wicked woman, not the matchless joys
Of life itself had made me wish to live   110
With any saint but thee; deceitful creature,
How hast thou mocked my hopes, and in the shame
Of thy lewd womb even buried me alive!
I did too dearly love thee.

Vas.   This is well;   *Aside* [*to him*].
Follow this temper with some passion, be brief and   115
moving: 'tis for the purpose.

Sor. Be witness to my words thy soul and thoughts,
And tell me, didst not think that in my heart
I did too superstitiously adore thee?

Ann. I must confess, I know you loved me well.   120

Sor. And wouldst thou use me thus? O Annabella,
Be thou assured, whatsoe'er the villain was
That thus hath tempted thee to this disgrace,
Well he might lust, but never loved like me: √
He doted on the picture that hung out   125

114–16.] *so this ed.;* I . . . well; / Follow . . . passion, / Bee . . . purpose.
Q; as prose Weber.   117. words thy] *Q;* words, my *Dodsley.*   122. thou]
Gifford; thus *Q.* whatsoe'er] *Q;* whoe'er *Gifford.*

101–2. *were of any credit*] deserved any reward (cf. I. ii. 174).
102. *distractions*] fits of mental disturbance.
105. *extremities*] hardships.
106–8. *in this . . . heart*] Cf. Matthew VI. 19–21.
110. *life*] 'the state of existence of the souls of the blessed departed'
(*O.E.D.*, 2); cf. I. i. 68, II. ii. 11.
115. *temper*] calmness.
passion] outburst of feeling (*O.E.D.*, *sb* 6 c).
119. *superstitiously adore*] 'idolize'.

    Upon thy cheeks, to please his humorous eye:
    Not on the part I loved, which was thy heart,
    And as I thought, thy virtues.
Ann.   O my lord!
    These words wound deeper than your sword could do.
Vas. Let me not ever take comfort, but I begin to weep   130
    myself, so much I pity him; why, madam, I knew when
    his rage was overpassed what it would come to.
Sor. Forgive me, Annabella: though thy youth
    Hath tempted thee above thy strength to folly,
    Yet will not I forget what I should be,   135
    And what I am, a husband; in that name
    Is hid divinity. If I do find
    That thou wilt yet be true, here I remit
    All former faults, and take thee to my bosom.
Vas. By my troth, and that's a point of noble charity.   140
Ann. Sir, on my knees—
Sor.   Rise up, you shall not kneel;
    Get you to your chamber, see you make no show
    Of alteration; I'll be with you straight.
    My reason tells me now, that 'tis as common
    To err in frailty as to be a woman.   145
    Go to your chamber.   *Exit* ANNABELLA.
Vas. So, this was somewhat to the matter; what do you think
    of your heaven of happiness now, sir?
Sor. I carry Hell about me, all my blood
    Is fired in swift revenge.   150

144–5. 'tis . . . woman] *italic in Q* ('*Tis*).

---

    126. *humorous*] capricious.
    140. *point*] instance (*O.E.D.*, *sb* 5).
    142–3. *make . . . alteration*] give no sign of disturbance (*O.E.D.*, *s.v.* alter 3).
    144–5. '*tis . . . woman*] Cf. 'Frailty, thy name is woman!' (*Hamlet*, I. ii. 146); also 'To err is human' and 'Woman is the weaker vessel' (Tilley, E179, W655).
    147. *matter*] purpose.

Vas. That may be, but know you how, or on whom? Alas, to
marry a great woman, being made great in the stock to
your hand, is a usual sport in these days; but to know
what ferret it was that haunted your cony-berry—there's
the cunning.   155

Sor. I'll make her tell herself, or—

Vas. Or what? You must not do so, let me yet persuade
your sufferance a little while; go to her, use her mildly,
win her if it be possible to a voluntary, to a weeping
tune; for the rest, if all hit, I will not miss my mark. Pray   160
sir, go in; the next news I tell you shall be wonders.

Sor. Delay in vengeance gives a heavier blow.   *Exit.*

Vas. Ah sirrah, here's work for the nonce! I had a suspicion
of a bad matter in my head a pretty whiles ago; but after

---

154. ferret] *Dodsley; Secret Q.*   haunted] *Q.; hunted Dodsley.*

151–4. *to marry . . . cony-berry*] a chain of puns. 'Great woman' means
both 'woman of rank' and 'woman great with child'. 'Stock' means (1) butt
or handle, (2) body, (3) rabbit-burrow (not thus recorded before 1741) and
(4), as a verb used of breeding animals, to impregnate (O.E.D., *sb*¹ 28, 5,
46, *vb*¹ 17). Thus 'great in the stock to your hand' might idiomatically
mean 'the right size for you to hold', but here takes on the meaning 'ready
impregnated for you'; and 'stock' finally suggests the metaphor of the
woman's body as a rabbit-hole invaded by a ferret.

154. *what ferret . . . cony-berry*] Cf. *Fancies*, IV. i, where Secco, pro-
claiming himself a cuckold, says 'this sucking ferret hath been wriggling
in my old cony-burrow' (Dyce, II, 292).

haunted] frequented. Dodsley's emendation gives a more vigorous and
perhaps (for a single burrow) a more logical reading; but 'haunted',
implying frequent visits by the lover, fits in well with Vasques's technique
of subtly adding fuel to Soranzo's rage (cf. 88).

cony-berry] rabbit-burrow. Land was set aside for rabbits to breed
in; when sport or meat was needed they could be bolted from their holes
into nets by muzzled ferrets (George Turbervile, *The Noble Art of Venerie*,
1576, repr. 1908, pp. 179–80), or trapped, or caught by dogs or trained
hawks (*Shakespeare's England*, II, 364). The ferret of Vasques's metaphor
may be wild, or belong to a poacher.

155. *cunning*] skill.

159. *voluntary*] piece of music played or sung at the performer's choice
(O.E.D., *sb* 2 b; cf. *Lover's Melancholy*, I. i, Dyce, I, 15).

160. *if all hit*] if everything goes right.

163. *nonce*] time being, occasion.

my madam's scurvy looks here at home, her waspish   165
perverseness and loud fault-finding, then I remembered
the proverb, that where hens crow and cocks hold their
peace there are sorry houses. 'Sfoot, if the lower parts
of a she-tailor's cunning can cover such a swelling in
the stomach, I'll never blame a false stitch in a shoe   170
whiles I live again. Up, and up so quick? and so
quickly too? 'Twere a fine policy to learn by whom;
this must be known: and I have thought on 't—here's
the way, or none.

Enter PUTANA.

—What, crying, old mistress? alas, alas, I cannot blame   175
'ee: we have a lord, Heaven help us, is so mad as the
devil himself, the more shame for him.

Put. O Vasques, that ever I was born to see this day! Doth
he use thee so too sometimes, Vasques?

Vas. Me! why, he makes a dog of me; but if some were of   180
my mind, I know what we would do. As sure as I am
an honest man, he will go near to kill my lady with un-
kindness; say she be with child, is that such a matter for
a young woman of her years to be blamed for?

Put. Alas, good heart, it is against her will full sore.   185

Vas. I durst be sworn, all his madness is for that she will not
confess whose 'tis; which he will know, and when he
doth know it, I am so well acquainted with his humour
that he will forget all straight. Well I could wish she
would in plain terms tell all, for that's the way indeed.   190

167–8. where . . . houses] *italic in* Q (*Where*).   172–3. whom; this] *Gifford;*
whom this Q; whom. This *Weber.*   known] Q; done *Dodsley.*   174.1.]
so Weber; Q *places after* 177.   189. Well I] Q; Well, I *Dodsley.*

167–8. *where hens . . . houses*] 'They are sory houses, where the
Hennes crowe, and the cock holdes his peace', *Florio his Firste Fruites*
(1578), f. 33ᵛ; cf. IV. i. 72–3 and notes.

172. *policy*] piece of craft.

176. *mad*] furious.

188. *humour*] peculiarity of temperament.

Put. Do you think so?

Vas. Foh, I know 't; provided that he did not win her to 't
by force. He was once in a mind that you could tell, and
meant to have wrung it out of you, but I somewhat
pacified him for that; yet sure you know a great deal.   195

Put. Heaven forgive us all, I know a little, Vasques.

Vas. Why should you not? who else should? Upon my conscience, she loves you dearly, and you would not betray
her to any affliction for the world.

Put. Not for all the world, by my faith and troth, Vasques.   200

Vas. 'Twere pity of your life if you should; but in this you
should both relieve her present discomforts, pacify my
lord, and gain yourself everlasting love and preferment.

Put. Dost think so, Vasques?

Vas. Nay, I know 't; sure 'twas some near and entire friend.   205

Put. 'Twas a dear friend indeed; but—

Vas. But what? Fear not to name him; my life between you
and danger; faith, I think 'twas no base fellow.

Put. Thou wilt stand between me and harm?

Vas. Ud's pity, what else? You shall be rewarded too; trust   210
me.

Put. 'Twas even no worse than her own brother.

Vas. Her brother Giovanni, I warrant 'ee!

Put. Even he, Vasques; as brave a gentleman as ever kissed
fair lady. O, they love most perpetually.   215

Vas. A brave gentleman indeed; why, therein I commend
her choice. [*Aside*] Better and better. [*To her*] You are
sure 'twas he?

Put. Sure; and you shall see he will not be long from her too.

Vas. He were to blame if he would: but may I believe thee?   220

217. S.D.'s] *Gifford* (*Q has long dashes*).

---

205. *entire*] perfectly devoted and beloved; intimate; perhaps also 'not
castrated' (*O.E.D.*, adj 3c, 4b).

206. *dear*] both 'well-loved' and 'costly' (for a similar pun see *Twelfth
Night*, III. ii. 49–52).

210. *Ud's*] God's.

214. *brave*] fine.

Put. Believe me! why, dost think I am a Turk or a Jew? No,
Vasques, I have known their dealings too long to belie
them now.

Vas. Where are you? there within, sirs!

Enter Banditti.

Put. How now, what are these?   225

Vas. You shall know presently: come sirs, take me this old
damnable hag, gag her instantly, and put out her eyes.
Quickly, quickly!

Put. Vasques, Vasques!

Vas. Gag her I say, 'sfoot d'ee suffer her to prate? what d'ee   230
fumble about? Let me come to her, I'll help your old
gums, you toad-bellied bitch! [*He gags* Putana]. Sirs,
carry her closely into the coal-house and put out her eyes
instantly, if she roars slit her nose; d'ee hear, be speedy
and sure.   235

Exeunt [Banditti] *with* PUTANA.

Why, this is excellent and above expectation. Her own
brother? O horrible! To what a height of liberty in
damnation hath the devil trained our age; her brother,
well! There's yet but a beginning, I must to my lord,
and tutor him better in his points of vengeance; now I   240
see how a smooth tale goes beyond a smooth tail—but

---

224. you? there] *Q; you there? Dyce.*   226–8.] *so Weber;* You . . .
presently, / Come . . . *hagge,* / Gag . . . quickly. *Q.*   232. S.D.] *this
ed.; they gag her Gifford.*   235.1. S.D.] *Gifford; Exit with* Putana *Q*
(*after* expectation *236*).   241–2. goes . . . soft] *on separate line in Q.*

---

222. *belie*] tell lies about.

224.1. 'It may appear singular, that Vasques should have a body of
assassins awaiting his call; before he had any assurance that they would be
needed; the circumstance serves, however, to illustrate the savage nature
of this revengeful villain' (Gifford).

226. *presently*] at once.

230. *'sfoot*] 'by God's foot'.

233. *closely*] secretly.

238. *trained*] enticed; probably also 'educated'.

241. *goes beyond*] outwits, 'gets round'.

tail] lower parts; presumably a synecdoche for 'woman' generally
rather than for Annabella or Putana. 'Smooth' may imply deceitfulness, as
in 'smooth-tongued', 'smooth-faced'.

soft: what thing comes next?

Enter GIOVANNI.

Giovanni! as I would wish; my belief is strengthened,
'tis as firm as winter and summer.

Gio. Where's my sister?   245

Vas. Troubled with a new sickness, my lord; she's somewhat ill.

Gio. Took too much of the flesh, I believe.

Vas. Troth sir, and you I think have e'en hit it; but my
virtuous lady—   250

Gio. Where's she?   [*Gives him money.*]

Vas. In her chamber; please you visit her? She is alone,
your liberality hath doubly made me your servant, and
ever shall, ever—   *Exit* GIOVANNI.

Enter SORANZO.

Sir, I am made a man, I have plied my cue with cunning   255
and success; I beseech you, let's be private.

Sor. My lady's brother's come, now he'll know all.

Vas. Let him know 't: I have made some of them fast enough.
How have you dealt with my lady?

Sor. Gently, as thou hast counselled: O, my soul   260
Runs circular in sorrow for revenge!
But Vasques, thou shalt know—

242. what . . . next] *on separate line in Q, with S.D. on right.*   243-4.
Giovanni! . . . summer] *so Weber;* Giouanni! . . . strengthned, / 'Tis
. . . Summer. *Q.*   249-50.] *so Weber;* Troth . . . it, / But . . . *Lady.*
Q.   251. S.D.] *Weber.*   252. her?] *this ed.;* her; *Q.*   254. ever shall,]
Gifford; euer shal *Q;* shall *Dodsley.*   258-9.] *so Weber;* Let . . . enough,
/ How . . . Lady? *Q.*

---

248. *Took . . . flesh*] (1) 'Ate too much meat'; (2) 'had too much sex'
(a sense obviously unintended by Giovanni).

253. *liberality*] generosity; perhaps also 'licentiousness' (*O.E.D.*, liberal
adi 2, 3).

255. *made a man*] perhaps a misprint for 'a made man', i.e. one whose
success is assured; cf. *Queen*, 3051.

plied my cue] played my part.

Vas. Nay, I will know no more: for now comes your turn to
    know; I would not talk so openly with you. Let my
    young master take time enough, and go at pleasure; he   265
    is sold to death, and the devil shall not ransom him. Sir,
    I beseech you, your privacy.
Sor. No conquest can gain glory of my fear.   *Exeunt.*

268. *Exeunt*] *Reed; Exit Q.*

268.] Perhaps: 'No victory of mine can win glory if the matter is as I
fear', implying that Soranzo's suspicions have been alerted by Vasques's
last remark. Alternatively, 'Whatever defeats I may suffer, the victor shall
not have the glory of seeing me show fear'. For *conquest* in an unusual
sense see *Perkin Warbeck*, v. iii. 94.

Act V

Enter ANNABELLA *above.*

Ann. Pleasures farewell, and all ye thriftless minutes
  Wherein false joys have spun a weary life;   *Boethius - false felicities*
  To these my fortunes now I take my leave.
  Thou precious Time, that swiftly ridest in post
  Over the world, to finish up the race   5
  Of my last fate; here stay thy restless course,
  And bear to ages that are yet unborn
  A wretched woeful woman's tragedy.
  My conscience now stands up against my lust
  With depositions charactered in guilt,   10

Enter Friar.

  And tells me I am lost; now I confess,
  Beauty that clothes the outside of the face
  Is cursèd if it be not clothed with grace.
  Here like a turtle, mewed up in a cage

---

v. i. Act V] *Actus Quintus. Q.*   10. depositions] *Dodsley;* dispositions *Q.*
10.1.] *Qᵇ; not in Qᵃ.*   12–13.] *italic in Q.*

---

v. i. 1 ff.] Annabella's part in this scene, like the Friar's in III. vi, has
echoes of Ford's penitential poem *Christes Bloodie Sweat* (1613).
  4. *in post*] at full speed (like a despatch-rider).
  9–10.] Conscience appears in court as a counsel who reads out the
written testimony (depositions) supplied by guilt.
  10. *charactered in guilt*] a pun: the phrase could mean 'in gold letters',
as of words deserving display.
  12–13.] Semi-proverbial: cf. 'Beauty is but skin-deep' and 'Beauty
without goodness is worth nothing' (Tilley B170, B175.)
  14. *turtle*] dove; a bird proverbially devoted to its mate (Tilley T624).
  mewed] cooped.

99

Unmated, I converse with air and walls,   15
And descant on my vile unhappiness.
O Giovanni, that hast had the spoil
Of thine own virtues and my modest fame,
Would thou hadst been less subject to those stars
That luckless reigned at my nativity!   20
O, would the scourge due to my black offence
Might pass from thee, that I alone might feel
The torment of an uncontrollèd flame!
Fri. [*Aside*] What's this I hear?
Ann.   That man, that blessed friar,
Who joined in ceremonial knot my hand   25
To him whose wife I now am, told me oft
I trod the path to death, and showed me how.
But they who sleep in lethargies of lust
Hug their confusion, making Heaven unjust,
And so did I.
Fri. [*Aside*]   Here's music to the soul!   30

24. *Aside*] *Weber.*   28–9.] *italic in Q.*   30. *Aside*] *Weber.*

---

16. *descant*] sing; discourse; complain (*O.E.D.*, *vb* 1–2).

17–18. *had the spoil Of*] both 'plundered' and 'destroyed'.

19–20. *stars . . . nativity*] perhaps an echo of *Dr. Faustus*, xix. 157
(ed. Jump, 1962).

23.] Though the main idea is probably 'the unquenched fire of Hell'
(cf. III. vi. 11; also Luke XVI. 24, 'I am tormented in this flame'), *uncontrolled flame* also suggests ungoverned passion (for *flames* in this sense cf.
I. ii. 222). Thus the line can mean 'the torment of unsatisfied desire',
possibly in the present (cf. 14–15) but more probably prolonged in Hell
as a punishment for lechery (a traditional belief: cf. III. vi. 21–3; *Christes
Bloodie Sweat*, sig. E1ᵛ; *Paradise Lost*, IV. 509–11). Also, *scourge* (21) suggests providential chastisement rather than damnation; in this light 23
could mean 'the torment of conscience which follows ungoverned passion'. Ideas of present and future pains, fires of lust and of Hell, seem
vaguely combined.

28–9 Cf. *Christes Bloodie Sweat*, sigs. F1ᵛ and esp. H4ᵛ: 'Inchanting
sinne, that with it's cunning charmes Luls men in death-full sleepes, . . .
Rockes them in Lethargies, and neuer wakes Reason, to feele the bane-impotion'd wrath, Which by such dead securitie it hath'.

29. *confusion*] destruction, damnation.

making Heaven unjust] believing that Heaven will not deal justly with
them (*O.E.D.*, make *vb* 49 c).

Ann.   Forgive me, my good genius, and this once
     Be helpful to my ends: let some good man
     Pass this way, to whose trust I may commit
     This paper double-lined with tears and blood;
     Which being granted, here I sadly vow   35
     Repentance, and a leaving of that life
     I long have died in.

Fri.   Lady, Heaven hath heard you,
     And hath by providence ordained that I
     Should be his minister for your behoof.

Ann.   Ha, what are you?

Fri.   Your brother's friend the friar;   40
     Glad in my soul that I have lived to hear
     This free confession 'twixt your peace and you.
     What would you, or to whom? fear not to speak.

Ann.   Is Heaven so bountiful? then I have found
     More favour than I hoped. Here, holy man: 45

                                Throws a letter.

     Commend me to my brother, give him that,
     That letter; bid him read it and repent.
     Tell him that I—imprisoned in my chamber,
     Barred of all company, even of my guardian,
     Who gives me cause of much suspect—have time   50
     To blush at what hath passed; bid him be wise,
     And not believe the friendship of my lord.
     I fear much more than I can speak: good father,
     The place is dangerous, and spies are busy,

50. Who] *Q;* Which *Gifford.*

---

31. *Forgive . . . genius*] The same phrase occurs in *Love's Sacrifice*,
v. i (Dyce, II, 93). For *genius* see note to II. ii. 159.

32. *ends*] purposes.

34. *double-lined*] inter-lined.

37. *died*] i.e. spiritually; cf. I. i. 58, and the corresponding use of 'life'
at I. i. 68, IV. iii. 110.

39. *behoof*] advantage.

50. *Who*] which (see Abbott, sect. 264; cf. *Fame's Memorial*, Dyce, III,
296).

suspect] suspicion; fear (*O.E.D.*, sb[1]).

I must break off—you'll do 't?

Fri.   Be sure I will,   55
     And fly with speed; my blessing ever rest
     With thee, my daughter; live to die more blest!   *Exit.*

Ann. Thanks to the heavens, who have prolonged my breath
     To this good use; now I can welcome death.   *Exit.*

[v. ii]
                     Enter SORANZO *and* VASQUES.

Vas. Am I to be believed now? First, marry a strumpet that
     cast herself away upon you but to laugh at your horns?
     To feast on your disgrace, riot in your vexations, cuckold
     you in your bride-bed, waste your estate upon panders
     and bawds?   5

Sor. No more, I say no more!

Vas. A cuckold is a goodly tame beast, my lord.

Sor. I am resolved; urge not another word,
     My thoughts are great, and all as resolute
     As thunder; in mean time I'll cause our lady   10
     To deck herself in all her bridal robes,
     Kiss her, and fold her gently in my arms.
     Begone—yet hear you, are the banditti ready
     To wait in ambush?

Vas. Good sir, trouble not yourself about other business than 15
     your own resolution: remember that time lost cannot be
     recalled.

Sor. With all the cunning words thou canst, invite
     The states of Parma to my birthday's feast;

55.] *long space follows dash in Q.*   57. blest] *Dodsley;* blessed *Q.*
v. ii. 1. Am ... now?] *on separate line in Q.*   7.] *italic in Q.*

---

     v. ii. 2. *your horns*] It was a traditional joke that horns grew (invisibly)
from a cuckold's forehead.
     3. *riot in*] revel in, delight in (*O.E.D., vb* 1 c, not recorded earlier than
1741).
     19. *states*] persons of high rank or office.

Haste to my brother rival and his father,   20
Entreat them gently, bid them not to fail;
Be speedy and return.

Vas. Let not your pity betray you till my coming back; think
upon incest and cuckoldry.

Sor. Revenge is all the ambition I aspire,   25
To that I'll climb or fall: my blood's on fire.   *Exeunt.*

[V. iii]

Enter GIOVANNI.

Gio. Busy opinion is an idle fool,
That, as a school-rod keeps a child in awe,
Frights the unexperienced temper of the mind.
So did it me; who ere my precious sister
Was married, thought all taste of love would die   5
In such a contract: but I find no change
Of pleasure in this formal law of sports.
She is still one to me, and every kiss
As sweet and as delicious as the first
I reaped, when yet the privilege of youth   10
Entitled her a virgin. O, the glory
Of two united hearts like hers and mine!
Let poring book-men dream of other worlds,
My world, and all of happiness, is here,
And I'd not change it for the best to come: 15

23–4.] *so Weber;* Let . . . backe, / Thinke . . . *Cuckoldry.* Q.   23. you]
Dyce; you, Q. back;] *Reed;* backe, Q.

v. iii. 3. the unexperienced] Q (vnexperienc't); th'unexperienc'd *Dodsley.*

---

25. *aspire*] ardently desire (*O.E.D.*, *vb* 4).

v. iii. 1. *Busy*] meddlesome.
opinion] common or received opinion.
idle] futile, ineffective.
6, 7. *In*] as a result of.
7. *formal*] merely conventional (*O.E.D.*, 7).
law of sports] Cf. 'law of any game' (I. ii. 56), where *law* means 'accepted
code, rules'; cf. also 'belly-sports' (IV. iii. 12).

A life of pleasure is Elysium.

Enter Friar.

Father, you enter on the jubilee
Of my retired delights: now I can tell you,
The Hell you oft have prompted is nought else
But slavish and fond superstitious fear;   20
And I could prove it, too—
Fri.   Thy blindness slays thee;
Look there, 'tis writ to thee.   *Gives the letter.*
Gio. From whom?
Fri. Unrip the seals and see;
The blood's yet seething hot, that will anon   25
Be frozen harder than congealed coral.
Why d'ee change colour, son?
Gio.   'Fore Heaven, you make
Some petty devil factor 'twixt my love
And your religion-maskèd sorceries:
Where had you this?
Fri.   Thy conscience, youth, is seared,   30
Else thou wouldst stoop to warning.
Gio.   'Tis her hand,
I know 't; and 'tis all written in her blood.

16.] *italic in* Q.

---

16. *Elysium*] in classical mythology, the region in which blessed souls
dwelt after death.

17. *jubilee*] exultant joy (*O.E.D.*, *sb* 5), or perhaps 'period of rejoicing'
(*sb* 4); cf. *Perkin Warbeck*, I. ii. 140–1, 'thou grow'st upon my heart like
peace, Creating every other hour a jubilee'.

18. *retired*] secluded, private.

19. *prompted*] put into my mind.

26. *congealed coral*] Q has 'congeal'd'; possibly *coral* is accented on the
second syllable, as in Chaucer. Sturgess points out that coral was formerly
believed to be an underwater plant which hardened on exposure to air.

28. *factor*] act as agent: cf. P. Fletcher, *Purple Island* (1633), 'A carrion
crow he is . . . the devil's factoring knave' (cited by *O.E.D.*).

30. *seared*] made incapable of feeling, as by cauterization: cf. 'having
their conscience seared with a hot iron', 1 Timothy IV. 2.

31. *stoop to*] humble yourself before; obey (perhaps with metaphor of
the trained hawk coming under control by 'stooping' to its lure).

She writes I know not what—death? I'll not fear
An armèd thunderbolt aimed at my heart.
She writes we are discovered—pox on dreams   35
Of low faint-hearted cowardice! Discovered?
The devil we are! which way is 't possible?
Are we grown traitors to our own delights?
Confusion take such dotage, 'tis but forged!
This is your peevish chattering, weak old man.   40

Enter VASQUES.

Now sir, what news bring you?

Vas. My lord, according to his yearly custom keeping this
day a feast in honour of his birthday, by me invites you
thither; your worthy father, with the Pope's reverend
Nuncio and other magnificoes of Parma, have promised   45
their presence: will't please you to be of the number?

Gio. Yes, tell them I dare come.

Vas. Dare come?

Gio. So I said; and tell him more, I will come.

Vas. These words are strange to me.   50

Gio. Say I will come.

Vas. You will not miss?

Gio. Yet more? I'll come! Sir, are you answered?

Vas. So I'll say; my service to you.   *Exit.*

Fri. You will not go, I trust.

Gio.   Not go! for what?   55

Fri. O do not go, this feast, I'll gage my life,
Is but a plot to train you to your ruin;
Be ruled, you sha'not go.

40.1] *so Dyce; Q places after* 41.   47. them] *Q;* him *Gifford.*   53. come!
sir, are] *Q* (come;)*;* come, sir. Are *Gifford.*

---

39. *Confusion*] destruction, damnation.
dotage] nonsense.
40. *peevish*] senseless; spiteful.
52. *miss*] fail.
56. *gage*] pledge, stake.
57. *train*] entice.

Gio.   Not go? Stood Death
        Threat'ning his armies of confounding plagues,
        With hosts of dangers hot as blazing stars,   60
        I would be there: not go! yes, and resolve
        To strike as deep in slaughter as they all,
        For I will go.

Fri.   Go where thou wilt, I see
        The wildness of thy fate draws to an end,
        To a bad, fearful end; I must not stay   65
        To know thy fall; back to Bononia I
        With speed will haste, and shun this coming blow.
        Parma farewell; would I had never known thee,
        Or aught of thine! Well, youngman, since no prayer
        Can make thee safe, I leave thee to despair.   *Exit.*   70

Gio. Despair, or tortures of a thousand hells,
        All's one to me: I have set up my rest.
        Now, now, work serious thoughts on baneful plots;
        Be all a man, my soul; let not the curse
        Of old prescription rend from me the gall   75
        Of courage, which enrols a glorious death.
        If I must totter like a well-grown oak,

71. *Gio.*] *Dodsley; not in Q.*

---

60. Cf. *Queen*, 2581, 'To meet whole hosts of dangers'.
blazing stars] comets, thought to be not only ominous but dangerous,
because of their fiery tails.

69. *youngman*] in regular use as a single word, probably stressed on the
first syllable.

72. *set up my rest*] committed my last stakes; taken a final resolution. To
'set up one's rest' in primero was to venture one's reserve stakes, to lose
which was to lose the game.

75. *prescription*] custom and its binding force.
gall] an organ receiving the 'fiery superfluity' of choler from the liver
(Browne, *Pseudodoxia Epidemica*, III. ii); the bitter secretion of this organ;
hence, anger or fierceness. Another kind of gall, found on oak-trees, was
used in making ink (*O.E.D.* *sb*³); perhaps *gall* has here the additional
meaning 'ink' by a synecdoche.

76. *enrols*] honourably records: cf. George Herbert, 'Praise (II)', 25–6,
'Small it is, in this poore sort To enroll thee'. One kind of gall animates
the hero to meet a worthy death, another records it (see last note).

Some under-shrubs shall in my weighty fall
Be crushed to splits: with me they all shall perish.

Exit.

[v. iv]
Enter SORANZO, VASQUES *and* Banditti.

Sor. You will not fail, or shrink in the attempt?

Vas. I will undertake for their parts: be sure, my masters, to
be bloody enough, and as unmerciful as if you were prey-
ing upon a rich booty on the very mountains of Liguria.
For your pardons, trust to my lord; but for reward you   5
shall trust none but your own pockets.

Ban. omnes. We'll make a murder.

Sor. Here's gold, here's more; want nothing, what you do
Is noble, and an act of brave revenge:
I'll make ye rich, banditti, and all free.   10

Ban. omnes. Liberty! Liberty!

Vas. Hold, take every man a vizard. When ye are withdrawn,
keep as much silence as you can possibly: you know the
watchword, till which be spoken, move not, but when
you hear that, rush in like a stormy flood; I need not   15
instruct ye in your own profession.

Ban. omnes. No, no, no.

Vas. In, then; your ends are profit and preferment—away!

Exeunt Banditti.

Sor. The guests will all come, Vasques?

v. iv. 18.1. *Exeunt*] *Reed; Exit Q.*

---

79. *splits*] splinters.

v. iv. 2. *undertake for*] answer for.

4. *Liguria*] a region in N.W. Italy where the lower Alps join the Appe-
nines; these mountains run between Parma and Genoa.

5. *pardons*] perhaps for earlier crimes, as well as that now to be committed (see 11 and note).

8. *want*] lack.

10. *free*] acquitted; perhaps 'restored to civil rights and liberties'
(*O.E.D.*, 7, 1).

12. *vizard*] mask.

Vas. Yes sir, and now let me a little edge your resolution: 20
      you see nothing is unready to this great work, but a great
      mind in you. Call to your remembrance your disgraces,
      your loss of honour, Hippolita's blood, and arm your
      courage in your own wrongs; so shall you best right those
      wrongs in vengeance which you may truly call your own.   25
Sor. 'Tis well; the less I speak, the more I burn,
      And blood shall quench that flame.
Vas. Now you begin to turn Italian! This beside, when my
      young incest-monger comes, he will be sharp set on his
      old bit: give him time enough, let him have your cham-   30
      ber and bed at liberty; let my hot hare have law ere he
      be hunted to his death, that if it be possible he may post
      to Hell in the very act of his damnation.

Enter GIOVANNI.

Sor. It shall be so; and see, as we would wish,
      He comes himself first.—Welcome, my much-loved   35
        brother,
      Now I perceive you honour me; y' are welcome.

20. Yes sir] *on separate line in Q.* 20. and . . . resolution] *on separate line in Q.*

---

    29. *sharp set*] 'keen'; hungry; hence, eager for sexual intercourse (*O.E.D.*, 2 b).

    30. *bit*] morsel of food (*O.E.D.*, sb^2 2); hence, something to tempt the sexual appetite. Cf. 'she's a juicy Bit, a mettl'd Wench', *Don Quixote*, p. 576.

    31. *hot hare*] Besides being noted for 'its foecundity and superfetation', the hare symbolized 'unnatural venery and degenerous effemination' because of its supposed bisexuality (Browne, *Pseudodoxia Epidemica*, III, xvii).

    law] time to get away, a 'start' (*O.E.D.*, sb^1 20).

    32–3. *that if . . . damnation*] The notion of a revenge that would destroy soul as well as body, originating probably in the *novelle*, was well established on the English stage by Ford's day (e.g. *Hamlet*, III. iii. 87–95; Webster, *White Devil*, ed. Brown, 1960, v. i. 72–4). After discussing 26 examples of this device Eleanor Prosser concludes that it was 'morally revolting to Shakespeare's audience, even as it is today' (*Hamlet and Revenge*, Stanford and London, 1967, p. 275).

    32. *post*] speed.

But where's my father?

Gio.   With the other states,
Attending on the Nuncio of the Pope
To wait upon him hither; how's my sister?

Sor. Like a good housewife, scarcely ready yet;   40
Y' are best walk to her chamber.

Gio.   If you will.

Sor. I must expect my honourable friends;
Good brother, get her forth.

Gio.   You are busy, sir.   *Exit.*

Vas. Even as the great devil himself would have it! Let him
go and glut himself in his own destruction.   45
                                          Flourish.

Hark, the Nuncio is at hand; good sir, be ready to
receive him.

    Enter Cardinal, FLORIO, DONADO, RICHARDETTO *and*
                    Attendants.

Sor. Most reverend lord, this grace hath made me proud
That you vouchsafe my house; I ever rest
Your humble servant for this noble favour.   50

Car. You are our friend, my lord; his Holiness
Shall understand how zealously you honour
Saint Peter's Vicar in his substitute:
Our special love to you.

Sor.   Signiors, to you
My welcome, and my ever best of thanks   55
For this so memorable courtesy.
Pleaseth your grace to walk near?

Car.   My lord, we come

45.1.] *so Gifford; in margin opposite* let him goe ... receiue him *Qᵃ; in
margin opposite* 'Enter ... Attendants' *Qᵇ.*   57. Pleaseth] *Q;* Please
Weber.   grace to walk] *Q;* grace walk *Gifford.*

---

42. *expect*] wait for.
53. *St. Peter's Vicar*] the Pope.

To celebrate your feast with civil mirth,
As ancient custom teacheth; we will go.

Sor. Attend his grace, there! signiors, keep your way.   60

Exeunt.

[V. v]

Enter GIOVANNI *and* ANNABELLA *lying on a bed.*

Gio. What, changed so soon? Hath your new sprightly lord
Found out a trick in night-games more than we
Could know in our simplicity? Ha, is 't so?
Or does the fit come on you, to prove treacherous
To your past vows and oaths?

Ann.   Why should you jest   5
At my calamity, without all sense
Of the approaching dangers you are in?

Gio. What danger's half so great as thy revolt?
Thou art a faithless sister, else thou know'st
Malice, or any treachery beside,   10
Would stoop to my bent brows; why, I hold fate

---

58. *civil mirth*] well-behaved merry-making.

60. *keep your way*] keep going in that direction.

V. v. 0.1 Enter . . . bed] Cf. '*Enter the* Admirall *in his bed*', Marlowe, *Massacre at Paris*, in *Works*, ed. Brooke (1910), 256/7; '*Enter* ANNE *in her bed*', T. Heywood, *Woman Killed with Kindness*, ed. van Fossen (1961), xvii. 38.1. 'Enter' need mean no more than that the persons are disclosed within the inner stage, coming forward if necessary later. But other S.D.'s call for a bed to be 'thrust out' on to the main stage with a person in it (e.g. Middleton, *Chaste Maid*, ed. Parker, 1969, III. ii. 0.1; *Late Lancashire Witches*, cited by van Fossen, *loc. cit.*), and that may have happened here. No S.D. specifies a bed on the upper stage, though whatever structure was used in *Antony and Cleopatra*, IV. xv, might well have accommodated one.

4. *fit*] capricious impulse; cf. II. i. 48.

6. *calamity*] state of distress, affliction (*O.E.D.*, I).

8. *revolt*] disloyalty; change of sides (*O.E.D.*, *sb*[1] I c, citing Warner, *Albions England*, 1596, 'his soone Reuolt from friend to friend').

11. *stoop to my bent brows*] yield to my frown.

11-12. *I hold . . . fist*] an echo of Marlowe, *I Tamburlaine*, 369-70 (*Works*, ed. Brooke): 'I hold the Fates bound fast in yron chaines, And with my hand turne Fortunes wheel about'.

Clasped in my fist, and could command the course
Of time's eternal motion; hadst thou been
One thought more steady than an ebbing sea.
And what? You'll now be honest, that's resolved?   15
Ann. Brother, dear brother, know what I have been,
And know that now there's but a dining-time
'Twixt us and our confusion: let's not waste
These precious hours in vain and useless speech.
Alas, these gay attires were not put on   20
But to some end; this sudden solemn feast
Was not ordained to riot in expense;
I that have now been chambered here alone,
Barred of my guardian, or of any else,
Am not for nothing at an instant freed   25
To fresh access: be not deceived, my brother,
This banquet is an harbinger of death
To you and me, resolve yourself it is,
And be prepared to welcome it.
Gio.   Well then,
The schoolmen teach that all this globe of earth   30
Shall be consumed to ashes in a minute.

---

v. v. 17. dining-time] *Q*ᵇ (dyning time)*; dying time *Q*ᵃ.

---

17. *a dining-time*] long enough to eat a dinner; the period of the mid-day meal.
18. *confusion*] destruction, damnation.
21. *solemn*] ceremonious; sumptuous (*O.E.D.*, 3, 4).
22. *riot*] indulge profusely; perhaps 'revel' (*O.E.D.*, vb 1 a, c).
25–6. *freed To fresh access*] allowed to see company again.
28. *resolve yourself*] be assured.
30. *schoolmen*] mediaeval theologians.
30–3. *all this globe . . . waters burn*] The problem concerns the interpretation of some passages in Revelation xx and xxi. St Augustine writes: 'So then they that were not in the book of life being judged, and cast into eternal fire . . ., then shall this world lose its form by worldly fire, as it was formerly destroyed by earthly water. . . . But for that which follows, "There was no more sea," whether it imply that the sea should be dried up by that universal conflagration, or be transformed into a better essence, I cannot easily determine.' (*City of God*, trans. Healey, revd. Tasker, 1945, Bk. xx, ch. xvi.)

Ann. So I have read too.

Gio.   But 'twere somewhat strange
To see the waters burn: could I believe
This might be true, I could believe as well
There might be Hell or Heaven.

Ann.   That's most certain.   35

Gio. A dream, a dream: else in this other world
We should know one another.

Ann.   So we shall.

Gio. Have you heard so?

Ann.   For certain.

Gio.   But d'ee think
That I shall see you there, you look on me;
May we kiss one another, prate or laugh,   40
Or do as we do here?

Ann.   I know not that,
But good, for the present, what d'ee mean
To free yourself from danger? Some way, think
How to escape; I'm sure the guests are come.

Gio. Look up, look here; what see you in my face?   45

Ann. Distraction and a troubled countenance.

Gio. Death, and a swift repining wrath—yet look,
What see you in mine eyes?

Ann.   Methinks you weep.

39–40.] *so Reed;* That . . . there, / You . . . mee, / May . . . another, /
Prate or laugh, *Q.*   42. good,] *Sherman;* good *Q;* good brother,
Dodsley; brother, *Gifford.*   what] *Q;* how *Dodsley.*   46. countenance]
Q; conscience *Dodsley.*

---

40. *prate*] prattle, talk idly.

41. *do as we do here*] 'Do' has both its general and its specifically sexual
meaning, 'make love', as at IV. iii. 20.

42. *good*] Though editorial repunctuation often disguises the fact,
'good' is used as a term of address more than a dozen times in Ford's
plays: see e.g. *Lover's Melancholy*, I. i, II. i, II. ii, v. i (Dyce, I, 14, 40, 43,
99); *Lady's Trial*, I. i (Dyce, III, 13); *Perkin Warbeck*, IV. ii. 40; *Queen*,
1810. Cf. the more common vocative use of 'sweet', 'dear'.

mean] intend.

45–7. Cf. *1 Tamburlaine*, 1889–93.

47. *repining*] discontented, angered.

Gio. I do indeed: these are the funeral tears
         Shed on your grave; these furrowed up my cheeks   50
         When first I loved and knew not how to woo.
         Fair Annabella, should I here repeat
         The story of my life, we might lose time.
         Be record all the spirits of the air,
         And all things else that are; that day and night,   55
         Early and late, the tribute which my heart
         Hath paid to Annabella's sacred love
         Hath been these tears, which are her mourners now.
         Never till now did Nature do her best
         To show a matchless beauty to the world,   60
         Which in an instant, ere it scarce was seen,
         The jealous Destinies required again.
         Pray, Annabella, pray; since we must part,
         Go thou white in thy soul, to fill a throne
         Of innocence and sanctity in Heaven.   65
         Pray, pray my sister.
Ann.   Then I see your drift;
         Ye blessed angels, guard me!
Gio.   So say I.
         Kiss me. If ever after-times should hear
         Of our fast-knit affections, though perhaps
         The laws of conscience and of civil use   70

51. woo] *Q^b*; woe *Q^a*.   62. required] *Q^b*; require *Q^a*.

---

51. *woo*] Q^a's 'woe' was a possible spelling of 'woo'.

54. *spirits of the air*] 'Aerial Spirits or Devils are such as keep quarter most part in the air, cause many tempests, thunder, and lightnings, tear oaks, fire steeples, houses, strike men and beasts. . . . *tempestatibus se ingerunt* [they make their presence known by storms] saith *Rich. Argentine*; as when a desperate man makes away himself, which by hanging or drowning they frequently do, . . . dancing and rejoicing at the death of a sinner' (Burton, I, 217–18).

64. *white in thy soul*] Ford may have in mind the Neoplatonic doctrine that the soul is immaculate and cannot be defiled by the sins of the body (cf. Spenser, *An Hymne in Honovr of Beavtie*, 159–61).

66. *drift*] intention.

70. *civil use*] civilized custom.

May justly blame us, yet when they but know
Our loves, that love will wipe away that rigour
Which would in other incests be abhorred.
Give me your hand; how sweetly life doth run
In these well-coloured veins! how constantly   75
These palms do promise health! but I could chide
With Nature for this cunning flattery.
Kiss me again—forgive me.

Ann.   With my heart.

Gio. Farewell.

Ann.   Will you be gone?

Gio.   Be dark, bright sun,
And make this midday night, that thy gilt rays   80
May not behold a deed will turn their splendour
More sooty than the poets feign their Styx!
One other kiss, my sister.

Ann.   What means this?

Gio. To save thy fame, and kill thee in a kiss.

                                        Stabs her.

Thus die, and die by me, and by my hand: 85
Revenge is mine; honour doth love command.

Ann. O brother, by your hand?

Gio.   When thou art dead
I'll give my reasons for 't; for to dispute
With thy—even in thy death—most lovely beauty,
Would make me stagger to perform this act   90

86.] *italic in* Q.

---

72. *wipe away that rigour*] remove the shame of that violence of passion (*O.E.D.*, *s.v.* wipe *vb* 6ᵇ, rigour 4). 'Rigour' could express any extremity of weather, e.g. excess of heat or violence of storms; for this metaphorical use cf. *Lady's Trial*, II. iv (Dyce, III, 41), 'The rigour of an uncontrollèd passion'.

75. *constantly*] confidently (*O.E.D.*, 1 b).

80. *gilt*] golden.

82. *Styx*] In Greek mythology, a poisonous river which flowed nine times round the underworld.

84. *kill thee in a kiss*] Cf. *Othello*, V. ii. 361–2.

90. *stagger*] hesitate, waver.

- death & dignity

Which I most glory in.

Ann. Forgive him, Heaven—and me my sins; farewell,
   Brother, unkind, unkind—mercy, great Heaven!—O—O!

                                        Dies.

Gio. She's dead; alas, good soul; the hapless fruit
   That in her womb received its life from me,   95
   Hath had from me a cradle and a grave.
   I must not dally. This sad marriage-bed,
   In all her best, bore her alive and dead.
   Soranzo, thou hast missed thy aim in this,
   I have prevented now thy reaching plots,   100
   And killed a love, for whose each drop of blood
   I would have pawned my heart. Fair Annabella,
   How over-glorious art thou in thy wounds,
   Triumphing over infamy and hate!
   Shrink not, courageous hand; stand up, my heart,   105
   And boldly act my last and greater part!

                                  Exit with the body.

[v. vi]

   A Banquet. Enter Cardinal, FLORIO, DONADO, SORANZO,
RICHARDETTO, VASQUES *and* Attendants; *they take their places.*

---

98. *In all her best*] in her best condition, at her highest point (*O.E.D.*,
best *adj* 8 c). Annabella's bridal robes seem not to be in question, as the
sense 'in one's best clothes' is not recorded earlier than 1790.
   100. *reaching*] far-reaching.
   102. *pawned*] pledged; put at risk.
   103. *over-glorious*] beautiful beyond all measure ('glorious' has possible
implications of 'richly adorned' and 'shining': *O.E.D.*, *s.v.* glorious 4,
over- 25).

   v. vi. o.1. A Banquet] Cf. IV. i. o.1 and note. Probably Soranzo and his
guests are now sitting down to begin their meal; flexible stage-time permits sc. v and the subsequent dismemberment of Annabella to take place
while the party moves from one room into another. It is difficult to
suppose the guests have reached dessert (for which they might adjourn)
without Annabella having been sent for.
   o.2. places] seats.

Vas. [*Aside to Sor.*] Remember sir, what you have to do; be
    wise and resolute.
Sor. [*Aside to Vas.*] Enough, my heart is fixed. [*To Car.*]
      Pleaseth your grace
    To taste these coarse confections? Though the use
    Of such set entertainments more consists   5
    In custom than in cause, yet, reverend sir,
    I am still made your servant by your presence.
Car. And we your friend.
Sor. But where's my brother Giovanni?

    Enter GIOVANNI *with a heart upon his dagger.*

Gio. Here, here Soranzo! trimmed in reeking blood   10
    That triumphs over death; proud in the spoil
    Of love and vengeance! Fate, or all the powers
    That guide the motions of immortal souls
    Could not prevent me.
Car.   What means this?
Flo. Son Giovanni!
Sor. [*Aside*]   Shall I be forestalled?   15
Gio. Be not amazed: if your misgiving hearts
    Shrink at an idle sight, what bloodless fear
    Of coward passion would have seized your senses,
    Had you beheld the rape of life and beauty
    Which I have acted? My sister, O my sister!   20

v. vi. 1. *Aside to Sor.*] *Weber.*   3. *Aside to Vas.*] *Dyce.*   4. confections?] *Walley;* Confections; *Q.*   15. *Aside*] *Gifford.*

---

    4. *coarse confections*] homely dishes. A 'confection' was a prepared
delicacy of any kind (*O.E.D.*, *sb* 5 d); most often a dessert, but see note
to 0.1.
    4–6. *the use . . . cause*] 'though such formal entertainments are held
more for the sake of keeping up a custom than for any more logical
purpose'.
    10. *trimmed in*] decorated with.
    reeking] steaming.
    11. *spoil*] Both 'destruction' and 'plunder' (cf. v. i. 17).
    16. *misgiving*] apprehensive, fearful.
    17. *idle sight*] mere spectacle.

Flo. Ha! what of her?

Gio.   The glory of my deed
    Darkened the mid-day sun, made noon as night.
    You came to feast, my lords, with dainty fare;
    I came to feast too, but I digged for food
    In a much richer mine than gold or stone   25
    Of any value balanced: 'tis a heart,
    A heart my lords, in which is mine entombed.
    Look well upon 't; d'ee know 't?

Vas. What strange riddle's this?

Gio. 'Tis Annabella's heart, 'tis; why d'ee startle?   30
    I vow 'tis hers: this dagger's point ploughed up
    Her fruitful womb, and left to me the fame
    Of a most glorious executioner.

Flo. Why, madman, art thyself?

Gio. Yes father, and that times to come may know   35
    How as my fate I honoured my revenge,
    List, father, to your ears I will yield up
    How much I have deserved to be your son.

Flo. What is 't thou say'st?

Gio.   Nine moons have had their changes,
    Since I first throughly viewed and truly loved   40
    Your daughter and my sister.

Flo.   How! alas,

41-2. How ... madman] *so McIlwraith; as one line in* Q; How ...
lords, / He is ... madman *Weber.*

---

26. *balanced*] estimated after weighing.

30. *startle*] start; take fright.

31-2. *dagger's . . . womb*] In the context of 'fruitful womb' the
ploughing would normally be a sexual metaphor, as might the dagger: cf.
'She made great Caesar lay his sword to bed. He ploughed her, and she
cropp'd' (*Antony and Cleopatra*, II. ii. 231-2). Their effect here is to make
the murder seem a sadistic version of the sexual act.

38. *How much . . . son*] directly, and through his relationship with
Annabella. Giovanni saw himself as Annabella's husband (II. vi. 35-41),
and 'son' was commonly used for 'son-in-law' (*O.E.D.*, 1 c, and cf.
'father' at v. iv. 37).

40. *throughly*] thoroughly, properly.

My lords, he's a frantic madman!

Gio.   Father, no.
For nine months' space, in secret I enjoyed
Sweet Annabella's sheets; nine months I liv'd
A happy monarch of her heart and her.   45
Soranzo, thou know'st this: thy paler cheek
Bears the confounding print of thy disgrace;
For her too fruitful womb too soon bewrayed
The happy passage of our stol'n delights,
And made her mother to a child unborn.   50

Car. Incestuous villain!

Flo.   O, his rage belies him!

Gio. It does not, 'tis the oracle of truth;
I vow it is so.

Sor.   I shall burst with fury;
Bring the strumpet forth!

Vas. I shall, sir.   *Exit.*

Gio.   Do, sir; have you all no faith   55
To credit yet my triumphs? Here I swear
By all that you call sacred, by the love
I bore my Annabella whilst she lived,
These hands have from her bosom ripped this heart.

Enter VASQUES.

Is 't true or no, sir?

Vas.   'Tis most strangely true.   60

Flo. Cursèd man!—have I lived to—   *Dies.*

Car.   Hold up Florio;
Monster of children, see what thou hast done,

59.1] *so Weber; Q places on* 60 *after* 'sir?'   61. up] *Q;* up, *Dodsley.*

---

42. *frantic*] frenzied.
47. *confounding*] shaming, discomfiting.
51. *rage*] fit of violent madness.
belies him] makes him speak falsely.
61. *Hold up Florio*] As Q regularly omits commas before vocatives this
may be addressed to Florio and mean 'Bear up!'; but cf. III. ii. 67, also
Queen, 3506, 'Hold up the *Queen*, she swouns'.

Broke thy old father's heart! Is none of you
Dares venture on him?

Gio.   Let 'em; O, my father,
How well his death becomes him in his griefs!   65
Why, this was done with courage: now survives
None of our house but I, gilt in the blood
Of a fair sister and a hapless father.

Sor. Inhuman scorn of men, hast thou a thought
T' outlive thy murders?

Gio.   Yes, I tell thee yes;   70
For in my fists I bear the twists of life.
Soranzo, see this heart which was thy wife's:
Thus I exchange it royally for thine,   [*Stabs him.*]
And thus, and thus; now brave revenge is mine.

                                        [*Soranzo falls.*]

Vas. I cannot hold any longer: you sir, are you grown   75
insolent in your butcheries? have at you!   *Fight.*

Gio. Come, I am armed to meet thee.

Vas. No, will it not be yet? if this will not, another shall.—
Not yet? I shall fit you anon.—Vengeance!

                          Enter Banditti.

Gio. Welcome! come more of you, whate'er you be,   80
I dare your worst.—   [*They surround and wound him.*]
O, I can stand no longer; feeble arms,
Have you so soon lost strength?   [*Falls.*]

73. S.D.] *Sherman; Fight. Weber.*   74.1] *Weber.*   78–9.] *so Weber;* No
... shall, / Not. ... anon— *Q (with 'Vengeance.' after space and at end of
line).*   81. S.D.] *Gifford.*   83. S.D.] *Gifford.*

67. *gilt in*] smeared with (cf. *Macbeth*, II. ii. 55–7); decorated with.
71. *twists of life*] threads of life. In Greek mythology lives were represented as threads spun and cut off by the Fates or Parcae; cf. *Fame's
Memorial* (Dyce, III, 302), 'fate had weaven The twist of life, and her of
life bereaven'.
79. *fit you anon*] pay you back or 'fix you up' soon.
Vengeance!] the agreed signal (v. iv. 13–15).

Vas. Now you are welcome, sir! Away my masters, all is done,
    shift for yourselves, your reward is your own; shift for   85
    yourselves.

Ban. Away, away!   *Exeunt* Banditti.

Vas. How d'ee, my lord? See you this? How is 't?

Sor. Dead; but in death well pleased, that I have lived
    To see my wrongs revenged on that black devil.   90
    O Vasques, to thy bosom let me give
    My last of breath; let not that lecher live—O!   *Dies.*

Vas. The reward of peace and rest be with him, my ever
    dearest lord and master.

Gio. Whose hand gave me this wound?   95

Vas. Mine sir, I was your first man; have you enough?

Gio. I thank thee; thou hast done for me
    But what I would have else done on myself.
    Art sure thy lord is dead?

Vas.   O impudent slave,
    As sure as I am sure to see thee die.   100

Car. Think on thy life and end, and call for mercy.

Gio. Mercy? Why, I have found it in this justice.

Car. Strive yet to cry to Heaven.

Gio.   O, I bleed fast;
    Death, thou art a guest long looked-for, I embrace
    Thee and thy wounds: O, my last minute comes.   105
    Where'er I go, let me enjoy this grace,
    Freely to view my Annabella's face.   *Dies.*

Don. Strange miracle of justice!

Car. Raise up the city, we shall be murdered all!

Vas. You need not fear, you shall not: this strange task being 110
    ended, I have paid the duty to the son which I have
    vowed to the father.

84–6. *so Weber;* Now . . . Sir, / Away . . . done, / Shift . . . owne, / Shift
. . . selues. *Q.*   88. See you this] *Gifford adds S.D. 'Pointing to Gio.'*
93–4.] *so Weber;* The . . . him, / My . . . Maister. *Q.*   97–100.] *so*
Reed; as prose in Q.   97. thee;] *Q* (thee,)*; thee, Vasques, conj. Dyce.*
100. thee] *Dodsley;* the *Q.*

Car. Speak, wretched villain, what incarnate fiend
    Hath led thee on to this?

Vas. Honesty, and pity of my master's wrongs. For know, 115
    my lord, I am by birth a Spaniard, brought forth my
    country in my youth by Lord Soranzo's father; whom
    whilst he lived I served faithfully; since whose death I
    have been to this man, as I was to him. What I have done
    was duty, and I repent nothing but that the loss of my 120
    life had not ransomed his.

Car. Say fellow, know'st thou any yet unnamed
    Of counsel in this incest?

Vas. Yes, an old woman, sometimes guardian to this mur-
    dered lady. 125

Car. And what's become of her?

Vas. Within this room she is; whose eyes after her con-
    fession I caused to be put out, but kept alive, to confirm
    what from Giovanni's own mouth you have heard. Now,
    my lord, what I have done you may judge of, and let 130
    your own wisdom be a judge in your own reason.

Car. Peace! First, this woman, chief in these effects,
    My sentence is that forthwith she be ta'en
    Out of the city, for example's sake,

---

116. *a Spaniard*] 'The Spaniards are subtle, wrapping their drifts in
close secresie, expressing suretie in their words, but keeping their intentions dissebled vnder disguised assurance of amity, betraying the inno-
cency of their friendes, in malice infinite . . .' (Robert Johnson, *Essaies*,
edit. 1607, quoted by F. T. Bowers, *Elizabethan Revenge Tragedy*,
Gloucester, Mass., edit. 1959, p. 56).

123. *Of counsel in*] in the secret of.

124. *sometimes*] formerly, 'some time'; cf. *Perkin Warbeck*, I. iii. 49–50.

127. *this room*] presumably pointing towards the coal-house; see IV.
iii. 233.

131. *in your own reason*] of your own justice (*O.E.D., sb*[1] 15).

132. *this woman*] Putana, whose guilt has just been disclosed. It has been
suggested that the Cardinal might mean 'the corpse of Annabella'; but it
is hard to see why her corpse should be burned and not Giovanni's.

chief in these effects] 'the person who played a leading part in these
doings' (*O.E.D.*, effect *sb* 3, 7).

There to be burnt to ashes.

Don.   'Tis most just.   135

Car. Be it your charge, Donado, see it done.

Don. I shall.

Vas. What for me? If death, 'tis welcome: I have been
   honest to the son, as I was to the father.

Car. Fellow, for thee: since what thou didst was done   140
   Not for thyself, being no Italian,
   We banish thee for ever, to depart
   Within three days; in this we do dispense
   With grounds of reason, not of thine offence.

Vas. 'Tis well: this conquest is mine, and I rejoice that a   145
   Spaniard outwent an Italian in revenge.   *Exit.*

Car. Take up these slaughtered bodies, see them buried;
   And all the gold and jewels, or whatsoever,
   Confiscate by the canons of the Church,
   We seize upon to the Pope's proper use.   150

Rich. [*Discovers himself*] Your grace's pardon: thus long
            I lived disguised
   To see the effect of pride and lust at once
   Brought both to shameful ends.

Car. What, Richardetto, whom we thought for dead?

Don. Sir, was it you—

Rich.   Your friend.

Car.   We shall have time   155
   To talk at large of all; but never yet
   Incest and murder have so strangely met.

---

144. reason, not] *Dodsley;* reason not *Q.*   151. S.D.] *Weber.*

143–4. *we do . . . offence*] 'we grant a dispensation [of the letter of the
law], in consideration of your motives, not of the nature of the offence'
(*O.E.D.*, dispense *vb* 4, reason *sb*[1] 5).

150. *proper*] personal.

156. *at large*] fully.

    Of one so young, so rich in Nature's store,
    Who could not say, *'Tis pity she's a whore?*

                                       Exeunt.

FINIS.

    The general commendation deserved by the actors in their   1
presentment of this tragedy may easily excuse such few faults
as are escaped in the printing: a common charity may allow
him the ability of spelling, whom a secure confidence assures
that he cannot ignorantly err in the application of sense.   5

158. *Nature's store*] the gifts of abundant Nature; natural wealth.

1–5. This apology for misprints was probably added by Ford himself
after most of the play had passed through the press. Its second sentence
especially recalls the style of his 'Epistle'—balanced, stilted, abstract,
obscure, and somewhat unconvincing. Cf. too the request in *Christes
Bloodie Sweat*, sig. A4: '*And* (kind Reader) *this is my request, that faults in
Printing may be charitably corrected; that the sence of the matter may be
wisely (and herein truely) construed, and so shall yee both approue your owne
Iudgements, and right the Authour in his hopes*'.

3–5. *a common . . . sense*] presumably: 'it may be assumed without extraordinary charity that one who knows himself to be using words in their
right meanings also knows how to spell them'.

APPENDIX I

Extracts from François de Rosset, 'Des Amours Incestueuses d'vn frère & d'vne soeur, & de leur fin malheureuse,
& tragique', in *Les Histoires Tragiques de Nostre Temps*
(Paris, 1615). (Editor's translation)

[pp. 174–84] One need not now go to Africa to see some new mon-
strosity: our Europe produces only too many of them today. The
scandals which occur daily would not surprise me if I were living
among the heathen. But when I see Christians polluted with
abominable crimes such as those who are ignorant of the Gospel
would not dare commit, I am forced to confess that our age is the
sewer for all the vices of the others, as the following stories bear
witness, especially that which I am about to relate.

In one of the finest provinces of France, formerly called Neustria,[1]
lived a gentleman of good family who married an honest lady, the
daughter of a neighbouring gentleman. They had a number of fine
children, among them a girl whom we shall call Doralice, and a son
some eighteen months younger whom we shall name Lyzaran. This
daughter and son were so beautiful that it seemed Nature had
delighted in shaping them, so as to display one of her miracles. They
were so perfectly alike that Ariosto's Bradamante was never more
like her brother Richardetto.[2] In due time their father took pains to
have them taught all kinds of worthy accomplishments, such as to
play the spinet, to dance, to read, to write and to paint. They
profited so well by their lessons that they surpassed the wishes of
their teachers. In addition, these two young children, brought up
side by side, loved each other with such love that neither could live
without the other. They were happy only in each other's sight, and
did not care to roam abroad or to spend their time with other
children of their own age. In that time of innocence everything was
permitted them. They usually slept together, and perhaps went on
doing so for too long. Fathers and mothers should take care of this,
and be wise by their example. Our age, as I have already said, is only

---

[1] Normandy.

[2] 'Richardet'. A mistake, as Koeppel points out (see Introduction,
pp. xxvii–xxviii): in *Orlando Furioso* Bradamante's brother is Rinaldo;
the name Richardetto does not occur.

too corrupt. Children just taken from the breast know more mischief than children of twelve would have known in less sophisticated times. I firmly believe that the evil sprang from this too long familiarity, which continued from day to day until, Doralice being now ten or eleven years old and Lyzaran nine or ten, he was sent away to a college to study. This separation was so grievous to them that each shed a thousand tears. Nothing but sobs and broken sighs on the one side and on the other, which their father and mother set down to fraternal affection. But shameful, abominable love was no doubt already intermingled with it; or so it strongly appears, as we shall see from the story that follows.

Having been put to college in one of the finest towns in the province, Lyzaran soon made himself so capable that he outstripped all his companions. When he had been at his studies for four years his father desired to see him again. He therefore sent for his son, and was delighted to see him so handsome, so learned, and already tall. But this was nothing compared with the happiness of Lyzaran's sister, who gave him embraces and kisses without end. Nevertheless, they no longer enjoyed the familiarities which had been permitted during their childhood; moreover, both were restrained by shame, and by the hatefulness of the sin which they were picturing. But neither could curb their damnable passion so well, but that it sometimes escaped the control of reason. Meanwhile their father sent Lyzaran back to college to finish his studies, and at the same time formed the plan of procuring him an ecclesiastical benefice.[1] He had several other sons, and was pleased to be able to save expense by finding the youngest some good place in the Church. And this he did, while at the same time the beauty and grace of Doralice drew many brave and honest gentlemen to pay her their attentions. She was sought after by an infinite number of gallants of great merit, and of an age suitable to her own. Nevertheless her father, putting wealth above all other considerations, bestowed her upon a neighbouring gentleman whose riches were great, but whose hair was already grey. O cursed avarice, what harm thou causest in the world! He who called thee the root of all evil well knew thee and thy fruits. In our story we shall name this gentleman Timandre. A happy man would he have been, if he had passed the rest of his days without linking himself to a beauty who was too young for him, and who made him suffer a thousand indignities (*luy faisoit mille affronts*) when he paid his addresses. At least when two parties agree, the goodwill they bear each other can do something to make up for the difference of age. For all her lamentations and tears, Doralice was

---

[1] 'vne Abbaye', benefice held from an abbey or monastery.

forced in the end to obey her father's will. The marriage was arranged, and Lyzaran was summoned from his studies to attend the wedding. As soon as his sister saw him and could speak without being overheard, she uttered these pitiful words: 'Dear brother, how wretched I am! Must I spend the flower of my youth with a person I detest more than death itself? Is not my father cruel to give me into the hands of a deadly enemy? Am I to pass the rest of my days in a subjection so contrary to my age and disposition? What use are riches if they bring no happiness? Give me your advice, I beg, in this great affliction. I am brought almost to that extremity of meeting death by my own hand.' When Lyzaran had heard these lamentations, he replied in the following manner. 'Dear sister, I pity you in this calamity. Your misfortune is my own, I feel it as much as you do. I cannot help blaming my father's cruelty in matching you so much against your liking, and to a man whose age is so different from yours. Nevertheless, since the power that fathers have over their children is absolute, I advise you to be patient. Fortune may still have something better in store for you. Be assured, at least, that once you are married to Timandre I shall hardly let you out of my sight. I will make my home with you. It is almost impossible for me to live without seeing you.' Breaking off this talk, they embraced and closely kissed, and had it not been for shame and for fear of being seen they would have performed their abominable desires. Consoled by Lyzaran's promise—whom she loved, not only as a brother, but also with a violent love, beyond all other men—Doralice now concerned herself little about marriage to an old man, who would henceforth serve as a screen for her vile pleasures. And so she was wedded, and Timandre gathered the fruit he had longed for. After the celebrations were over he took his wife back to his house, a country mansion near that of his father-in-law. Lyzaran, whose knowledge already was only too great, did not return to college but enjoyed a good living his father had procured for him. His disorderly passion for his sister did not allow him to wait long before visiting her in her new household, which he made his regular abode, spending all his time at her side.

This being frequently together kindled their desires in such a way that often they would have indulged them completely, had it not been for the shame of such a great and detestable sin. The fearfulness of such a crime was often in their minds, especially in that of Doralice, who communed with herself thus: 'Ah! cruel Love, that makest me madly to love one whose immodest glance I should flee because of our close kinship, with a mad and incestuous passion, the discovery of which by any other than myself I ought to dread: what hast thou in store for me? Must I commit so abominable a sin?

Let us throw off this accursed fantasy before it takes a deeper hold, and think of the woe which could follow such a detestable crime.' Often these good impulses would almost have turned her aside from her mad thoughts when they were opposed and instantly destroyed by the beauty and charm of her brother, and the love she had for him. 'And who,' she would then ask herself, 'can prevent me from loving? Is it not a natural thing? Were such matters considered in the time of innocence, and in the golden age? Men have given laws to their pleasures: but Nature is stronger than all those scruples. I will follow her, since she is a kind and sure guide for our life.' In such a manner would this abominable woman speak, while at the same time her brother underwent the same conflicts. In short, I dread to record here their damnable and perverse reasonings. Such is not my intention. My aim is to depict vice in all its filthiness, not to defend it. I shall only say, therefore, that after being swayed many times first one way and then another they took as their precedent the custom practised by the accursed pagan gods, Jupiter and Juno.

They went on with their vile pleasures for some time without being suspected. Even if they were found lying together on a bed, or if they openly kissed, or went roaming in woods and lonely places, who would ever have supposed that such an intimacy existed between them? But Heaven could not suffer this horrible and incestuous adultery for long, and brought it about that one day a servant woman caught them in the act. She crossed herself a thousand times, and shut her eyes so as not to see the abominable thing. Not wishing at once to make it public, she merely remonstrated with her mistress in private upon the great crime she was committing, and the great scandal which would result if it were discovered. Instead of taking this warning in good part, Doralice treated the woman in the most shameful manner possible: for having first given her insulting words, and then a good beating, she turned her out of doors. The servant, outraged by the wrong done her in return for the good she intended, secretly informed Timandre of the cause for which his wife had dismissed her, and warned him to have a care of her; for there was no doubt but that the brother was enjoying the shameful embraces of his own sister. The husband, astounded by this news, knew neither what to say nor do. At one moment the thirst for vengeance possessed his soul so completely that he was for revenging himself on them without any further delay; then, reflecting that it might perhaps be a slander, he concealed his just grief and pain, and spied on the actions of his wife and brother-in-law in so many ways that he became only too well assured of their incestuous behaviour.

The love he bore his wife, together with some opinion he entertained that perhaps it was not true even though he had seen all the signs of it that could be noticed, led him to content himself with forbidding his brother-in-law the house: a most lenient course of action from a husband so shamefully wronged. Thus our lovers were deprived of each other's sight, to the great displeasure of both. Doralice, feigning the part of an upright woman, asked her husband what grudge he had against her brother that he should forbid him the house ? Timandre then told her of their abominable filthiness, and of how he might justly resent it if it were not that he preferred gentle dealing to revenge; and promised to bury everything in oblivion, on condition that she would live henceforth a better life, and ask God's pardon for such a horrible and hateful crime; otherwise he would be forced to punish them as they deserved. Doralice, hearing her husband's reasons, burst into tears. Lamentations and regrets then poured from her mouth, together with terrible oaths which might have made Timandre believe the opposite of what he knew to be true, if his soul had not already been completely possessed by jealousy. . . . To conclude, he utterly refused to allow Lyzaran to return to his house, and swore that if he found him there he would do him a mischief.

[By a concerted plan of action the lovers flee the district. Timandre takes the news to their father, who falls prostrate with grief. After many wanderings the pair seek refuge in Paris, where they are taken in bed by a magistrate and constables. Doralice is four months pregnant by her brother. They are condemned to death.]

[p. 194] 'Courage, brother,' then said Doralice, 'since we must die, let us die with patience. It is time that we should be punished as we deserve. Let us not fear to confess our sin before men: we shall soon have to render account of it to God. His mercy is great, dear brother, and he will pardon us if we truly repent of our faults. Alas, gentlemen,' said she then to the judges, 'I confess that I have justly deserved to die; but I beg you to give me the most cruel death imaginable, if you will only grant life to this poor gentleman. It is I who have caused all the harm; I alone must receive the punishment. . . .' [But both the lovers are executed, winning compassion and admiration from all the spectators by their youth, courage and beauty.]

APPENDIX II
Sannazaro's Encomium on Venice
(see II. ii. 12–15)

Ford may have come across these verses, and the story of Sanna-zaro's reward, in *Coryat's Crudities* (1611); or he may have seen James Howell's letter supposedly written to Robert Brown of the Middle Temple (where Ford was in residence), and dated from Venice on 12 August 1621. Coryat writes:

'I heard in Venice that a certaine Italian Poet called Jacobus Sannazarius had a hundred crownes bestowed upon him by the Senate of Venice for each of these verses following. I would to God my Poeticall friend Mr. Benjamin Johnson were so well rewarded for his Poems here in England, seeing he hath made many as good verses (in my opinion) as these of Sannazarius.

> Viderat Adriacis Venetam Neptunus in undis
>   Stare urbem, & toto ponere jura mari:
> Nunc mihi Tarpeias, quantumvis Juppiter, arces
>   Objice, & illa tui moenia Martis, ait.
> Si pelago Tybrim praefers, urbem aspice utramque,
>   Illam homines dicas, hanc posuisse Deos.'

([Thomas] *Coryat's Crudities*, Glasgow, 1905, I, 301–2.)

Howell gives the same verses (with *dices* for *dicas*) and adds a translation and comment:

> '*When* Neptune *saw in* Adrian *Surges stand*
> Venice, *and give the Sea Laws of Command:*
> *Now* Jove, *said he, object thy* Capitol,
> *And* Mars' *proud Walls: this were for to extol*
> Tiber *beyond the* Main; *both Towns behold:*
> Rome, *Men thou' lt say,* Venice *the Gods did mould.*

Sannazaro had given him by St. *Mark* a hundred *Zecchins* for every one of these Verses, which amounts to about 300*l*. It would be long before the City of *London* would do the like; witness that cold

Reward, or rather those cold Drops of Water which were cast upon my Countryman, Sir *Hugh Middleton,* for bringing *Ware* River thro' her Streets, the most serviceable and wholesomest Benefit that ever she receiv'd.'

(*Epistolae Ho-Elianae: the Familiar Letters of James Howell*, ed. J. Jacobs, 1890, [I,] 80; first published in 1645.)

Criticism of '*Tis Pity She's a Whore*, 1661–1932

1661: SAMUEL PEPYS

9 [September]. . . . But I drank so much wine that I was not fit for business; and therefore, at noon I went and walked in Westminster-hall a while; and thence to Salsbury Court play-house, where was acted the first time *Tis pitty shee's a Whore*—a simple [i.e. foolish] play and ill acted; only, it was my fortune to sit by a most pretty and most ingenious lady, which pleased me much.

(*Diary*, ed. Robert Latham and William Matthews, II, 1970, p. 175.)

1691: GERARD LANGBAINE

'*Tis pity she's a whore* . . . equalls any of our Author's Plays; and were to be commended, did not the Author paint the incestuous Love between *Giovanni*, and his Sister *Annabella*, in too beautiful Colours.

(*An Account of the English Dramatick Poets*, Oxford 1691, p. 222.)

1764: DAVID ERSKINE BAKER

I cannot help considering this play as the masterpiece of this great author's works. There are some particulars in it both with respect to conduct, character, spirit, and poetry, that would have done honour to the pen of the immortal Shakespeare himself. Langbaine has, however, pointed out a fault, which I must, though unwillingly, subscribe to, and which relates to a very essential point, viz. the morals of the play; which is, his having painted the incestuous love between Giovanni and his sister Annabella, in much too beautiful colours; and, indeed, the author himself seems by his title to have been aware of this objection, and conscious that he had rendered the last-mentioned character, notwithstanding all her faults, so very lovely, that every auditor would naturally cry out to himself, '*Tis Pity she's a Whore*. In consequence of this incestuous passion also, on which the whole plot of the play turns, the catastrophe of it is too shocking for an audience to bear, notwithstanding every recollection of its being no more than fiction.

(*Biographica Dramatica*, edit. 1782, II, 373–4.)

1797: CHARLES DIBDIN

Nothing can be more revolting than the subject; and, therefore, the warmer and more glowing the pictures of love are worked up, the more reprehensible is the author . . . . It is not the province of a dramatic writer to seek for monsters, and to record prodigies; it is his duty to reprehend such vices as are commonly known, and often practised, in which catalogue, for the honour of human nature, incest without a motive has no place; but if it had, it ought to be introduced as a deed of darkness which could not be pleaded for or argued on, even by the wretches themselves, therefore, all we can say in favour of Ford is, to wish he had employed his beautiful writing to a more laudable purpose.

(*A Complete History of the English Stage*, 1797–1800, III, 279–80.)

1808: CHARLES LAMB

Ford was of the first order of Poets. He sought for sublimity, not by parcels in metaphors or visible images, but directly where she has her full residence in the heart of man; in the actions and sufferings of the greatest minds. There is a grandeur of the soul above mountains, seas, and the elements. Even in the poor perverted reason of Giovanni and Annabella . . . we discern traces of that fiery particle, which in the irregular starting from out of the road of beaten action, discovers something of a right line even in obliquity, and shows hints of an improveable greatness in the lowest descents and degradations of our nature.

(*Specimens of English Dramatic Poets who lived about the Time of Shakespeare*, ed. E. V. Lucas [1903], p. 218. The extracts Lamb gave from '*Tis Pity* were I. i, I. ii. 204–64, and, with cuts, V. v.)

1811: HENRY WEBER

Few dramatic authors have commenced their career with a production which more strongly breathes the very soul of poetry; but few have chosen a more unfortunate subject for the display of their talents. The vivid glow of passion with which the incestuous intercourse of Giovanni and Annabella is delineated has justly been termed by Langbaine 'too beautiful' for the subject, and the utter wreck and degradation of two characters which are held up to our admiration in the commencement; the one gifted with every qualification of a generous and philosophical soul, the other interesting for every thing which can render a female mind amiable, assails our feelings too powerfully, and renders the perusal of one of the finest plays, in point of pathetic effect, even painful. The conduct of the principal plot is skilfully interwoven with the subordinate one, the interest is not suffered to cool, a defect too frequent in the plays of that age, and the catastrophe is brought about with much dramatic art. With regard to the characters, none of them are amiable without alloy of baseness except the Friar, (a well-drawn copy of Friar Lawrence in Romeo and Juliet,) and the insipid husband of Hippolita.

(*The Dramatic Works of John Ford*, Edinburgh and London, 1811, Introduction, I, xi–xii.)

1811: WILLIAM GIFFORD

A play founded upon the incestuous and adulterous intercourse of a brother and sister, carries with it insuperable obstacles to its appearance upon a modern stage, nor could the beauty of its poetry have long supported, in any age, a representation so pregnant with horror. The exquisite language uttered by Giovanni and Annabella has, we suspect, beguiled [Weber] into a higher eulogium on the principal characters, than an examination of their claims will entitle them to. The fate of Giovanni and his sister would interest us more but for the alacrity with which she enters into, and even anticipates, his incestuous wishes, and for the total absence of remorse after the consummation of their unholy loves. There is also a flippant insensibility in Annabella's first conference with Soranzo, altogether incompatible with the amiable qualities which [Weber] would attribute to her; and her audacious taunting of her husband after her pregnancy is discovered, could only be the result of native and determined wickedness. In the character of Giovanni, we discover little to praise. His only estimable quality, his education, is prostituted to the delusions of perverted reasoning in furtherance of his designs: when his purposes are gained he hardens his heart and justifies his crimes with sophistical arguments; and after destroying the partner of his iniquities, in a scene of inimitable beauty, he rushes upon death with the gestures of a lunatic, and the insensibility of an atheist. There is indeed a want of discrimination and propriety in all the characters, each of which recommends itself in its turn by elevated sentiments and conduct, the effect of which is utterly effaced in some subsequent scene, till at length they all become unprincipled and wicked, and sink into an undistinguishable and common debasement. In addition to what we have observed, we think there is too little relief to the sombre character of the piece, which is so predominant that every reader, before he has finished the perusal, will be tempted to exclaim with Macbeth, that he is 'full of horrors'.

(*Quarterly Review*, VI, 1811, 466–7; written in collaboration with Barron Field. Some of these criticisms are repeated in severer terms in the Introduction to Gifford's own edition of Ford's *Works* in 1827: 'Giovanni comes upon the scene a professed and daring infidel, and . . . a shameless avower and justifier of his impure purpose: Annabella is not a jot behind him in precocity of vice . . . . After all, her repentance is of a very questionable nature'; while the poetry 'flings a soft and soothing light over what in its natural state would glare with salutary and repulsive horror.')

1819: WILLIAM HAZLITT

Ford is not so great a favourite with me as with some others, from whose judgment I dissent with diffidence. It has been lamented that the play of his which has been most admired ('Tis Pity She's a Whore) had not a less exceptionable subject. I do not know, but I suspect that the exceptionableness of the subject is that which constitutes the chief merit of the play. The repulsiveness of the story is what gives it its critical interest; for it is a studiously prosaic statement of facts, and naked declaration of passions. It was not the least of Shakespear's praise, that he never tampered with unfair subjects. His genius was above it; his taste kept aloof from it. I do not deny the power of simple painting and polished style in this tragedy in general, and of a great deal more in some few of the scenes, particularly in the quarrel between Annabella and her husband, which is wrought up to a pitch of demoniac scorn and phrensy with consummate art and knowledge; but I do not find much other power in the author (generally speaking) than that of playing with edged tools, and knowing the use of poisoned weapons. And what confirms me in this opinion is the comparative inefficiency of his other plays. Except the last scene of the Broken Heart (which I think extravagant—others may think it sublime, and be right) they are merely exercises of style and effusions of wire-drawn sentiment. Where they have not the sting of illicit passion, they are quite pointless, and seem painted on gauze, or spun of cobwebs.

(*Lectures on the Dramatic Literature of the Age of Elizabeth*, no. IV; *Works*, ed. P. P. Howe, 1930–4, VI, 268–9.)

1840: HARTLEY COLERIDGE

He disowned all courtship of the vulgar taste; we might therefore
suppose that the horrible stories which he has embraced in ' 'Tis
Pity She's a Whore', 'The Broken Heart', and 'Love's Sacrifice',
were his own choice, and his own taste. But it would be unfair from
hence to conclude that he delighted in the contemplation of vice
and misery, as vice and misery. He delighted in the sensation of
intellectual power, he found himself strong in the imagination of
crime and agony; his moral sense was gratified by indignation at
the dark possibilities of sin, by compassion for rare extremes of
suffering. He abhorred vice—he admired virtue; but ordinary vice
or modern virtue were, to him, as light wine to a dram drinker. His
genius was a telescope, ill-adapted for neighbouring objects, but
powerful to bring within the sphere of vision, what nature has
wisely placed at an unsociable distance. Passion must be incestuous
or adulterous; grief must be something more than martyrdom,
before he could make them big enough to be seen. Unquestionably
he displayed great *power* in these horrors, which was all he desired;
but had he been 'of the first order of poets', he would have found
and displayed superior power in 'familiar matter of to-day', in fail-
ings to which all are liable, virtues which all may practise, and sorrow
for which all may be the better.

(*The Dramatic Works of Massinger and Ford* [1840], Introduction,
p. xlviii.)

1871: ALGERNON CHARLES SWINBURNE

Nothing is more noticeable in this poet than the passionless reason
and equable tone of style with which in his greatest works he treats
of the deepest and most fiery passions, the quiet eye with which he
searches out the darkest issues of emotion, the quiet hand with which
he notes them down. At all times his verse is even and regular,
accurate and composed; never specially flexible or melodious,
always admirable for precision, vigour, and purity. . . .

   The subtleties and varieties of individual character do not usually
lie well within the reach of Ford's handling; but in the part of
Giovanni we find more of this power than elsewhere. Here the poet
has put forth all his strength; the figure of his protagonist stands
out complete and clear. . . . His sister is perhaps less finely drawn,
though her ebbs and flows of passion are given with great force,
and her alternate possession by desire and terror, repentance and
defiance, if we are sometimes startled by the rough rapidity of the
change, does not in effect impair the unity of character, obscure the

clearness of outline. She yields more readily than her brother to the curse of Venus, with a passionate pliancy which prepares us for her subsequent prostration of mind at the feet of her confessor, and again for the revival of a fearless and shameless spirit under the stroke of her husband's violence. . . .

Of all the magnificent scenes which embody their terrible story the last is (as it should be) the most noble; it is indeed the finest scene in Ford. . . . That swift and fiery glance which flashes at once from all depths to all heights of the human spirit, that intuition of an indefinable and infallible instinct which at a touch makes dark things clear and brings distant things close, . . . [Ford] has shown here at least; witness the passionate subtlety and truth of this passage, the deepest and keenest of his writing, as when taken with the context it will assuredly appear [v. v. 26–37]. All the horror of this wonderful scene is tempered into beauty by the grace and glow of tenderness which so suffuses it as to verify the vaunt of Giovanni [v. v. 68–77].

('John Ford', *Complete Works of Swinburne*, ed. E. Gosse and T. J. Wise, 1925–7, XII, 372–6.)

1888: HAVELOCK ELLIS

In his second extant play, *'Tis Pity She's a Whore*, Ford touched the highest point that he ever reached. He never after succeeded in presenting an image so simple, passionate, and complete, so free comparatively from mixture of weak or base elements, as that of the boy and girl lovers who were brother and sister. The tragic story is unrolled from first to last with fine truth and clear perceptions. . . .

The burden of a passionate and heavy-laden heart—that is the centre of every picture that Ford presents to us; on the painting of it he lavishes all his care. The rest of the canvas is filled in with a rapid and careless hand. . . . The conflict between the world's opinion and the heart's desire he paints and repaints, not as a moralist browbeating the cynical or conventional world, but as an artist, presenting problems which he does not undertake to solve save by the rough methods of the tragic stage. It is the grief deeper than language that he strives to express. . . . He is a master of the brief mysterious words, so calm in seeming, which well up from the depths of despair. . . . When we think of Ford we think of Giovanni and Annabella, passionate children who had given the world for love; of the childish sophistry with which they justified themselves, and of their last marvellous dialogue through which pierced a vague sense of guilt—a lurid shadow cast from the world they had contemned.

Ford is the most modern of the tribe to whom he belonged. . . .
He was an analyst; he strained the limits of his art to the utmost; he
foreboded new ways of expression. Thus he is less nearly related to
the men who wrote *Othello*, and *A Woman killed with Kindness*, and
Valentinian, than to those poets and artists of the naked human
soul, the writer of *Le Rouge et le Noir*, and the yet greater writer of
Madame Bovary.

(*The Best Plays of . . . John Ford*, Mermaid Series, 1888, Introduction, pp. x–xvii.)

1895: MAURICE MAETERLINCK

Ford . . . is at times almost like Racine; and amid the excited and
noisy barbarian beauties who surround them, his heroines—
Annabella, Calantha, Penthea, Bianca—possess an inner life which
is gentle, strong and silent. Without exactly knowing why one feels
that a soul is there, as in Bérénice and Andromaque; and this is a
very rare and mysterious gift. . . . Annabella is a girl like every other
girl, with no inward or outward traits to differentiate her from
ordinary womankind. No character could be more simple, colourless
and general. In everyday life she shows a rather narrow and vulgar
mind. She exchanges feeble jokes with her governess and her
suitors; and yet, once her love is aroused, this conventional person-
age effortlessly displays all the deepest, gentlest, most heroic and
most delicious aspects of feminine nature. She is pure, she is tender,
and all that is subtle and noble in the depths of the soul blossoms in
her, because she loves; and because no tongue in the world can
number the riches which are born and reborn unceasingly in the
heart of a woman, whoever she may be, when she loves—especially
when she must love in darkness, in weeping and in fear. . . .

Annabella [Maeterlinck's name for *'Tis Pity*, and for the French
play which he founded on its main plot] is the terrible, simple and
bloody poem of merciless love. It is carnal love in all its strength, in
all its beauty, and in all its almost supernatural horror. Giovanni
and Annabella are brother and sister. They have been in love for a
long while without telling of it, perhaps without knowing it. Then
suddenly, in one of those moments when for no reason the eyes are
opened to all the truth that has been making its way into the heart
for days, weeks and months, they meet trembling in a room in their
father's house; and love bursts forth, harsh, cruel, wild, groping,
and already shuddering beneath the hand of death. The words
which declare this love have already, on their lips, the dark and
bitter taste of death. . . . [In V. iii] Annabella defies [Soranzo] with
magnificent words torn up, like precious stones in a tempest, from

the eternal abyss of the human soul. . . . [Of V. v:] I do not believe there is any scene in literature more beautiful, more sweet, more tender, more cruel or more desperate. They bid each other goodbye; Giovanni kills her gently while kissing her and, dagger in hand, goes down bloody and frenzied to the banqueting hall; and the play ends with one of those fast and furious butcheries in which the old English tragedians often took delight.

(Preface to *Annabella*, Paris, 1895, pp. xii–xvii; editor's translation.)

1915: S. P. SHERMAN

'Tis Pity is extremely interesting both as a play and as a psychological document; for it represents the height of Ford's achievement as a dramatist and the depth of his corruption as an apostle of passion. . . . He approaches the theme not with the temper of a stern realist bent on laying bare the secret links of cause and effect in a ferocious and ugly story of almost unmentionable lust and crime, but with the temper of a decadent romanticist bent on showing the enthralling power of physical beauty and the transfiguring power of passion. He accordingly makes the ill-starred Giovanni and Annabella the well-bred offspring of a prosperous gentleman of Parma. . . . But like their author they have been nourished on that great mass of Renaissance literature which in Italy and in England establishes the religion and theology of earthly love. In the opening scene Giovanni, already in the throes of passion, fortifies himself with philosophical authority, casuistical argument, and Platonic nonsense quite in the vein of Spenser's hymns. Shocking as it is, we must recognize that this blossomed corruption is rooted in the fair garden of Elizabethan romance. To Giovanni, as to the youthful Spenser, love is the supreme thing in the world, beauty the unquestioned object of adoration. Since he finds this adorable beauty in his sister, his soul conforming to its celestial nature must bow and worship. . . . By making her yield at once with an abandon equal to Giovanni's Ford plainly intends to show that the souls of the brother and sister were predestined for union in that Platonic heaven of lovers whence they came. . . . As the fatal net closes around the lovers, Ford seems to summon all his powers to represent their misery as the price of their devotion to the highest ends of which their souls are capable. . . .

Ford's theory of the inviolability of the soul has much in common with Maeterlinck's. It seems, however, much more startling because it is clothed in very human flesh and blood, and set upon a realistic stage. Ford presents his hero and heroine, for such they must be called, in the light of common day. He prepares us for a tragedy in which we should witness the operation of the laws of this world; but he presents us a tragedy in which the protagonists are emancipated from the laws of this world, and act in accordance with the laws of a Platonized Arcadia. They are idealists in one world, but criminal degenerates in the other. . . .

After a generation of great dramatists had spoken, [Ford] had still something to say. He had to say that the essence of tragedy is the defeat of the ideal by the real world. In order to explain the idea dramatically he had to invent the problem play. If he could have supported his theory of tragedy by a series of such fine and effective illustrations as *The Broken Heart*, he would have made himself a large and secure place in literature. Unfortunately, however, his experience, judgment, and common sense were unequal to the task. His talent was limited by a morbid temperament. His intellectual grasp was weak when he wrote *Love's Sacrifice*. When he wrote *'Tis Pity*, though every artistic faculty was alert, he was deserted by common-sense.

(*'Tis Pity She's a Whore and The Broken Heart*, Belles-Lettres Series, Boston and London [1915], Introduction, pp. xxxiv–lv.)

1932: T. S. ELIOT

To the use of incest between brother and sister for a tragic plot there should be no objection of principle: the test is, however, whether the dramatic poet is able to give universal significance to a perversion of nature which, unlike some other aberrations, is defended by no one. . . . Ford handles the theme with all the seriousness of which he is capable, and he can hardly be accused here of wanton sensationalism. . . . Ford does not make the unpleasant appear pleasant; and when, at the moment of avowed love, he makes Annabella say

> Brother, even by our mother's dust, I charge you,
> Do not betray me to your mirth or hate . . .

he is certainly double-stressing the horror, which from that moment he will never allow you to forget; but if he did not stress the horror he would be the more culpable. . . . When all is said, however, there are serious shortcomings to render account of. The sub-plot of Hippolita is tedious, and her death superfluous. More important, the passion of Giovanni and Annabella is not shown as an affinity of temperament due to identity of blood; it hardly rises above the purely carnal infatuation. . . . Giovanni is merely selfish and self-willed, of a temperament to want a thing the more because it is forbidden; Annabella is pliant, vacillating and negative: the one almost a monster of egotism, the other virtually a moral defective. Her

rebellious taunting of her violent husband has an effect of natural-
ness and arouses some sympathy; but the fact that Soranzo is himself a bad lot does not extenuate her willingness to ruin him. In
short, the play has not the general significance and emotional depth
(for the two go together) without which no such action can be
justified; and this defect separates it completely from the best plays
of Webster, Middleton and Tourneur. . . .

Ford's poetry, as well as Beaumont and Fletcher's, is of the
surface: that is to say, it is the result of the stock of expressions of
feeling accumulated by the greater men. . . . But Ford, as dramatic
poet, as writer of dramatic blank verse, has one quality which
assures him of a higher place than even Beaumont and Fletcher;
and that is a quality which any poet may envy him. The varieties of
cadence and tone in blank verse are none too many, in the history of
English verse; and Ford, though intermittently, was able to mani-
pulate sequences of words in blank verse in a manner which is quite
his own.

('John Ford', *Selected Essays*, edit. 1951, pp. 196–8, 204.)

Glossarial Index to the Commentary

An asterisk before a word indicates information which supplements that given in *O.E.D.* The index lists most words in the form in which they appear in the text, but for words that occur more than once the basic form is sometimes given.

142

Date Due

Douglas Library 2 OCT 21 1977
DISCH.

Douglas Library DEC 1 0 1980
DISCH. 801201

Douglas Library APR 27 1981
810424

Douglas Library MAY 1 5 1984
DISCH. 840512

Douglas Library JAN 2 5 1985
DISCH. 8412 05

Douglas Library OCT 29 1992
DISCH 102092

Douglas Library FEB 1 8 1993
MAR 04 '93

FORM 109